Approaches to Teaching the Works of Naguib Mahfouz

I0894095

Approaches to Teaching World Literature

For a complete listing of titles,
see the last pages of this book.

Approaches to Teaching the Works of Naguib Mahfouz

Edited by

Waïl S. Hassan

and

Susan Muaddi Darraj

The Modern Language Association of America

New York 2012

Library of Congress Cataloging-in-Publication Data

Approaches to teaching the works of Naguib Mahfouz /
edited by Waïl S. Hassan and Susan Muaddi Darraj.
p. cm.—(Approaches to teaching world literature, ISSN 1059-1133 ; 119)
Includes bibliographical references and index.
ISBN 978-1-60329-108-8 (hardcover : alk. paper)—
ISBN 978-1-60329-109-5 (pbk. : alk. paper)
1. Mahfuz, Najib, 1911–2006—Study and teaching.
I. Hassan, Waïl S. II. Darraj, Susan Muaddi.
PJ7846.A46Z5775 2012
892.7'36—dc23 2011040247

Approaches to Teaching World Literature 119
ISSN 1059-1133

Published by The Modern Language Association of America
26 Broadway, New York, New York 10004-1789
www.mla.org

CONTENTS

PREFACE

The Approaches to Teaching World Literature series has yet to include a volume focused on an Arab author or Arabic literature. It seemed a natural choice to make the first such volume a study of ways to approach teaching the works of the Arab world's best-known writer, Naguib Mahfouz.

Since he was awarded the Nobel Prize in 1988, Mahfouz has been increasingly featured on North American university syllabi as the focus of study in courses devoted to literature (both in Arabic and English translation), Middle East studies, and other subjects. This progress brings with it several concerns, which we hope this volume will address: many undergraduates and graduates do not comprehend the major literary influence of Mahfouz on Arabic literature and even politics; there are inherent difficulties in teaching translations of Mahfouz; in survey courses, he is often included as an author representative of Arabic literature as a whole; many instructors teaching him (e.g., in a survey course on world literature) are not familiar with his work; and it is difficult to know how to approach the many stylistic and thematic aspects of that work. As Mahfouz steadily enters the North American classroom, instructors have voiced a need for critical studies, syllabi, and other teaching resources. This volume addresses these needs as well as the many concerns related to the presentation of Mahfouz and his work in North American and European classrooms.

In the introduction under part 1, "Materials," we offer some discussion of Mahfouz's background, influence, and critical reception. In part 2, "Approaches," thirteen scholars share their insights into teaching Mahfouz, in the hope that teachers will glean useful information and resources about Mahfouz's oeuvre as well as concrete suggestions for introducing it in their classrooms. No matter in which environment Mahfouz is taught (the world literature survey course, the history class, a Middle East studies seminar, or an Arabic-language class), these essays should help teachers think creatively and innovatively about including Mahfouz in their syllabi. Many essays in the first section, "Contexts," also discuss pedagogy; many in the second section, "Teaching Specific Texts," also discuss various contexts of Mahfouz's work—a neat, clean division is neither possible nor desirable. The overlap should promote a fuller, broader perspective on the texts' many facets.

Several factors have changed since we began assembling the volume, including the ways in which we considered presenting the material. One significant change is that, when we began our work, Mahfouz was still alive; he passed away on 30 August 2006, at the age of ninety-four. The death of the Arab world's literary giant was remarked on around the world and generated retrospectives of his work and influence.

As his appearance in university syllabi increases in the future, the need for this volume will become all the more pressing.

Note on Transliteration of Arabic Words

In the United States, there are two standard systems for rendering Arabic words into the Latin alphabet, that of the Library of Congress and that used by the *International Journal of Middle East Studies.* But Arabic words and names are also more informally spelled, in a variety of ways. For example, depending on how it is pronounced in different regions and languages, one common name is spelled as Muhammad, Mohammad, Mohammed, Mohamed, Mohamet, Mahomet, and Mehmet. The editors have chosen to allow such variation across the volume. The transliteration system chosen by each contributor has been retained, while names are rendered the way their owners have written them or in the way they most commonly appear in English (e.g., Naguib rather than Najib, Mahfouz rather than Mahfuz).

WSH and SMD

Part One

MATERIALS

Early Years

Naguib Mahfouz (or Najib Mahfuz) was the preeminent Arab novelist in the twentieth century. He had achieved stature in the Arab world before the award of the Nobel Prize in Literature brought him international fame in 1988. Until then, only nine of his novels were translated into English and French; since the award, about five hundred editions of his works have been made available in forty languages. By virtue of his extremely long and prolific career, stretching from the 1930s to his death, Mahfouz was also the single most important chronicler and analyst of twentieth-century Egypt.

Mahfouz was not the first novelist in the Arabic language. As distinct from compilations of tales like كليلة و دمنة (Kalila wa Dimna; "Kalila and Dimna") and *The Thousand and One Nights*, the picaresque narratives of the مقامات (*maqamat*), and oral sagas and epics such as those of Sayf Ibn Dhi-Yazan and Abu-Zayd al-Hilali, modern Arabic fiction emerged in the late nineteenth century as a direct result of new Arabic translations and adaptations of French novels. By some accounts, now disputed, the first Arabic novel was Muhammad Husayn Haykal's زينب (Zaynab; "Zaynab") (written in Paris in 1911 and published in Cairo in 1913). That fiction was considered an inferior genre at the time is perhaps best illustrated by the fact that Haykal felt compelled to publish *Zaynab* under a pseudonym for fear that his reputation as a lawyer would suffer if he became known as the author of a novel. This fear quickly proved to be unfounded; major writers like Taha Hussayn, ʿAbbas Mahmud al-ʿAqqad, and Tawfiq al-Hakim also wrote novels, although their literary endeavors remained concentrated on other genres. Mahfouz was the first Arab writer to devote his energies to the novel, and he single-handedly brought it to maturity and established it as a serious genre of Arabic literature. Over the course of seven decades, thirty-six novels and fourteen collections of short stories (not to mention seven one-act plays, a score of film scripts, a memoir, and seven volumes of collected journalistic articles) poured out of Mahfouz's pen. A civil servant for roughly four decades, he wrote his meticulously crafted works in his spare time. Moreover, because an eye condition prevented him from working during the summer months, he could write only between September and April of every year. He set a heroic example of self-discipline and dedication in the face of personal, professional, and political obstacles.

Mahfouz was born in 1911 to a middle-class family in the district of al-Gammaliyyah near downtown Cairo, the youngest of seven children. His father was employed in the Ministry of Religious Endowments and Islamic Affairs, where Mahfouz himself would later begin his own civil service career. He remembered a happy childhood, and although there was no library in the family's apartment to satisfy the boy's voracious reading appetite, his mother, who had a passion for antiquities, took him to visit museums and ancient Egyptian sites. At the age of seven, he witnessed the demonstrations held during the 1919 revolution from a window in the family residence, and they made a lasting impression on him. When he was twelve, the family moved to the new suburb of al-ʿAbbasiyyah. Mahfouz missed the old neighborhood, which later provided the setting for many of his novels, but he quickly settled in. A few years later, he attended Fuʾad I University (now Cairo University), majoring in philosophy, but he also attended lectures on Egyptology and literature, reading widely in all three fields. At first, he wanted to pursue a graduate degree in philosophy, but when he was denied a government scholarship to study abroad, he left the university, entered the civil service, and turned his intellectual ambition to literature. Fearing that marriage and family life would divert his time and energy from writing, he remained a bachelor until 1954. He had finished his trilogy in 1952 and, as he recounts, despaired of writing fiction again. During that period, he wrote only film scripts and did not begin another novel until 1958. He reported that his marriage proved to be helpful, rather than detrimental, to his literary career, and the couple had two daughters.

Novels and Short Stories

While studying philosophy at Fuʾad I University, Mahfouz published his first book, a translation into Arabic of James Baikie's *Ancient Egypt* (1912). This choice signaled an interest in a topic that would inspire Mahfouz to plan a series of forty novels, all set in ancient Egypt. He would write only three pharaonic novels, however, between 1939 and 1944: عبث الأقدار (ʿAbath al-aqdar; *Khufu's Wisdom*), رادوبيس (Radubis; *Rhadopis of Nubia*), and كفاح طيبة (Kifah Tiba; *Thebes at War*), the last an allegory of Egypt's struggle against British colonialism.

Abandoning the grand scheme of historical novels, Mahfouz turned to realism as a more direct mode to examine contemporary society, publishing eight novels between 1945 and 1957 that firmly established him as a major novelist. Those include زقاق المدق (Zuqaq al-midaqq; *Midaq Alley*), perhaps his most widely read novel in English translation, and, his most important work, the trilogy (بين القصرين [Bayn al-qasrayn; *Palace Walk*], قصر الشوق [Qasr al-shawq; *Palace of Desire*], and السكرية [Sukkariyah; *Sugar Street*]). A family saga tracing the fortunes of three generations between the First and Second World Wars, the trilogy captures the tension between the seemingly timeless world of a family patriarch, Ahmad Abd al-Jawwad, which comes to an abrupt end during the 1919 revolution, and the rapid social and political changes that followed. The trilogy ends with the emergence of the new ideologies of communism and Islamic fundamentalism, which, on the eve of the 1952 revolution, lead the patriarch's two grandsons to prison. Although completed before that historic moment, this massive work was not published until 1956–57. Mahfouz did not write anything new for several years, using that period of silence to observe the changes brought on by the first Egyptian regime to rule the country in two thousand years. He considered himself a child of the 1919 revolution, but the revolution of 1952 seemed for a moment to realize the country's dreams of independence, social justice, and democracy.

His first commentary on the regime of Colonel Gamal Abdel Nasser was the allegorical novel أولاد حارتنا (1959; Awlad haritna; *Children of the Alley*), a politicoreligious allegory depicting Adam, Moses, Jesus, and Muhammad that became highly controversial. His most widely read short story in English translation, "Zaabalawi," from the collection دنيا الله (1963; Dunya Allah; *God's World*), brought the same spiritual, philosophical, and existential concerns into the twentieth century, albeit still in an unmistakably allegorical mode. In the novels written during the 1960s, most notably اللص و الكلاب (1975; Al-liss wa al-kilab; *The Thief and the Dogs* [1984]), and ميرامار (1967; Miramar; *Miramar*), Mahfouz made more extensive use of techniques like stream of consciousness, multiple narrators, episodic and fragmentary plots, while also occasionally writing conventional, realistic novels such as السمان والخريف (Al-samman wa al-kharif; *Autumn Quail*), الطريق (Al-tariq; *The Search*), الشحاذ (Al-shahhadh; *The Beggar*), and ثرثرة فوق النيل (Thartharah fawq al-Nil; *Adrift on the Nile*). In all those novels, he registered the failures of the Nasser regime—political repression and the corruption, opportunism, hypocrisy, and nihilism it breeds—and further developed the existential and Sufi themes that would preoccupy him throughout his career. Allegorical novels like قلب الليل (1975; Qalb al-layl; *The Heart of the Night*) and عصر الحب (1980; Asr al-hubb; *The Age of Love*) pick up on those themes, while realistic novels like الحب تحت المطر (1973; Al-hubb tahat al matar; *Love in the Rain*) and الكرنك (1974; Al-Karnak; *Karnak*), written after Nasser's death in 1970, treat the failures of his regime and the magnitude of its defeat in the 1967 war with Israel with more openness than would have been possible during the president's lifetime. The defeat led Mahfouz to a two-year period of silence that ended in 1969, when he published four collections of short stories between then and 1971. The first novel after that war, المرايا (Al-maraya; *Mirrors*) published in 1972, is in the form of fifty-five vignettes that represent a social panorama—an attempt, it seems, to take stock of the forces that shaped Egyptian society from the early twentieth century until around 1970. Several other episodic novels followed, including most notably الحرافيش (Al-harafish; *The Harafish*), a saga that evokes the world of strongmen and thugs he depicted earlier in *Children of the Alley*; *Arabian Nights and Days*, a sequel to the great medieval work that begins in the one-thousand-and-second night, but with a cynical and bitter Sharazade and a repentant yet ever cruel Shahrayar; and رحلة ابن فطومة (Rihlat Ibn Fattouma; *The Journey of Ibn Fattouma*), which evokes another great medieval Arabic work, تحفة النظار في غرائب الأمصار وعجائب الآسفارt (Tuḥfat an-naẓār fī gharā'ib al-amṣār wa ʿajā'ib al-asfār; *The Travels of Ibn Battuta*).

Mahfouz returned to ancient Egypt in two more works. In the ambitious أمام العرش (1983; Amam al-ʿarsh; *Before the Throne*), he put on trial (before Osiris,

Egyptian god of the underworld and judge of the dead) Egypt's rulers from Menes to Anwar Sadat (whose assassination in October 1981 became the subject of his next novel, يوم قتل الزعيم (1985; Yawma qutila al-zaʿim; *The Day the Leader Was Killed*). In العائش في الحقيقة (1985; Al-ʿaʾish fi al-haqiqah; *Akhenaten: Dweller in Truth*), the second pharaonic novel of the late period and fifth of his career, Mahfouz dealt with the reign of Akhenaten, who introduced monotheism and banned the worship of Egypt's traditional gods. Mahfouz's award of the Nobel Prize in 1988 revived the controversy over *Children of the Alley*, which the Swedish Academy mentioned in its citation. The controversy coincided with the Salman Rushdie affair, which erupted the following year, earning Mahfouz his own fatwa, from the extremist cleric Omar Abd al-Rahman. Acting on that fatwa, a young fanatic stabbed the eighty-two-year-old Mahfouz in the neck, on 14 October 1994. Mahfouz survived, but the damaged nerves of his right arm and hand left him unable to write for more than a few minutes a day, even after several years of physical therapy. His last major work, أصداء السيرة الذاتية (Asdaʾ al-sira al-dhatiyya; *Echoes of an Autobiography*), was published in 1994, followed a decade later by أحلام فترة النقاهة (2004; Ahlam fatrat al-naqahah; *The Dreams*).

Memoirs, Interviews, and Articles

Besides the highly condensed and aphoristic *Echoes of an Autobiography* and *The Dreams*, some of Mahfouz's novels are believed to be autobiographical, notably *Mirrors* and حكايات حارتنا (Hakayat haretna; *Fountain and Tomb*). *Naguib Mahfouz at Sidi Gaber: Reflections of a Nobel Laureate, 1994–2001: From Conversations with Mohamed Salmawy* offers fascinating insights into Mahfouz's views on a wide range of topics. Mahfouz also gave hundreds of interviews on politics, society, and literature throughout his life, some of which have been collected in Arabic. The most notable among those collections are أتحدث إليكم (Atahaddath ilaykum; "I Speak to You"), edited by Sabri Hafiz in 1977, and نجيب محفوظ يتذكر (1980; Naguib Mahfouz yatadhakkar; "Naguib Mahfouz Remembers"), based on interviews given to the novelist and disciple Gamal al-Ghitani, who edited the volume, in which Mahfouz speaks about his early life, literary influences, family, daily habits, and so on. In 2006, al-Ghitani published another volume based on interviews, which was translated into English as *The Mahfouz Dialogs* (2007). In the wake of the Nobel Prize, Mahfouz gave countless interviews to the foreign press that are widely available, many in English-language publications, although they have not been collected.

Following his retirement from the civil service in the 1970s, Mahfouz contributed a weekly column to Cairo's daily newspaper, *Al-Ahram*. Many of those articles have been collected and classified thematically in nine volumes: حول الدين والديمقراطية (1990; Hawl al-din wa al-dimuqratiyyah; "On Religion and Democracy"), حول الثقافة والتعليم (1990; Hawl al-thaqafah wa al-taʿlim; "On Culture and Education"), حول الشباب والحرية (1990; Hawl al-shabab wa al-hurriyyah; "On Youth and Freedom"), 1996) حول العلم العمل; Hawl al-ʿilm wa al-ʿamal; "On Knowledge and Work"), حول التدين والتطرف (1996; Hawl al-tadayyun wa al-tatarruf; "On Religiosity and Extremism"), حول العدل والعدالة (1996; Hawl al-ʿadl wa al-ʿadalah; "On Justice and Fairness"), حول التحرر والتقدم (1996; Hawl al-taharrur wa al-taqaddum; "On Liberation and Progress"), and حول العرب والعروبة (1996; Hawl al-ʿarab wa al-ʿurubah; "On Arabs and Arabness"). When he became unable to write as a result of the attack he suffered in 1994, he dictated his weekly column to Salmawy.

Mahfouz and Cinema

According to Hashim al-Nahhas, an Egyptian film critic, Mahfouz's influence on Egyptian cinema, the largest in the Middle East, is as great as, if not greater than, his influence on modern Egyptian literature. The reasons, in al-Nahhas's judgment, are that, first, Mahfouz was the first Egyptian litterateur to write film scripts, beginning with Salah Abu-Sayf's *The Avenger* (1947) and *The Adventures of ʿAntar and ʿAbla* (1948). Second, Mahfouz wrote scripts for, and saw his own short stories and novels turned into, sixty films by 1988. Of those films, he wrote or collaborated on writing the scripts of about twenty-four, none of which were based on his own works. He refused to adapt his own works, leaving the production of thirty-six films based on his novels and short stories to others, never once interfering with the decisions of directors, producers, and scriptwriters. To illustrate the magnitude of this contribution, al-Nahhas points out that the novelist Ihsan Abd al-Quddus, who did not write film scripts himself, comes in a distant second, with twenty-two films based on his fiction. Third, Mahfouz's films were shot by the most prominent directors in Egypt—Abu-Sayf, Youssef Chahine, Kamal al-Shaykh, ʿAtif Salim, Hussam al-Din Mustafa, Hassan al-Imam, and Hussayn Kamal—and were often among those directors' most successful films. Fourth, Mahfouz's career in the civil service was directly connected to cinema from 1959 until his retirement in 1971: he was the only novelist to be appointed, in turn, director of censorship on cinema, director and chairman of the board of the Cinema Foundation, president of that foundation, then adviser to the minister of culture for cinema affairs (al-Nahhas 15–17). At least ten of Mahfouz's novels have also been adapted for the theater, some more than once, and for television.

Two Mexican films have been based on Mahfouz's novels: Arturo Ripstein's *Principio y fin* (1993; "Beginning and End"), an adaptation of بداية و نهاية (1949; Bidaya wa nihaya; *Beginning and End*) that won fifteen international awards, and Jorge Fons's *El callejón de los milagros* (1995; "The Alley of Miracles"), based on

Midaq Alley (1947), which received forty-nine international awards, making it the most awarded Mexican film ever. Starring Salma Hayek, a Mexican American film star of Lebanese descent, and widely available in the United States under the title *Midaq Alley*, the second film makes an interesting companion to the novel. Both films are set in Mexico City and, while closely following the plots of the novels, adapt the story and characters to their Mexican setting.

Mahfouz in Translation

Roughly two years after Mahfouz won the Nobel Prize, Edward Said reported on an exchange that he had with a prominent New York publisher who had asked him for suggestions of major works of world literature to translate. When Said listed the names of Mahfouz and other Arab novelists among his recommendations, the editor declined to pursue the translation of the Arabic works because, he said, Arabic was "a controversial language" ("Embargoed Literature" 97). This odd explanation prompted Said to describe Arabic literature as "embargoed," a reference to the politicization of Arab culture in the United States as a result of the Arab-Israeli conflict. This politicization has not dwindled, but the embargo has now been lifted, thanks to several factors, including the Nobel award, which drew the world's attention to Mahfouz and to modern Arabic literature in general; the efforts of numerous translators and editors; and the increased interest of the reading public in all things Arab and Islamic in the post-9/11 period.

Before 1988, about a dozen of Mahfouz's novels were available in English and French translations. The Nobel committee based its decision on only six texts: Trevor LeGassick's translation of زقاق المدق (Zuqaq al-midaqq) as *Midaq Alley* (1966), Philippe Vigreux's French translation of the first two volumes of the trilogy as *Impasse des deux palais* (1985; "Cul-de-Sac of Two Palaces") and *Le palais du désir* (1987), Philip Stewart's translation of أولاد حارتنا (Awlad haritna) as *Children of Gebelawi* (1981), and a collection of short stories selected and translated by Akef Abadir and Roger Allen under the title *God's World* (1973). The committee also mentioned ثرثرة فوق النيل (Tharthara fawq al-Nil; *Adrift on the Nile*), which had not yet been translated. In 1972, the American University in Cairo Press, which had already published *Midaq Alley*, signed an agreement with Mahfouz to publish translations of eight more novels: *Miramar* (1978), *The Thief and the Dogs* (1984), أفراح القبة (1984; Afrah al-qubbah; *Wedding Song*), *Autumn Quail* (1985), *The Beginning and the End* (1985), *The Beggar* (1986), حضرة المحترم (1987; Hadrat al-muhtaram; *Respected Sir*), and *The Search* (1987). Roger Allen, whose translation of *Mirrors* had also already been published by Bibliotheca Islamica (1977), reports that the press commissioned a translation of the trilogy during the mid-1970s that was found to be so poor, it was discarded ("Impact" 88). In 1985, the American University in Cairo Press obtained worldwide rights to publish Mahfouz's remaining work in English and control over the rights to their translation into all other languages. Naturally, translation accelerated at a rapid pace after the Nobel award, so that by now almost all of Mahfouz's fiction has become available in English. According to the press Web site, there are currently five hundred editions of Mahfouz in forty languages, and *Midaq Alley* alone appears in thirty editions in fifteen languages (*Naguib Mahfouz*). In the United States, Doubleday (and its imprint Anchor Books) has published editions simultaneous with those of the American University in Cairo Press, while Passeggiata Press has published Stewart's updated version of *Children of Gebelawi* (1997), which is based on his earlier translation but takes account of the numerous variations between the version of the novel serialized in the newspaper *Al-Ahram* in 1959 and the unauthorized version published in Beirut in book form in 1967 (Stewart 37–38). This is the only novel by Mahfouz for which there are two English translations, the other one being Peter Theroux's *Children of the Alley*, published by Anchor Books in 1996. For a discussion of some of the difficulties of translating Mahfouz, see Allen's "The Impact of the Translated Text."

Resources for Teachers

The two volumes of translated interviews mentioned above, Salmawy's *Naguib Mahfouz at Sidi Gaber* and al-Ghitani's *The Mahfouz Dialogs*, offer useful insights into Mahfouz's background and his views on a wide range of topics. His Nobel lecture is also significant in that in it Mahfouz articulates his sense of cultural and civilizational identity in a direct, yet highly nuanced, address to Europe (and the "West"), stressing at once his reproach for the part it has played in the crises of developing nations and his gratitude for the prize ("Nobel Lecture"). Francka Mouloudi's documentary film *Naguib Mahfouz: The Passage of the Century* (1999), which contains excerpts from interviews with Mahfouz and a host of other writers, actors, and students, lends itself well to classroom viewing and discussion. In 2007, Rasheed el-Enany published the only English-language biography of Mahfouz to date, *Naguib Mahfouz: Egypt's Nobel Laureate* (the American University in Cairo Press edition of the book is entitled *Naguib Mahfouz: His Life and Times*).

There is now a large number of academic articles and book-length studies of Mahfouz. Among the most useful overviews of Arabic literature and the Arabic novel are M. M. Badawi's *A Short History of Modern Arabic Literature* (1993), which has a chapter on Mahfouz and other Egyptian novelists; Allen's *The Arabic Literary Heritage* (1998) and *The Arabic Novel* (1995); and Sabry Hafez's *The Genesis of Arabic Narrative Discourse* (1993). Mona Mikhail's *Studies in the Short Fiction of Mahfouz and Idris* focuses on existential themes in the short stories, while Samia Mehrez's *Egyptian Writers between History and Fiction* (1994) treats the relation between the writers and political authority and their role as historians, especially since the 1960s. Several of the essays collected in Michael Beard and Adnan Haydar's *Naguib Mahfouz: From Regional Fame to Global Recognition* (1993) reflect on the significance of the Nobel Prize, and other essays treat the topics of time and place in Mahfouz's fiction, history, politics, gender, dreams, and the reception of Mahfouz by Arab critics. There is also an extract from al-Ghitani's "Naguib Mahfouz Remembers." The most comprehensive study of Mahfouz's fiction remains el-Enany's *Naguib Mahfouz: The Pursuit of Meaning* (1993). Departing from conventional surveys of Mahfouz's work, which divide it into periods duplicating the history of the European novel, el-Enany classifies the novels thematically (e.g., the use of ancient Egypt, the conflict between past and present, time, and disappointments of the 1960s–70s) as well as formally (episodic novels are grouped in one chapter, short stories and plays in another). A chapter is devoted to a detailed study of one novel, *Respected Sir.* Matti Moosa's *The Early Novels of Naguib Mahfouz* (1994) is a detailed study of Mahfouz's first twelve novels, ending with *Children of the Alley* and focusing on social, political, and religious themes. Instead of treating each novel in turn, as most other critics have done, Menahem Milson divides his *Najib Mahfuz: The Novelist-Philosopher of Cairo* (1998) into chapters on Mahfouz's background, recurrent images and themes in his fiction, and the political aspects of his work. Two insightful chapters discuss his deliberative choice of character names. El-Enany's *Naguib Mahfouz: His Life and Times* is an informative and concise biography that would be a useful companion to Mahfouz's works.

Part Two

APPROACHES

Introduction

In awarding the Nobel Prize in Literature to Naguib Mahfouz, the Swedish Academy's Sture Allén noted, "In Arabic literature, the novel is actually a 20th-Century phenomenon, more or less contemporary with Mahfouz. And it was he who, in due course, was to bring it to maturity." It is doubtful that any other writer can claim to have developed an entire genre of literature in his or her own cultural environment.

The Arab literary legacy is an old and rich one, but it is dominated by poetry. In the Middle East today, poets continue to enjoy important social status. The Palestinian poet Mahmoud Darwish used to draw crowds by the thousands to his poetry readings, and the last few years have seen the rise of poetry competitions, à la *American Idol*, airing on several Arabic-language television networks. The novel was not adopted by Arab writers until the late nineteenth century, and its early practitioners did not pen works with any degree of success. Indeed, the novel as a literary genre did not gain popularity in Arabic-speaking countries until Naguib Mahfouz dedicated himself to this genre and carved out a place for it in the Arabic literary canon. Mahfouz himself said, "There was no legacy of the novel [in Arabic] that I could depend on. . . . I arrived on a scene that was nearly empty. It was incumbent on me to discover things and to lay the ground by myself" (qtd. in el-Enany, *Naguib Mahfouz: His Life* 23–24).

It is often difficult for those new to the work of Mahfouz to comprehend the deep and resounding impact he had on Arabic literature. The Nobel Academy's description of his impact may seem like an overstatement, but anyone who has studied Arabic literature knows it to be true: "In Egypt, each new publication [by him] is regarded as a major cultural event and his name is inevitably among the first mentioned in any literary discussion from Gibraltar to the Gulf" (*Naguib Mahfouz: Biography*). Because the last thirty years have seen a deemphasis on the humanities and a decline in the importance of literature in the United States, students may not understand how a modern literary writer can attain the status of a celebrity, as Mahfouz did.

Instructors may also find it helpful to inform their students about various elements of Mahfouz's intellectual and political life. We offer a review of them here but strongly encourage instructors to read further, using the secondary materials cited in part 1 of this volume.

Readers and teachers should consider the ways in which they approach a writer whose life spanned many decades and whose writing encompassed various styles and trends. The coeditors of this volume adhere to the belief that there is no single, simple way to approach the work of Naguib Mahfouz. His career is multifaceted, composed of phases that may seem distinct at times while recurrent at others. Most of all, Mahfouz was also an intellectual whose work demands consideration of cultural, linguistic, religious, philosophical, political, and historical influences. And yet, we understand that someone new to Mahfouz may need grounding in the general themes that are important in considering his oeuvre. Therefore, what follows are some broadly outlined features of his writing that emerge from the essays in this volume.

Place and Identity

As a writer, Mahfouz is inspired by his immediate setting, which is the city of Cairo (al-Qahira, "the victorious"), founded in 969 by the Fatimids and established over the ruins of ancient Egyptian and Roman settlements and the settlements of earlier Islamic dynasties. One of the most overpopulated urban centers in the world (it teems with approximately 18 million people by day), Cairo spans both sides of the Nile River and gives the impression that it is in a constant frenzy of activity. It is not surprising that such a modern city, built on ancient roots and shaped by numerous influences, inspired the writer. Mahfouz was born and lived all his life in Cairo and hardly ever left it. Gamal al-Ghitani writes:

> I have never come across anyone more attached to his place of birth than Naguib Mahfouz. He lived in the Gamaliyya Quarter for the first twelve years of his life and then moved to the ʿAbbasiyya Quarter, but he has always remained drawn to the quarters and the narrow streets of al-Husayn and al-Gamaliyya. He has remained attached to the people he came to know and who came to know him. This place has become the setting for his most important and greatest works.
>
> ("From *Naguib Mahfouz Remembers*" 37)

Mahfouz writes about Cairo (and occasionally about Alexandria, another major Egyptian metropolis) in a highly specific way, using actual streets and place-names. As Caroline Williams points out, "An understanding of the place is thus important for the non-Cairene readers of Naguib Mahfouz's writings" (52). For example, she notes, the "spatial setting" in which Mahfouz's characters move is relatively small and clearly definable (53). Others have asserted that one can track the characters' movements through the various novels on a map of the city. Of course, the pre–World War I Cairo in which Mahfouz was born and spent his youth differs from the Cairo of today. Places and locations have changed; shops, schools, and other buildings have been torn down or replaced with others. So it is important to realize that Mahfouz writes about Cairo in a certain time period. But other issues of time may not be apparent to the reader new to Mahfouz. Williams adds:

> What Mahfouz does not make clear . . . is the temporal environment . . . [which] the foreign reader who has never been to Al-Qahira, never walked the streets of these quarters, and never breathed in its atmosphere of

> continuing time will find difficult to visualize. The foreign reader has to appreciate that, although this area is relatively tiny by the urban limits of today's Cairo, the richest architectural heritage in the Middle East lies within its confines. (54)

There are many features of the Cairene landscape that one sees again and again in Mahfouz's work, such as the *qahwa* ("café") and the *hara* ("alley or street"). Rasheed el-Enany likens the *qahwa* to the British pub, a place for mostly men to hang out and discuss the news of the day: "There is hardly a novel by Mahfouz in which the café does not represent a significant part of the scene, and there are several in which the café is the most important element in the setting" (*Naguib Mahfouz: His Life* 38). Mahfouz says, "For me, the café is the place where I used to meet my closest friends. Later, as a writer, the café became a place to meet other writers and intellectuals. But I also go to the café to be alone, to watch passersby and meditate" (Mahfouz, *Naguib Mahfouz at Sidi Gaber* 53). The *hara* is more of a relic of Mahfouz's childhood, and when it appears, it is usually a rendering of the Gamaliyya Quarter in which he was born. In the writer's youth, the *hara* was an area occupied by a variety of socioeconomic classes (the Mahfouz family itself was of the lower middle class) rather than by the lower classes that occupy it today. For Mahfouz, connecting with the *hara* was a way of connecting with reality, a way of keeping his writing rooted in the lives of everyday people. He said, "It seems to me that [a man of letters] must have a tie with a certain place or a certain object to form a point of departure for his emotions. . . . What really moves me is the *hara* world. . . . It is my favourite world" (el-Enany, *Naguib Mahfouz: The Pursuit* 2).

For Mahfouz, setting is paramount, and writing about Cairo and the *hara* represents Egyptian identity and embodies his nationalist sense. Much has been made of the fact that he rarely left Egypt (he did not even attend the Nobel ceremony in Europe). Egypt served as a well of inspiration for him during his entire writing career, and he often reflected on what it meant to be Egyptian. Of his Egyptian identity, he once wrote:

> In my opinion, our homeland is the source of our identity, something that has nothing to do with race. Egyptians represent an integral culture, formed by races of different civilizations—Arabs, Sudanese, Turks, and Moors, as well as ancient Egyptians. The common denominator has been our homeland, which has made one people of migrants of many races and civilizations, fusing their traits to form our national and cultural identity.
> (*Naguib Mahfouz at Sidi Gaber* 101)

To understand Mahfouz's setting is also to understand what inspired Mahfouz in his everyday environment and what filtered into his writing. As a denizen of Cairo for so many years, he wove into his work the many threads of the city's influence.

Religion and Humanism

Mahfouz was born into a Sunni Muslim family, and by his own accounts, his family was religiously observant. One of the dominant institutions in Cairo is al-Azhar, the mosque and university established by the Fatimids in the late tenth century. Its scholars are the world's foremost authorities on Islamic questions, and its Supreme Council often issues rulings and judgments on these questions. Mahfouz always stepped carefully with al-Azhar and its legal scholars, working with them whenever possible. In 1959, when the serial publication of أولاد حارتنا (Awlad haritna; *Children of the Alley*) outraged many for its depiction of God and the prophets, Mahfouz promised al-Azhar never to allow the manuscript to appear in book format (although it was published outside Egypt without his permission). Later Mahfouz wrote about the controversial novel:

> Ironically, the novel for which I was accused of blasphemy ends with the triumph of faith. . . . *Children of the Alley* was intended as an Islamic novel. I refused to have it published in Egypt until it had the approval of al-Azhar, a refusal that is based on the fact that I am against neither religion nor al-Azhar. (*Naguib Mahfouz at Sidi Gaber* 81)

Finally, shortly before his death in 2006, the novel was published in book form for the first time in Cairo with al-Azhar's consent.

Mahfouz often asserted his belief that one can be an intellectual and a Muslim:

> Islam is a religion that appeals to the intellect: it exalts knowledge, and accords scientists a preeminent place. It has drawn on some of the most humanistic elements of other civilizations, prohibiting discrimination on the basis of color or economic and social status. (110)

It is impossible (and not especially useful) to say that Mahfouz did or did not live as an observant Muslim, but one can say that his writings demonstrate his strong humanist and rationalist sense. Concerned with the human condition, he never allowed his intellect to be constricted by religious dogma. Instead, philosophy was the foundation for most of his work.

He often bemoaned the rise of religious extremism. He grappled with the rise of Islamic fundamentalism more than with orthodox Islam. The Muslim Brotherhood and other hard-line Islamists never appeared positively in his writing. Of course, extremist Muslims made his personal life difficult later. In the 1990s, according to a short essay of his, "An Uninvited Courtship," Islamists waged a short-lived campaign (much as they did against the feminist Egyptian doctor Nawal al-Saadawi) to have Mahfouz forcibly divorced from his wife on the grounds that he was an apostate and therefore could not be married to a Muslim (Mahfouz, *Naguib Mahfouz at Sidi Gaber* 80). The attempted assassination of the elderly writer in 1994 signaled the extent of the anger his writings had roused in those with extremist religious views.

In the middle of his career, Mahfouz seems to have embarked on a study and deliberation of Sufism, a branch of Islam that adopts a mystical approach to the understanding of religion and universal truth. In Sufism, attaining the truth is a lifelong endeavor that requires purification of various sorts and constant focus on the goal. One can imagine that Sufism attracted Mahfouz because it is a process analogous to writing. He said, in a short essay entitled "Sufism and Poetry":

> Aside from the realism with which Western criticism has concerned itself, if there is a spiritual dimension to writing—arising, as it would be, from the Sufi ether in which life in the East is constantly immersed—I am certainly aware of it, yes, but that does not mean that it is intentional or premeditated. In fact, my aim has often been one of pure, unadulterated realism, but the inevitably poetic dramas of life in this part of the world, the poetry inherent to Arabic, and the poetry of the setting come through in spite of me. (*Naguib Mahfouz at Sidi Gaber* 61)

Mahfouz uses Sufi characters in his works to emphasize internal conflicts as well as struggles of characters with their society. El-Enany writes:

> The sufi as a character type with a symbolic role was introduced for the first time in Mahfouz's *The Thief and the Dogs*. . . . In the author's work generally, the sufi character type is used to probe in symbolic terms the role of the absolute in the life of both individual and society.
> (*Naguib Mahfouz: The Pursuit* 163)

Sufi practice varies widely, and in addition Mahfouz filters its influences according to his own creative needs. Nadine Gordimer, in the introduction to Mahfouz's *Echoes of an Autobiography*, notes:

> Faith, no matter what its doctrine, takes on the contours of individual circumstance, experience, and the meditation upon these of the adherent. We therefore may take manifestations of Sufi religious philosophy that are to be discerned in Mahfouz's thinking as more likely to be his own gnosis, original rather than doctrinal. (xv)

The Sufi mystics or sheikhs who appear in his writing often represent an active engagement with society. In one of the short vignettes that appear in *Echoes*, a man requests entrance into the Sufi brotherhood:

> "What propels you toward us?" he asked me.
>
> Without hesitation, I said, "I have all but wearied of the world and wish to flee from it."

> He said distinctly, "Love of the world is the core of our brotherhood and our enemy is flight." (79)

Using Sufism as a theme in his writing may have allowed Mahfouz to focus on the human condition and on the process of understanding one's reality without forcing on himself or his readers any definitive conclusions.

Many readers new to Mahfouz overestimate the influence of Sufism on his life. The frequent inclusion of the short story "Zaabalawi" in American anthologies to the exclusion of his other work contributes to this assumption. Mahfouz did speak broadly about spirituality and its influence on his work, but Mona Mikhail asserts that it is probably the affinity between Sufism and Western existential philosophy that struck a chord with Mahfouz, who graduated from Cairo University with a degree in philosophy. As she states, "Sufism and existentialism place humanity at the center of all things" ("Existential Themes" 81).

Politics

Mahfouz once said, "In all my writing, you will find politics. You may find a story which ignores love, or any other subject, but not politics; it is the very axis of our thinking" (el-Enany, *Naguib Mahfouz: The Pursuit* 22–23).

As a child, Mahfouz was moved, as most young Egyptians were, by the revolution of 1919, the nationalist motivations of which inspired him and shaped his political views. He recounts his impression of watching the demonstrations and public protests that filled the streets of Cairo, as well as the sight of those killed and wounded (4). El-Enany asserts, "For the rest of his life, as his works attest, [Mahfouz] was to remain a child of that golden era of the national struggle and a spiritual follower of the liberal, democratic principles of the Wafd party which inherited the revolution" (4). Indeed, Gordimer states that Mahfouz, when asked later in his life what subject was closest to his heart, replied, "Freedom. Freedom from colonization, freedom from the absolute rule of kings, basic human freedom in the context of society and family. These types of freedom follow one from the other" (xvii).

The influence of the 1919 revolution can be seen in the depiction of colonialism in his work. The legacy of 1919, the ideal of freedom and democracy, caused him to become disillusioned by the revolution of 1952, during which Gamal Abdel-Nasser and his fellow officers overthrew the Egyptian monarchy. Though Mahfouz was sympathetic to the socialist underpinnings of the revolution (he was a firm believer in socialism's benefits) and its core values (e.g., improving the quality of life for the poor, condemning colonialism, giving a voice to the disenfranchised), he did not approve of the manner in which Nasser's regime maintained power. The most resounding dissent he offered was, ironically, his creative silence. He did not write novels for almost five years (the first work he published after this silence was *Children of the Alley*, in 1957), producing film scripts instead. Most of his fiction following that period allegorized the failure of the revolution to turn its principles into reality, to deliver to the people what had been promised, and its transformation into a police state that silenced intellectuals and dissenters.

The critic of Nasser was criticized himself for his support of Anwar Sadat's 1977 visit to Jerusalem and of Sadat's attempts to reach a peace treaty with Israel. Mahfouz was also criticized for defending Salman Rushdie's *Satanic Verses*—only to find himself linked to Rushdie as a blasphemer of Islam.

Controversy and Censorship

Mahfouz had a complicated relation with the political and religious establishment in Egypt. His reputation as the preeminent Arab novelist grew steadily from the late 1940s on, and his influence on later novelists has been enormous. He won many important literary awards in Egypt, beginning with his second novel and culminating with the Egyptian State Prize in 1957. The Nobel award in 1988 confirmed, on a world scale, the stature that he had already reached in Egypt and the rest of the Arab world. Even so, Mahfouz became controversial on several occasions. His works were banned in most Arab countries after he supported President Sadat's conclusion of the Camp David Accords with Israel in the late 1970s. Film producers deleted his name from the credits for fear of diminishing the distribution of their films in the Arab world. The ban was lifted after Mahfouz won the Nobel Prize. By that time, too, Egypt was welcomed back into the Arab League, from which it had been expelled for a decade.

On several occasions Mahfouz had a brush with authority. In 1946, he published القاهرة الجديدة (Al-Qahirah al-jadidah; *New Cairo*), the story of a government employee who prostitutes his wife to curry favor with his superiors. Coincidentally, a scandal involving high-ranking officials at the time of publication exposed Mahfouz to suspicion. He was called in for questioning but cleared (Mehrez 20). A more threatening incident occurred following the publication of ثرثرة فوق النيل (1966; Tharthara fawq al-Nil; *Adrift on the Nile*), which exposed Mahfouz to the anger of President Nasser and Vice-President ʿAbd al-Hakim ʿAmir. The novel depicts a group of men and women from a cross-section of society who regularly meet in a boathouse on the Nile to indulge in sex, drugs, and drunkenness—an escapist response to their existential sense of futility in a demoralized and bleak social environment. Under the influence of narcotics, they engage in rambling conversations about politics and in scathing criticism of the opportunism and rampant corruption among high government officials. At one point, a hallucinating character invokes an ancient Egyptian sage who sings a warning song to the pharaoh and accuses him of turning a blind eye to the misdeeds of his subordinates. The significance of this was not lost on Nasser, and ʿAmir is reported to have threatened to punish Mahfouz. However, as Mahfouz recounts, Nasser asked Tharwat ʿUkasha, minister of culture, his opinion of the book. ʿUkasha said to Nasser, "Mr. President, I tell you frankly that if art is not allowed this kind of freedom, it will not be art." Nasser replied, "Very well, consider the matter closed" (Mehrez 27). The novel proved to be an uncanny prediction of Egypt's 1967 defeat in the war with Israel, after which the regime's tolerance for criticism became minimal and censorship was imposed. In 1969, Nasser visited the offices of the semiofficial daily *Al-Ahram,* of which Muhammad Hasanayn Haykal, Nasser's close friend, was in charge and where Mahfouz himself was employed. Nasser joked about putting both Haykal and Mahfouz in prison.

It was not until after Nasser's death, in 1970, that Mahfouz could treat, in الحب تحت المطر (1973; Al-hubb tahat al matar; *Love in the Rain*) and الكرنك (1974; Al-Karnak; *Karnak*), thorny issues like repression by the state security apparatus; the torture of political detainees; and the general demoralization, apathy, and distrust of the regime. Nevertheless, an entire battlefront scene set in the 1967 war was censored when *Love in the Rain,* which had first been serialized in the newspaper *Al-Shabab,* was about to be published in book form. Mahfouz was tempted to withdraw the novel from publication, but the publisher threatened to charge him the printing costs, which Mahfouz could not afford. He laments that "the published novel was like a single-winged bird since we do not see the draftee [on the battlefront] to understand the reason for his anger" (Shukri, "Naguib Mahfouz" 55; our trans.).

The greatest controversy of all was occasioned by the serialized publication of *Children of the Alley* (1959), a philosophical and political allegory modeled on the Qurʾanic stories of the Fall, Moses, Jesus, and Muhammad. It concludes with the advent of the age of modern science and the death of God. The setting, however, is an alley near the Muqattam Hills at the eastern outskirts of Cairo, and the time of narration spans several generations in an unspecified, semimythic past. The story itself is about the conflict among the descendants of the mysterious God-figure Gabalawi over control of his وقف (*waqf*; "family endowment"), which often falls in the hands of rapacious فتوات (*futuwwat*; "strong-arm men"). Thus the spiritual history of humankind is brought to bear on the history of Egypt and its rulers from the beginning of time to the present.

The novel was first serialized in *Al-Ahram* under the editorial leadership of Haykal. Mahfouz said that the novel was the result of his intense reflection on the new situation after the coup led by Nasser in 1952, adding:

> I have always been sincere in my writing. There have never been any circumstances that made me lie to myself or to my readers. There were, however, circumstances when, in order to express my ideas, I had to employ subterfuges of which literature . . . has always availed itself, such as symbol and allegory. (qtd. in Jacquemont 283; our trans.)

In another interview, Mahfouz said:

> I started to feel that there were many faults and mistakes that worried me, actions of terrorism, torture and imprisonment. . . . [In the novel] I asked

> the men of the Revolution, do you want to follow the road of the prophets or the road of the *futuwwat*? The story of the prophets is the artistic frame, but the purpose of it was to criticize the Revolution and the prevailing social order. (qtd. in Stagh 162)

The use of allegory was a successful strategy to avoid censorship: the regime took no notice of the political significance of the book. But the religious establishment, represented by al-Azhar, began to attack it even before its serialization was completed, on the grounds that it blasphemed against the sacred history of the prophets. Haykal suggested to Nasser that the book be examined by a committee of al-Azhar sheikhs, who decided that the book should be banned. Mahfouz recounts:

> [S]everal petitions were sent to al-Azhar as soon as the novel appeared. For the first time the sheikhs of al-Azhar had to read a novel. And one must remember that the work was considered highly innovative even among the intellectual circles of the time. So the sheikhs cannot be blamed for their interpretation. The petitions had made reference to the Prophet Muhammad, and accordingly the sheikhs condemned the work as blasphemous and demanded that it be banned. (qtd. in Mehrez 21–22)

Interestingly, Mahfouz at that time was the director of censorship on art media—that is, cinema, theater, sound recordings, and so on. His office was in the same building as that of Hassan Sabri al-Khuli, who was the chief censor on print publications and hence Mahfouz's colleague. Al-Khuli came to Mahfouz and said, "We do not want a fight with al-Azhar. We will ban the book itself and anything written about it. But if you want to publish it outside Egypt you may do so." Mahfouz said that he "considered this a reasonable solution given the attacks on the book" (Mehrez 22). The matter was concluded without legal or adminstrative action. By then, however, the entire novel had been published in *Al-Ahram*, despite protests from al-Azhar, but Mahfouz refrained from publishing it in book form abroad out of respect for the decision by al-Azhar and the protection of Haykal and the state. As Samia Mehrez puts it, "[P]atronage shielded Mahfouz, and in turn he agreed to compromise rather than opt for an open confrontation with religious authorities" (22). In 1967, however, the novel, slightly expurgated, was published in book form in Beirut without Mahfouz's consent and became readily available on the black market in Egypt. The government turned a blind eye.

The matter was almost forgotten until the Swedish Academy announced that the novel was among the works it reviewed before reaching the decision to award Mahfouz the 1988 Nobel Prize in Literature. Attacks on Mahfouz were renewed, but this time they were made by the fundamentalists, not al-Azhar, which remained quiet. Several Egyptian intellectuals asked President Mubarak to lift the ban on the novel, but he declared that it had never been officially banned in the first place. When that became known, the daily *Al-Masa'* began to serialize the novel once more without Mahfouz's permission. It stopped publication at his request. Another newspaper, *Al-Ahali*, published the entire novel (also without his consent) in a special issue, which sold out in a few hours.

Matters became more complicated a few months later with Khomeini's fatwa condemning Rushdie's *The Satanic Verses.* Both Rushdie and the fundamentalists linked the two books, and Sheikh Omar ʿAbd al-Rahman, who was later to be convicted for his role in the 1993 World Trade Center bombing in New York, issued the following statement:

> Salman Rushdie has wronged Islam. He has wronged the wives of the Prophet and has abused the Qur'an. In doing this he found appreciation in the West. From an Islamic point of view, Salman Rushdie, like Naguib Mahfouz, is an apostate. Anyone who wrongs Islam is an apostate and the religious jurisdiction in this case is that they repent. If they do not repent, they must be killed, since the Prophet himself said, "Kill him who changes his religion." Accordingly, Khomeini's *fatwa* is correct. Salman Rushdie must be killed. Had this sentence been passed on Naguib Mahfouz when he wrote *Children of the Alley,* it would have served as a lesson to be heeded by Salman Rushdie. (qtd. in Mehrez 24)

Muhammad Sayyid Tantawi, mufti of the republic, responded to this fatwa:

> I am totally opposed to this *fatwa*, for it cannot have been decreed by a sane human being. . . . Mr. Naguib Mahfouz is an important literary figure. Should he do wrong, we must question him. But should he do right we must thank him.

Mahfouz commented:

> The Mufti of al-Azhar has responded to the *fatwa* of my death. This is the Islamic point of view. But the fundamentalists do not want to listen. And in the West they ignore what the mufti has said, and they use what has been said by the fundamentalists in order to abuse Islam. (25)

As to the association made between him and Rushdie, Mahfouz issued the following statement in *Al-Ahram*:

> I have condemned Khomeini's fatwa to kill [Salman Rusdie] as a breach of international relations and as an assault on Islam as we know it in the area of apostasy. I believe that the wrong done by Khomeini towards Islam and the Muslims is no less than that done by the author himself. As regards freedom of expression, I have said that it must be considered sacred and that thought can only be corrected by counter-thought. During the debate

> I supported the boycott of the book as a means of maintaining social peace, on condition that such a decision not be used as a pretext to constrain thought. Indeed, I even supported al-Azhar's request to ban *Awlad haritna* so long as the sheikhs have not changed their position concerning the book. I assured my interlocutor that my book contained nothing injurious to any religion or prophet and that to associate it with Rushdie's book is a grave mistake. I still have great hopes to convince those opposed to my book of its true signification. (qtd. in Mehrez 23–24)

The affair culminated with the attempt on Mahfouz's life by a follower of Abd al-Rahman; the assailant was apprehended, tried, and sentenced to death. In 2006, a few months before Mahfouz's death, the novel was finally published in book form in Egypt, with al-Azhar's approval.

A Final Word

The task of presenting Mahfouz's work to a classroom of American students may seem daunting to an instructor. How does one even begin to approach the work of so prolific an author, a novelist whose name and career are synonymous with the evolution of the Arab novel itself? Whether one is presenting a single story in the context of a world literature survey class or developing an entire course on Mahfouz, we hope that the essays of this volume will provide readers with the resources needed to envision and plan their courses.

Waïl Hassan opens the section "Contexts" by offering a framework for planning an entire course devoted to Mahfouz. The other contributors deal with the issues that permeate one or many of Mahfouz's texts. Michelle Hartman describes an approach that recenters the text as the focus of analysis; she reminds instructors of Mahfouz to be careful of relying on those few works that have been traditionally taught; they should include lesser-known works in their curriculum. Terri DeYoung gives the historical context of the 1919 revolution in Egypt and shows how it affected Mahfouz and other intellectuals of his generation as well as the complex ways in which it is portrayed in his work. Shaden Tageldin discusses the writer's literary influence and the lessons learned about Mahfouz's styles and themes through teaching بين القصرين (Bayn al-qasrayn; *Palace Walk*). Nouri Gana explores Mahfouz's vision of the failures of the Arab leftist intellectual after the 1952 revolution. Justin St. Clair contextualizes one of Mahfouz's lesser-known works and offers ways for instructors to approach it with their students.

The section "Teaching Specific Texts" contains essays that provide in-depth ways to present some of the most popular of Mahfouz's works, such as the novel زقاق المدق (Zuqaq al-midaqq; *Midaq Alley*) and the short story زعبلاوي (Zaʿbalawi; "Zaabalawi"), as well as examine significant elements in them. Barbara Harlow explores one of the most famous characters of *Midaq Alley* and how that character's hopes and ambitions reflect those of Egypt after World War II. Also using *Midaq Alley* as her focus, Maysa Hayward examines approaches to the nuances inherent in teaching works in translation, especially regarding language and cultural differences. Nabil Matar describes the controversy surrounding Mahfouz's *Children of the Alley*; he also examines Mahfouz's theological influences in creating the novel's characters, specifically the portrayal of Christ. Roger Allen offers instructors a conceptualization of the various ways in which they could approach teaching "Zaabalawi" in an American classroom. Michael Beard tackles the same short story, tracing the arc of its plot and offering instructors a helpful analysis of the allusion made to a twelfth-century Sufi poet. Elliott Colla considers the possible influence of William Faulkner on Mahfouz, especially on Mahfouz's experimentation with multiple perspectives. Hala Halim, in her discussion of ميرامار (Miramar; *Miramar*), focuses on the novel's "emphatic appeal to pluralism" and on how it represents a critique of the Nasserite period.

CONTEXTS

Teaching a Seminar on Mahfouz

Waïl S. Hassan

If Naguib Mahfouz was not responsible for establishing the Arabic novel as a literary form, he was the one who transformed it, almost single-handedly, from its hesitant beginnings into the preeminent genre it has become in modern Arabic literature. Over the course of seven decades, he published more than fifty novels and short story collections, many of which are landmarks in modern Arabic fiction, in addition to seven volumes of articles, several more of interviews, and twenty film scripts. In world literature at large, few writers have dominated a genre for such a long period of their country's literary history. A major-authors course on Mahfouz, therefore, needs no justification. In the fall of 2006, I taught such a course to some twenty-five seniors and graduate students enrolled in the Program in Comparative and World Literature and the Department of English at the University of Illinois, Urbana. The course was cross-listed between the program and the department and had both graduate and undergraduate designations. This essay outlines the literary-critical and pedagogical choices I made in designing the course.

At the initial phase of conception and planning, what had appeared as the generous space of an entire semester devoted to one writer quickly became cramped as I began to consider the design of the course and the selection of texts. How would the course be structured? Which eight or nine texts would I choose? What should be the basis for the selection? There were, of course, many possibilities. Taking courses on Shakespeare's tragedies or histories as models, one could concentrate on a subgenre like realism. In Mahfouz's case, this choice would be periodizing, since the critical consensus is that his realistic phase began with القاهرة الجديدة (1945; al-Qahirah al-jadidah; *New Cairo*) and culminated with السكرية

(1957; al-Sukkariyya; *Sugar Street*), the third part of the trilogy. Alternatively, one could use Stefan Meyer's designation of the Arabic novel in the second half of the twentieth century as experimental to examine Mahfouz's postrealistic work. Both choices would allow a more in-depth approach than a broad survey but also assume a certain familiarity on the part of the students not only with Mahfouz's work but also with the Arabic novelistic tradition in general. Indeed, similar courses are offered on a regular basis in Arabic literature departments in the Arab world (I myself attended such a course on the early Mahfouz, read in Arabic, at the American University in Cairo in the late 1980s). The course I was to offer, however, was intended for advanced undergraduate and MA-level students who were interested in reading what from their curricular perspectives were noncanonical texts by a "world literature," "Third World," or "postcolonial" writer new to them. Indeed, as it turned out, some of the students who registered for the course heard of Mahfouz for the first time from my course description, and only one of them had any familiarity with the language.

Under the circumstances, therefore, a survey seemed to be the appropriate approach. It would permit an overview of Mahfouz's career as well as of the history of Egypt in the twentieth century—an added benefit for students who knew little about the country or the Arab world in general. I wanted the course also to be an occasion for interrogating the construct of world literature in the United States, the politics of translation and international reception, and the mechanisms by which a writer like Mahfouz was included in anthologies and curricula. These were admittedly ambitious goals for a course that aimed at introducing students to an unknown writer from an unfamiliar culture, but the challenge was worth taking. Because of his exceptionally long and varied career, Mahfouz's work has often been divided into periods. Since I was to do a survey of his work, I quickly realized that the course could be structured in such a way as to interrogate rather than confirm the standard periodization of his lengthy career. Specifically, I wanted to explore with the students the ways in which Mahfouz's opus has been interpreted not so much in terms of how it reflects—thematically and formally—modern Egyptian history as in a framework derived from another tradition, that of the European novel. The course would expose that process and recontextualize Mahfouz's work in relation to the actual cultural, historical, and political conditions of its production, the conditions under which his craft developed.

Needless to say, the survey model raises a host of questions. A survey of any kind depends on a more or less accepted taxonomy. To survey anything, one must be able to divide it up according to some principle of classification. Surveys of national literary traditions tend to be divided chronologically into periods that reflect what are considered to be major trends or movements. Texts and authors are distributed under headings such as "Renaissance," "Enlightenment," "Romanticism," and so forth—or left out altogether if they do not seem to fit under an appropriate rubric or participate in a "major trend." In addition to formalistic and thematic criteria, gender, class, national origin, language, and ideology can play a role in determining the canonical status of an author or text. Critical scrutiny over the past several decades has demystified many of the power dynamics involved in canon formation in national literary traditions. In surveys of world literature, the balance of global power is often reflected in Eurocentric taxonomy and disproportionate distribution of space and time among literary traditions around the world (Hassan, "World Literature").

Writers like Mahfouz or Wole Soyinka enter into world literature anthologies in overdetermined ways, one of which is the award of a Nobel Prize. The Swedish Academy bestowed on Mahfouz literature's highest award in 1988 on the basis of no more than seven works that were available to the selection committee in English or French translation. In its sixth edition of 1992, and for the first time, *The Norton Anthology of World Masterpieces* included a short story by Mahfouz, زعبلاوي (Zaʿbalawi; "Zaabalawi"). The story has since been a fixture in editions of the Norton and in almost every other anthology of world literature published in the United States. In the aftermath of the Nobel Prize, English translations of Mahfouz began to appear at an increased pace.

Radical recontextualization always occurs when one attempts to read works as part of world literature. Although such reading aspires to a global perspective, it remains tied to the particular location of its production and therefore expresses a particular ideological worldview. Still, the effort to recontextualize often yields unexpected comparative insights. A risk of reading across national contexts is that one assumes the categories of one's own literary history to be universal and thus inadvertently imposes them on works from another tradition. Mahfouz, and Arabic literature in general, has been a victim of such imposition. Terms like *classical*, *neoclassical*, *Romantic*, *symbolist*, and *modernist* have been all too readily applied to Arabic poetry (DeYoung 159), while the stages of the Western European novelistic tradition—romance, realism, naturalism, modernism, and postmodernism—have often been applied to Mahfouz and other Arab novelists. In his 1983 preface to the English translation of Halim Barakat's عودة الطائر إلى البحر (ʿAwdat al-taʾir ila al-bahr; *Days of Dust*), Edward Said stated, "The Arabic novel in its history and development redistributes, or disperses, the conditions under which the Western European novel has existed" ("*Reflections*" 42). However, in a review first published in a 1988 issue of the *London Review of Books*, he wrote that Mahfouz's "work from the late 1930s on compresses the history of the European novel into a relatively short span of time. He is thus not only a Hugo and a Dickens, but also a Galsworthy, a Mann, Zola, and Jules Romain" (318). In 2000, Said reiterated the same idea: "Mahfouz . . . provid[es] in his novels a kind of history of the novel form, from historical fiction to the romance, saga, and picaresque tale, followed by work in realist, modernist, naturalist, symbolist, and absurdist modes" ("Cruelty" 46). In the first statement, Said asserts the specificity of Arabic literary history, as one would expect, but in the last two he echoes a widely held view among Mahfouz scholars that the Arabic novel repeats the history of its European counterpart.

This inconsistency is symptomatic of a broader tendency that is perhaps substantiated by Mahfouz's own account of how he became acquainted with the novel through John Drinkwater's *The Outline of Literature* and of how he proceeded systematically to read all the major novels mentioned in that literary history (el-Enany, *Naguib Mahfouz: The Pursuit* 16–20). Rasheed el-Enany writes:

> When [Mahfouz] started writing his realistic novels in the 1940s he was well aware that realism was already a spent force in Europe, . . . [but] he felt that since the novel was still a nascent form in Arabic without an established tradition in realism, he could not move straight away from romanticism to modernism: the Arabic novel and his own experience as a novelist in the making had to go through the *natural stages of evolution*.
>
> (18; emphasis added)

This strange formulation assumes, first, that the novel is a purely European form, having no antecedents in Japan or China (Murasaki Shikibu's *The Tale of Genji* and Cao Xueqin's *The Story of the Stone* [aka *The Dream of the Red Chamber*] are two well-known examples) or in ancient Greece, Rome, and possibly even Egypt, as Margaret Anne Doody argues in *The True Story of the Novel*. Second, it assumes that the history of the European novel in the past two centuries follows the only possible or "natural" course of development for the genre. Third, it assumes that therefore for the novel to flourish in non-European contexts, it must go through the same phases that it underwent in Europe, must relive or repeat European history, because skipping a "natural stage of evolution" would lead to something abnormal, a mutation, and not simply a new configuration of the genre in a different historical and cultural context. Roger Allen identifies the problem when he asks rhetorically, "Is the fate of the Arabic novel . . . (and by extension those of other non-Western / Third World cultures) to play a continuous and eventually unsuccessful game of 'catch-up' with the various subdivisions of the Western novel?" ("Literary History" 207). This is, of course, the literary-historical version of Eurocentric social theory.

Mahfouz was at one point interpellated by this ideology, as were many of his critics, but he eventually rejected it. For instance, when he was taken to task by Egyptian critics for writing in the realist mode, his response was quite revealing:

> As for the history of my style, it is related to my personal experience. I choose my style, or my style chooses me, according to the particular situation. . . . I remember that I wrote *Midaq Alley* the way I wrote it, though I had read Joyce, Kafka and Proust. Criticism was directed at me by Professors Badr al-Dib and Yusuf al-Sharidni, that I was writing in the style of the nineteenth century, but I found the courage to write *The Trilogy* in the same style because I felt that it was the style appropriate to the experience I was presenting. . . . After that, my feeling changed and I was no longer

> interested in the individual as an individual, possessed of particular characteristics in a particular time and place.
>
> (qtd. in Beard and Haydar, "Mapping" 5)

In a similar vein, he said, this time with reference to modernist techniques:

> The internal monologue is a method, a vision and a way of life; and even though I use it, you cannot say that I belong to its school as such. All that happens is that I sometimes encounter a Joycean moment in my hero's life, so I render it in Joyce's manner with some modification.
>
> (qtd. in el-Enany, *Naguib Mahfouz: The Pursuit* 20)

There were, then, two orientations in Arabic criticism of the novel during the 1930s–50s. Egyptian critics who were concerned that Arabic literature was behind the times preferred to see Mahfouz participate in the contemporary trends of the European novel. Another group of scholars believed that there were natural stages of evolution that the European novel had traversed and that non-European traditions had to follow in the same path. The first group believed that Arab novelists should imitate contemporary European novels; the second group held that Arabic fiction must pass through a period of apprenticeship by imitating nineteenth-century European novels before it could adopt contemporary European models. Both views were Eurocentric, but one wonders how it could have been otherwise at the time: Europe still cast a long military, political, economic, and cultural shadow over the Arab world, and the novel as a genre was still new and unsure of itself in the enormously long tradition of Arabic literature.

Yet Mahfouz speaks of his "courage" to follow his own sense of aesthetic necessity in the face of strong criticism. As el-Enany points out, Mahfouz

> informs us that he owes his training in the realistic school to its later developers rather than early masters: "I got to know realism through contemporary writers like Galsworthy, Aldous Huxley and D. H. Lawrence. After these, I was no longer able to read Dickens. Nor was I able to read Balzac having already read Flaubert and Stendhal."
>
> (*Naguib Mahfouz: The Pursuit* 17)

Moreover, despite his unreserved praise for William Shakespeare, Fyodor Dostoevsky, Guy de Maupassant, Marcel Proust, Herman Melville, Joseph Conrad, Rabindranath Tagore, and Hafiz, Mahfouz does not hesitate to criticize major writers he dislikes:

> *Ulysses* was a terrible novel. . . . As for Chekhov's theater, I found it flaccid and boring. . . . Out of Hemingway's work I only liked *The Old Man and the Sea*. His other work left me surprised at the fame he has acquired. I did not like Faulkner; he is too complicated. . . . *Le nouveau roman* is rubbish.

> It is as if you were saying, "life is boring therefore I will write for you an equally boring novel." The fact is that any expression of the boredom of life must be entertaining. (17)

Such statements reveal not so much a felt need to imitate the European novel in its various stages of development as a discerning and highly pragmatic assessment of its achievements and a determination to master its various modes. Mahfouz would not, therefore, abandon realism until he had exhausted its possibilities in the trilogy (19).

Even so, as many critics have noted, that work contains several Proustian and Joycean moments in which modernist techniques, like stream of consciousness, interrupt conventional narration—for example, the recounting of the death of Fahmy or Amina's thoughts after the death of her husband (*Cairo Trilogy*, chs. 70 and 153). (Note that whereas Mahfouz uses no typographic markers to set the interior monologues apart from the rest of the narration, the English translation encloses them in quotation marks, thus making less subtle the shift in narrative mode.) Here, Bergsonian notions of time that characterize modernist fiction intrude on chronological time. Even so, temporality, which Mahfouz himself emphasized in numerous statements, saying that time was the main character of his fiction, is not necessarily the most defining characteristic of his work: space is at least as important. As Said argues, "After Lukacs and Proust, we have become so accustomed to thinking of the novel's plot and structure as constituted mainly by temporality that we have overlooked the function of space, geography, and location" (*Culture* 84).

If space, geography, and location are always decisive coordinates in the literature of empire, whether explicitly, as in Conrad, or implicitly, as in Jane Austen, they play an even more central role in the work of postcolonial writers. The trilogy's three parts are given Cairene street names as titles, and the plot is structured around specific locations in the city. The narrative goes from the three residences of the ʿAbd al-Jawwad family in the lower-middle-class district of al-Gamaliyya to the upper-class district of al-ʿAbbasiyya, and it follows a major demonstration against the British from al-Azhar district to Ramses Square, then to Nubar Street and on to Ezbekiya Garden. In a specifically postcolonial chronotope, space and geography interrupt the seeming timelessness of the ʿAbd al-Jawwad family routine: British troops camp outside the family residence in Palace Walk and monopolize the entertainment district to the frustration of the patriarch, whose lifestyle comes to an abrupt end with the death of his son in a political demonstration. In brief, even while consciously writing in European narrative modes of realism and modernism and modulating the shifts in one of the major elements of the European novel, temporality, Mahfouz was nevertheless writing unmistakably postcolonial fiction that necessarily departed from his models in ways even he may not have been fully aware of at the time of composition.

Late in his career, in 1980, Mahfouz spoke of the development of his conception of the novel:

> When I started writing novels, I used to think that the European form of the novel was sacred. But as you grow older, your outlook changes; you want to free yourself from all that has been imposed on you, albeit in a natural and spontaneous way, and not just to break the rules and be different. You find yourself searching for [a certain] tune deep down, inside yourself. . . . As if you were saying to yourself: "Those forms which they [the Europeans] wrote in—were they not artistic molds that they created? Why can't I create a mold of my own?" . . . But I must make clear one important point: imitating the old [i.e., older Arabic narrative forms] is no different from imitating the new [i.e., European form]; both are acts of bondage.
> (qtd. in el-Enany, *Naguib Mahfouz: The Pursuit* 130)

The last sentence refers to his experimental novels from the 1970s on, in which he turned to earlier narrative forms in the Arabic tradition, such as biography, travel writing, and episodic fiction, models that he transformed to fit present circumstances. Thus his novels, especially late in his career, draw on and rework both European and Arabic forms.

Instead of the Eurocentric thesis of linear development, Gaber Asfour offers a spatial paradigm that allows us to see Mahfouz's fiction as

> contain[ing] within itself different schools and trends, ranging from critical realism to existential realism to socialist realism, and including naturalism, surrealism, and the absurd. It is as if the fictional world of Naguib Mahfouz were a museum exhibiting all the doctrines and trends the novel has known or a laboratory containing all the theories and methodologies known to criticism, starting with historicism and ending with structuralism.
> ("Naguib Mahfouz's Critics" 146)

A museum compresses historical time by juxtaposing objects belonging to different periods in a spatial field of synchronic relations; a museum also embalms those periods represented in it, sealing or bracketing securely in the past the objects it puts on display and the worlds they represent. Similarly, a laboratory contains tools, instruments, and specimens, each the product of a particular process, but all exist synchronically, side by side, ready to be used in a new experiment. In contrast to a museum, a laboratory expands the field of time into the future and toward the discovery of new relations and configurations. Thus to say that Mahfouz's opus is both a museum and a laboratory of the novel implies a relation between it and its European models radically different from what is postulated by the two Eurocentric theses mentioned above. It means, first, that Mahfouz's fiction comes after the end or completion of the tradition it supposedly mimics, and it seals or confines that tradition within itself. In that sense, Mahfouz evidences the death of the European novel, which survives only insofar as it is selectively represented in his work, the museum of the novel. The widespread view, echoed by Mahfouz himself (Mouloudi), that the most innovative novels since the 1960s have been written in Latin America, Africa, the Arab world, India, and Japan and by members of racial and ethnic minorities in the United States and Europe, lends support to that argument. By virtue of the extraordinary quantity and variety of his output, Mahfouz can be said to exemplify the non-European novel's superseding of the great European tradition.

Second, as laboratory, Mahfouz's work draws on the full spectrum of modes, strategies, and techniques that were developed in Europe and that Mahfouz had at his disposal from the beginning of his career. His use of modernist techniques in his early historical and realistic fiction demonstrates this view. He learned to use those techniques in what appeared to be straightforward imitations of European fiction, then experimented with them in new and sometimes unexpected ways once he felt confident of his mastery of the craft. It is therefore arguable that Mahfouz's career falls into only two stages, apprenticeship and innovation, although this division is hardly a useful way either to interpret or to assess the significance of individual works.

At any rate, this way of approaching the problem of periodization can help explain the formally innovative ways in which Mahfouz wrote novels after the trilogy, including the politicoreligious allegory أولاد حارتنا (1959; Awlad haritna; *Children of the Alley*); his reworking into novels of older Arabic narratives like الف ليلة و ليلة (Alf layla wa layla; *The Thousand and One Nights*) and تحفة النظار في غرائب الأمصار وعجائب الأسفار (Tuhfat al-nudhar fi ghara'ib al-amsar wa ʿaja'ib al-asfar; *The Travels of Ibn Battuta*), his return to pharaonic themes four decades after the end of the historical fiction phase in العائش في الحقيقة (Al ʿa'ish fi al-haqiqah; *Dweller in Truth*) and أمام العرش (Amam al-ʿarsh; *Before the Throne*); and his unusual autobiographical works, المرايا (Al-maraya; *Mirrors*), أصداء السيرة الذاتية (Asda' al-sira al-dhatiyya; *Echoes of an Autobiography*), and أحلام فترة النقاهة (Ahlam fatrat al-naqahah; *The Dreams*). The Arabic and the pharaonic are, of course, the two civilizations he claims as his own in his Nobel acceptance speech ("Nobel Lecture"). It is as if he had completed, over forty years of fiction writing, his own literary "migration to the North" (to use Tayeb Salih's iconic metaphor) and returned home to rediscover the Arabic narrative tradition and to reinvent the genre of the novel. El-Enany summarizes a 1987 interview in which Mahfouz speaks of his earlier belief that

> modern (European) civilization was the only viable one by dint of its assimilation of all past civilizations—Egyptian, Mesopotamian, Greek, Roman and Arab; and that as such it ought to be the universal civilization of mankind. More recently, he goes on to say, he came to believe that different civilizations upheld essentially different world views. He feels this has caused his enthusiasm for Western civilization to shift towards an enthusiasm for a universal human need such as science, which in turn can be used in the service of the world view of one's own culture. Mahfouz concludes by describing his present position as an eclectic one which seeks to benefit from the entire human legacy.
>
> (*Naguib Mahfouz: The Pursuit* 22)

It is noteworthy that Mahfouz's new interest in the entire human legacy remains limited by his intellectual formation, which, as Mahfouz came to realize, was deeply Eurocentric. There is no mention, for instance, of the civilizations of India, China, and Japan. Their worldviews, or at least their literary productions, do not seem to come within his purview, even at that late point in his career, so this shift in his thinking and the eclecticism it entails remain, as el-Enany argues, more theoretical than discernible in his work (22).

As such, Mahfouz's career encapsulates the history not so much of the European novel as of postcolonial literary consciousness. At the same time, it exhibits the epistemological limitations of that consciousness: from anticolonial resistance paradoxically steeped in colonial culture (historical and realistic novels) to the trials of the nationalist movement and independence (realistic, allegorical, and modernist novels), and from a growing awareness of Eurocentrism as a deep structure and intellectual orientation to the reevaluation of precolonial culture and openness to the entire world, including but no longer limited to Europe as a horizon of possibility (experimental novels, later pharaonic novels, and those reworking classical Arabic narratives).

Using the above-cited sources by Mahfouz and his critics to frame a survey course could be a provocative way of questioning the assumptions on which non-Western writers are interpreted and incorporated (or not) into a construct like world literature and of problematizing the standard periodization of Mahfouz's work. Selected reading from each of those periods and a pedagogy based on close reading would allow students to examine in detail textual instances that challenge the Eurocentric thesis, such as the Joycean moments in Mahfouz's historical and realistic novels. Close reading would be framed by historical contextualization and informed by insights from postcolonial theory and Mikhail Bakhtin's theory of the novel, especially regarding the chronotope and the relation between form and ideology. I assigned no additional theoretical readings, because seniors and graduate students in comparative literature and English can be expected to have some familiarity with concepts like discourse, ideology, hegemony, the canon, the chronotope, mimesis, and mimicry. I felt that I could, when necessary, elucidate and elaborate on such concepts in discussion.

The course I taught in the fall of 2006 had the following description:

> This course will focus on the work of Naguib Mahfouz, the major contemporary Egyptian novelist. Mahfouz, whose phenomenally long career spanned the 1930s–2000s, was little known outside of the Middle East until he won the Nobel Prize in 1988. Since then, most of his works have been published in English translation. Edward Said remarked that Mahfouz's career encompasses the history of the European novel: from historical to realist, modernist, and postmodern fiction. Through detailed readings of representative works, we will examine this thesis, at once incisive and symptomatic of the ways in which Mahfouz's work has been received by critics. Topics for discussion will include form and technique in Mahfouz's fiction; the influence on Mahfouz of Arabic literature, including

> the traditions of Islam and *The Thousand and One Nights*, and of European writers like Dickens, Balzac, Tolstoy, and Proust; the problematic of modernity in Arabic thought as reflected in his novels; the history and politics of the Middle East from colonial Egypt in the early twentieth century to the present; the politics of the Nobel Prize; the dynamics of literary and cultural translation; international literary reception; the production of categories such as "Third World," "postcolonial," and "world literature," and the packaging of writers so labeled for consumption in the English-speaking world—all with reference to Mahfouz.

The selected readings were from *Voices from the Other World*, *Thebes at War*, the Cairo Trilogy (read over a six-week period), "Zaabalawi," *The Thief and the Dogs*, *Mirrors*, *Arabian Nights and Days*, and *The Journey of Ibn Fattouma*.

Note that the reading list does not include the single most frequently taught novel by Mahfouz in the United States, *Midaq Alley*, or his most controversial text and the only one of which there are two English translations, *Children of the Alley*. Omission of the first was a strategic choice: if any of my students had read anything by Mahfouz in the past, it was likely to have been *Midaq Alley*, and since the entire trilogy was to occupy six weeks of the course, I did not want to devote more time to realistic novels, especially an early one. As for *Children*, its length and predictable structure did not suit my purposes, and the allegorical mode in which it is written could be discussed in the much more manageable short story "Zabalaawi." Nevertheless, the controversy that surrounded the novel and culminated in an assassin's attempt on Mahfouz's life was brought up in the documentary I showed on the first day of classes and at several other points in the semester. Nor does the syllabus include, for reasons of space, Mahfouz's late pharaonic novels, *Before the Throne* and *Akhenaten: Dweller in Truth*, which hark back to his early historical novels. These early novels are often dismissed by scholars as unaccomplished and preliminary to the major realistic work. The late pharaonic novels complicate the standard linear development of Mahfouz's career, but the point is driven home just as well with the last two "Arabist" novels on the syllabus, which have the added advantage of being more formally innovative.

The syllabus includes the little known, early short stories collected in *Voices from the Other World* as well as *Thebes at War*, the third of Mahfouz's historical novels, rarely taught in the United States but long required reading in Egyptian schools. The trilogy claims the lion's share of the course because it is arguably Mahfouz's most important work, putting on full display the panoramic scope of his sociohistorical vision and his mastery of realistic and modernist techniques. It is an ideal site for discussion of the changes in Egyptian society from the late nineteenth century through the first half of the twentieth as well as pondering the question of periodization. (One student told me that he found the 1,313-page narrative to be "economically written"; for an undergraduate to reach that conclusion was remarkable indeed.) *The Thief and the Dogs* is often described as marking the beginning of Mahfouz's modernist phase because of its heavy use of the stream of consciousness. The novel also announces Mahfouz's disillusionment with the 1952 revolution. The highly unusual *Mirrors*, of which there is still no American edition, comprises fifty-five vignettes of characters from the narrator's life (closely paralleling Mahfouz's own), represents Mahfouz at his most formally inventive, and at the same time signals his turn toward the narrative genres of classical Arabic literature. The last two novels of the course are inspired, as their titles indicate, by *The Arabian Nights* and *The Travels of Ibn Battuta*, the fourteenth-century Moroccan traveler and author of the book familiar to most Arab readers. Together with Mahfouz's late pharaonic novels, they show Mahfouz's career coming full circle, back to drawing on the heritage of the two civilizations from which he claimed descent in his Nobel Prize acceptance speech, with which I opened the course.

There are several important themes in that lecture worth touching on. Mahfouz's deftly controlled tone, which balances gratitude with reproach, pride with humility, philosophical solemnity with delicate irony, and his strategic juxtaposition of different notions of civilization (Lawall, "Naguib Mahfouz" 26–27) are rich entry points into the subject of his place in world literature, the significance of the Nobel Prize, and global power relations as reflected in the processes of canon formation. Encouraging the students to tease out those nuances served, first of all, to immerse them immediately in the complexities of the cultural politics of the prize, inseparable as it is from questions of global power. Second, it introduced them to some of the themes that preoccupied Mahfouz throughout his career: social justice, power, science, and truth. Third, it stressed the importance of close reading in interpreting the speech and as a pedagogical strategy to be followed throughout the semester. Sending the speech out by e-mail (along with the syllabus) to students or directing them to the Nobel Prize Web site, where it is posted together with other useful documents related to the prize, and asking them to read it before coming to class on the first day, makes for a better informed discussion of the speech.

Francka Mouloudi's 1999 film *Naguib Mahfouz: The Passage of the Century* was another effective way of launching the semester. (Since my course was taught as a seminar, with one weekly two-and-a-half-hour meeting, I could, after the usual introductions and explanation of course protocols, discuss Mahfouz's Nobel lecture and show important parts of the film on the same day. This can, of course, be spread out over the first week of the semester if the class meets more than once a week.) The film features too many people talking about Mahfouz—Egyptian students at the American University in Cairo, film and television directors, actors, journalists, and the novelists Gamal al-Ghitani and Yusuf al-Qa'id—and not nearly enough of Mahfouz himself. Nevertheless, the documentary contains a few key scenes in which Mahfouz recounts his discovery of reading as a third- or fourth-grader, his early interest in European novelists, his working habits, the writing of the trilogy, and the misfortunes he suffered every time he won a literary prize. He discusses religious and political freedom, the root causes of terrorism, and the end of Europe's "authority" (سطوة [*satwah*], as he puts it) in the field of the novel (in his view, Jean-Paul Sartre and Albert Camus were the last European greats). The film also touches on a number of important questions that are bound to accompany any discussion of Mahfouz's fiction and that became the subject of several term papers: gender and class relations, patriarchal and political authority, colonialism, historical change, and Cairo as topos.

It is not possible, in the space of this essay, to review the discussion of every story and novel on the syllabus, but I should mention how some of the less-taught texts contributed to the survey of Mahfouz's work. The short stories in *Voices from the Other World* brought up several of the themes that preoccupied Mahfouz throughout his life, thereby showing the unity of his work irrespective of period and narrative mode. The highly unusual "A Voice from the Other World" (1945) is a rare meditation on death, framed by Egyptian mythology and animated by a Sufi ethic of detachment from the material world. Narrated by a scribe who has just died, it expresses Mahfouz's view of the role of the writer as Mahfouz himself would play it throughout his life. "Evil Adored" (1936) and "King Userkaf's Forgiveness" (1938) are simple moral tales that introduce his themes of government, authority, and the abuse of power. "The Mummy Awakens" (1939) is framed by those dialectics of science and faith, rationality and the supernatural, justice and power, idealism and materialism, around which revolve Kamal's philosophical dilemmas in the trilogy. The dialectics also structure several other works, including *Children of the Alley*, "Zabalaawi," *Arabian Nights and Days*, and *The Journey of Ibn Fattouma*. In addition to offering an opportunity for comparison with Hollywood mummy flicks (an anticolonial tale vs. pop orientalism), "The Mummy Awakens" establishes a very concrete relation between Egypt's past and the narrative present when the country suffered from exploitation by both the Turko-Egyptian aristocracy and European colonialism.

Those two objects of criticism merge into the representation of the Hyksos in *Thebes at War*, Mahfouz's version of a national, anticolonial epic. Discussion of that novel benefited greatly from focusing on the novel's epic characteristics, which problematize György Lukács's famous description of the (European) novel as the epic of a world deserted by God: Whose world? Which God? What purpose do the two genres serve in different cultures and times? Students considered the solemnity of the tone, the lofty style Humphrey Davies comments on in his translator's introduction (ix–x), the flatness of the characters, and the unfulfilled love of Ahmose and Amenridis as formal characteristics of the epic genre instead of dismissing them facilely as weaknesses of an early novel (as, for example, el-Enany does [*Naguib Mahfouz: The Pursuit* 40–42], in concert with other critics before him). Investigating form as a correlative to the ideological project proved to be a fruitful way of complicating simple divisions of Mahfouz's work into phases that duplicate the history of the European novel, allowing us instead to consider how Mahfouz manipulates form to fit the purpose at hand.

Sabry Hafez makes a similar point with regard to Mahfouz's switch to realistic fiction during the 1940s, in the context of the rapid changes in Egyptian society during World War II, which necessitated a more immediate access to the present than the historical novel afforded (Introduction x–xi). It was also in response to contemporary circumstances, this time the tight censorship and suppression of criticism of Nasser's regime, that Mahfouz resorted to the allegorical mode in *Children of the Alley*. He intended that work—ironically, given the fallout with the religious establishment in the 1950s and the 1989 fundamentalist fatwa against him that led to the attempt on his life a few years later—as a political rather than religious allegory (el-Enany, *Naguib Mahfouz: The Pursuit* 99–100). "Zaabalawi" was also a politicoreligious allegory. Realism would have been a sure way to incur the wrath of the regime. As Menahem Milson points out, however, Mahfouz hints at the political uses of allegory in times of political repression already in the trilogy (132), which was written before the Nasser era but revised and published in its early years. Political conditions also spurred Mahfouz's turn to existential themes treated in his novels of the 1960s, notably *The Thief and the Dogs*: the alienation of the individual, the confrontation with authority, corruption, and the betrayal of revolutionary ideals. Mahfouz made extensive use of techniques that express alienation: the internal monologue, deemphasis of description, intensification of language, and greater reliance on symbol and imagery (el-Enany, *Naguib Mahfouz: The Pursuit* 101–04).

The defeat of Nasser's regime in the 1967 war with Israel was traumatizing, although many writers had been able to diagnose the social and political conditions leading up to the defeat before it occurred, even if they could not predict its magnitude. The 1970s witnessed great efforts to reexamine the past and reevaluate the Arabic cultural tradition in an attempt to formulate an answer to the question of what went wrong in the project of modernization begun in the nineteenth century. Mahfouz was among the novelists who participated in that examination; others were Halim Barakat, Sonallah Ibrahim, Gamal al-Ghitani, Emile Habibi, Elias Khoury, ʿAbd al-Rahman Munif, Yusuf al-Qaʿid, Tayeb Salih, and Sahar Tawfiq. Those novelists found that they had to reinvent the novel, each in his or her own way, since no established models were suited to the task at hand. Some writers, like al-Ghitani, Mahfouz, and Salih, reinvented the novel by using narrative genres indigenous to the Arabic tradition. Others experimented with different methods of storytelling.

Mahfouz wrote nothing for two years after the 1967 war, then published four collections of short stories between 1969 and 1971. *Mirrors* was the first full-length novel to appear after that, followed in quick succession by realistic novels that were much more explicitly critical of the Nasser era than his allegorical and existentialist works of the late 1950s and the 1960s. The relative freedom of expression that Anwar Sadat allowed in the first few years of his presidency (1970–81) rendered allegorical masking no longer necessary, especially when it came to criticizing the regime of his predecessor. *Mirrors* belongs to a group of Mahfouz's works that el-Enany distinguishes by their episodic structure and connects them, for that reason, to a long tradition of Arabic narratives that begins in the eighth century. That tradition includes كليلة و دمنة (Kalila wa Dimna; "Kalila and Dimna"), the animal fables that Ibn al-Muqaffaʿ translated into Arabic from the Persian translation of the Sanskrit *Panchatantra*; *The Thousand and One Nights*, with its stories of Chinese, Indian, Persian, and Arabic origin; the popular Arabic *siras* or epics of ʿAntara and Bani Hilal; and the *maqamat* of al-Hamadhani and al-Hariri, adventure narratives that appeared in the tenth century and are believed to have influenced the development of Spanish picaresque narratives later on (el-Enany, *Naguib Mahfouz: The Pursuit* 128). El-Enany puts *Children of the Alley*, *Arabian Nights and Days*, and *The Journey of Ibn Fattouma*, among others, in this group of works that have no European precedent.

But even in this constellation, *Mirrors* is a highly unusual text. It has no main plot other than the narrator's recollections of friends and acquaintances, who constitute a panorama of Egyptian society in the twentieth century. The fifty-five character sketches or vignettes of people Mahfouz has known from early childhood and at every stage of his life are mirrors not only of himself but also of Egyptian society over a period of more than half a century of rapid and turbulent transformations.[1] The vignettes are arranged not chronologically or thematically but alphabetically by first name, as is the practice in Arabic, so that, as the translator, Roger Allen (who wisely refrained from rearranging them according to the Latin alphabet), points out, the last vignette in the book is actually the earliest chronologically ("Translator's Introduction" 9). It is as if any other kind of organizational logic is impossible in such a sweeping survey. Other writers have resorted to techniques such as the fragmentation of voice and narration, the disintegration of form, hallucinatory dreams, and the breakdown of language in an effort to express the magnitude of the historical crisis, but Mahfouz, a die-hard rationalist, finds a way to impose order—if only alphabetically—on his material. In so doing, he is in effect applying the organizing principle of classical Arabic biographical dictionaries to the novel (Milson 254), demonstrating (in response to critics who objected that the work was not a novel) that a novel need not be constructed along the lines established in the European tradition of the genre.

In the 1980s, Mahfouz adapted two major Arabic narratives, *The Thousand and One Nights* and *The Travels of Ibn Battuta*. (It was also in the 1980s that he returned to ancient Egypt in *Before the Throne* and *Akhenaten: Dweller in Truth*.) The last two novels taught in the course, *Arabian Nights and Days* and *The Journey of Ibn Fattouma*, expand into the realm of myth the search for new cultural forms begun in *Mirrors*. Both ask the perennial questions that span Mahfouz's career—about the nature of evil, individual responsibility, freedom, science, social justice, corruption, the abuse of power—and also display his penchant for panoramic surveys of Egyptian and human history. *Arabian Nights and Days* contradicts the happily-ever-after ending of *The Thousand and One Nights* by depicting a repentant but despondent Shahrayar, an embittered Shahrazad, and a kingdom ravaged by crime and corruption. Shahrayar's tyrannical rule has created a condition in which the performance of social responsibility is often at odds with the instinct of self-preservation. Weaving together and refashioning selected tales from *The Thousand and One Nights*, Mahfouz turns that work into a modern-day myth in which supernatural elements like jinn, the cap of invisibility, and Solomon's ring become metaphors for the human capacity for good and evil and projections of desires and insecurities.

In *The Journey of Ibn Fattouma*, Mahfouz turns Ibn Battuta's journey across Africa and Asia into a journey through time (el-Enany, *Naguib Mahfouz: The Pursuit* 168). The novel surveys human social history from primitive times to feudalism, capitalism, and communism, and finds them all, along with the "lands of Islam," to be deficient in one way or another. The ending offers no fulfillment, unlike its historical model, in which Ibn Battuta at the conclusion expresses his satisfaction at a life well spent and knowledge attained. Instead, Mahfouz evokes Farid al-Din al-ʿAttar's منطق الطير (Mantiq al-tayr; *The Conference of the Birds*), an allegory of the soul's impossibly difficult journey toward perfect knowledge of its creator, thereby suggesting that humanity's search for the ideal form of social organization and government is far from over. Nevertheless, like the ending of "Zabalaawi," in which the search itself is validated even though its object remains elusive, *The Journey of Ibn Fattouma* ends with Mahfouz's characteristic optimism about humanity's gradual progress toward the distant ideal of social justice.

The remarkable thing about Mahfouz's career—and it bears repeating to students at every point in the semester—is how he constantly mixes, adapts, and transforms elements of the European and Arabic traditions to suit his creative needs at every stage of his country's history in the twentieth century—the only periodization that can do justice to Mahfouz's creative energy and his lifelong preoccupation with the country's cultural and political life. As Stefan Meyer argues:

> [S]tylistic devices can be borrowed or imitated. Instead of judging contemporary Arabic narrative by formal criteria alone, it is crucial also to inquire into the purpose to which formal innovation is employed and the literary precedent to which the writer is responding. (257)

This approach has the advantage of breaking down the facile Eurocentric narrative of Mahfouz's development as a novelist, along with tedious notions of what a novel is and is not, not to mention entirely pointless debates over the properties of "Western" and "non-Western" (another name for "oriental") novels, categories devoid of any analytic valence. Instead, that approach multiplies interpretive possibilities, especially of Mahfouz's rich albeit lesser-known texts. Perhaps most important, it allows us to see the Arabic novel—indeed, the novel in world literature generally—as a dynamic genre with limitless possibilities, constantly changing with the flux of its environment.

NOTES

I wish to thank Elliott Colla, Stephanie M. Hilger, and Nabil Matar for kindly reading and commenting on earlier drafts of this essay.

[1] The American University in Cairo Press edition of the translation includes the highly evocative portraits painted by the Egyptian artist Seif Wanli to accompany the character sketches as they were initially serialized in the Egyptian television magazine; those portraits were not included when the novel was published in book form in Egypt. They made for some fascinating student remarks and a perceptive term paper by a student of art history.

Teaching Mahfouz as World Literature

Michelle Hartman

Developing new approaches to working with Naguib Mahfouz's fiction is challenging, partly because of his canonical status in the Arabic literary pantheon and his standing as the exemplary figure of this canon in North America. In scholarly terms, this status has made Mahfouz a relatively fixed and stable figure. The vast output of criticism on his works since the 1980s has tended not to take many theoretical risks. As Elliott Colla has argued, "with the proliferation of texts that fix the meanings of Mahfouz it has become increasingly difficult for critics to produce new critical interpretations of his work" ("Multiplying"). This scholarly standstill also affects our teaching of his texts—particularly as innovative pedagogy tends to lag behind new theoretical approaches. Moreover, criticism and pedagogy often remain dissociated, especially when we teach texts removed from the areas that we engage most in our criticism. It is therefore important to think about how to invigorate our teaching of Mahfouz's texts in the North American classroom. This essay proposes how the framework of world literature can help in such a task.

World literature is a particularly well-suited approach to working with the fiction of Naguib Mahfouz, who is the most widely known and broadly disseminated Arab author outside the Arab world. At its best, world literature offers us a mode of reading that brings diverse literary texts together, makes connections between works in different ways, attends to aspects of literature often passed over or ignored, and expands our thinking about texts beyond national and linguistic borders. Reading and teaching Mahfouz in this framework allow us both to broaden our understanding of his works and to suggest some ways in which engaging with such texts can help modify the concept of world literature itself. To sketch out how this framework enhances approaches to Mahfouz in Arabic- and English-language classrooms in North America, I draw on my experience teaching graduate and undergraduate courses in Arabic and English in Canada, the United States, and Great Britain. One major issue resulting from the different emphases of teaching Mahfouz in the original Arabic and in English translation is the problematic separation of form and content. This dissociation is particularly damaging to the study of Arabic literature. Though it is difficult to teach about both form and content in translation, I argue that the concept of world literature can address some of these problems. David Damrosch's articulation of world literature is especially useful in this context; I build on and modify that articulation by integrating it with the concept of resistant translation.

With this modified world literature framework, I address two sets of problems related to teaching Mahfouz in North America and suggest specific ways in which it can help generate new approaches and pedagogical practices. I discuss the crucial question of form in teaching Mahfouz, exploring the tension between works considered world literature and works remaining national, labels that either sideline or highlight the formal and stylistic specificities of Mahfouz's fiction. Finally I consider the representation of women and gender relations in the Arab world—a question of content especially relevant to teaching in North America. I propose ways in which a world literature framework can enhance gendered readings of Mahfouz.

Mahfouz in Arabic- and English-Language Classrooms

The contrast between how Mahfouz's fiction is taught in Arabic- and English-language classrooms in North American universities accents both the possibilities and problems of the world literature framework. Instructors should formulate ways to bridge the gap between how and what we are likely to teach in courses where his works are read and discussed in Arabic and how and what we are likely to teach where they are read in translation and discussed in English. Differences in these classroom experiences point to the different expectations in the two languages of the work an Arabic novel is meant to do.

The foremost reason for the gap is the difference between reading the original text and reading a translation. One does not have to fetishize original texts to understand that the journey Mahfouz's novels have made from Arabic into English has changed them drastically. It can be difficult to teach the stylistic and formal features of Arabic novels when working with English translations, and it is all the more difficult to explain linguistic elements of these texts to students who do not know Arabic. Moreover, even those of us who know Arabic might consider it daunting to read and prepare two versions of a Mahfouz novel in the same semester. So then, what are our options if we wish to deal with language, style, and form while teaching Mahfouz in English translation? Is there a way to bring the kinds of issues commonly discussed in an Arabic-language course on Mahfouz's novels into an English-language classroom?

To begin with, it is clear that classrooms operating in Arabic and classrooms operating in English concentrate on different things. North American university courses that read Mahfouz's works in Arabic, even courses offered at the advanced level, are almost always focused on teaching the Arabic language. Where the language of instruction, reading, and discussion is English and students do not have the additional challenge of functioning in a second language, a more complex and sophisticated level of analysis of and discussion about the texts is likely.

The length of the works by Mahfouz included on the syllabus of an Arabic-language as opposed to an English-language course is the most obvious and most easily quantifiable difference between the courses. A class taught in Arabic will be more likely to use a shorter text whereas one using an English translation usually can accommodate a longer text, because of students' linguistic abilities. Often, of course, there is simply not enough time in a semester to read long works in any language, particularly in literature courses that assign many novels. These kinds of constraints and differences in classrooms should not be criticized per se. However, on the basis of my experience teaching both types of courses, I have found that the differences in texts used in Arabic- and English-language courses run deeper than these simple constraints. Even if it is not intended, the difference in approach and attitude to texts in the Arabic original and English translation is profound.

There is an ideological issue embedded in the seemingly innocuous matter of the length of the text. Two novels that I have taught in Arabic in university courses, for example, are among Mahfouz's shorter works: اللص و الكلاب (Al-liss wa'l-kilab; *The Thief and the Dogs*) and ليالي الف ليلة (Layali alf layla; *Arabian Nights and Days*). I have also used both works in courses teaching Mahfouz in English translation. In more cases, however, I—like most of my colleagues, I would guess—have selected different works. I have included the popular ثلاثية القاهرة (Thulathiyyat al-Qahira; *The Cairo Trilogy*) a number of times in several courses that I taught in English, sometimes teaching only the first work, بين القصرين (Bayn al-qasrayn; *Palace Walk*), and at other times all three volumes. Like many colleagues, in particular those who use Mahfouz's works in Middle East history courses (Leeke), I have also taught زقاق المدق (Zuqaq al-midaqq; *Midaq Alley*) in translation several times.

Aside from length, though perhaps linked to it, the differences between these works are notable. *The Cairo Trilogy* and *Midaq Alley* fit into the problematic but widely used category of Mahfouz's realistic fiction, for which he is renowned in the English-speaking world. The *Thief* and *Arabian Nights*, like many of his other shorter works, fall into other categories: existential, surrealist, magical realist, or experimental fiction. This simple example indicates a trend prevalent in teaching Mahfouz in North American universities. Mahfouz's longer novels are less likely to be taught in an Arabic-language course because of time constraints, but choosing shorter texts also dovetails with the greater attention in Arabic courses paid to stylistics and language. Such courses, because they teach language, are often willing to spend more time on formal features considered literary.

How we treat content and form in teaching Mahfouz boils down to ideology. The concerns that we focus on in our teaching are closely linked to the kinds of texts that we teach. This is a two-way process: the books we teach set the agenda of what we will discuss, but we also choose novels that illustrate the kinds of content that we are most interested in discussing. The content of our courses is where this difference is located. Many of us who teach Mahfouz in a course designed for students whose main academic interest is not Arabic literature per se—courses labeled "Third World literature," "world literature," "Arabic literature in translation," "postcolonial literature," or any course fulfilling a general non-Western requirement—know that despite our intentions, we usually end up spending a good deal of time teaching context. Thus, in teaching *Palace Walk*, we might devote considerable attention to the historical framework of the novel, to a specific issue like the meanings of head scarves, gender relations in contemporary Egypt, or to laws and customs related to divorce for Muslims. Linking texts to such issues is not wrong, nor am I asserting that we should divorce literary texts from their sociopolitical milieu. I merely note that expectations of students and exigencies of teaching in translation bring this phenomenon to light most starkly.

Students who have achieved a level of language sufficient to read a Mahfouz novel in the original will usually have less interest in discussing such topics. They also will be more likely to possess some relevant contextual and background knowledge related to Mahfouz's fiction. They are therefore more easily guided into a discussion of the formal, literary elements of the novel, a discussion in which most teachers of literature are eager to engage, rarely having this opportunity in their classes that teach Arabic literature in translation. I have found in my courses taught in Arabic that, although students seem initially to lack the linguistic skills to converse about literary texts in the formal Arabic that such classes require, when given the opportunity, they manage to express ideas as sophisticated as those in most of the discussions we have in my courses taught in English. The kinds of analyses they generate often have a subtlety and nuance unexpected at their level of language.

World Literature and Resistant Translation

Though working with original texts rather than translations does in some ways make teaching Mahfouz easier, I am neither idealizing teaching him in Arabic nor disparaging teaching him in English translation. Rather, I suggest a world literature approach, which can be useful to both, though here I focus on teaching in English. Because of its consciously inclusionary global perspective, world literature is a concept that can encompass the study of Arabic literary texts and allow us to read them alongside works of other traditions. But Arabic literature has rarely been so encompassed. The configuration of the world in the twenty-first century demands a greater engagement with the Arab world, an engagement that includes its creative production, its art and literature. As the exemplary figure of the Arabic literary tradition whose works have traveled throughout the world, Mahfouz is an ideal location to launch an exploration of how world literature as a framework can add to the understanding of his Arabic-language texts. Reading Mahfouz in this framework allows us to consider how his texts engage with other Arabic and non-Arabic texts and how they might transform our thinking about world literature itself.

In *What Is World Literature?*, Damrosch's compelling conceptualization of world literature is articulated in three parts. World literature is, first, texts that are an elliptical refraction of national literatures; second, texts that gain in translation. Third, world literature is a mode of reading—rather than a canon of texts—in which readers engage works beyond their own place and time (281).

Damrosch uses the metaphor of "elliptical refraction" in the first part of his definition to describe a double process at work in viewing literature through the space created between the host and source cultures of a traveling text (281). He suggests that world literature does not simply transcend the national to become world but is able to express itself well on both sides of the tension between the two. The second part of Damrosch's definition, translation, I explore in detail below. The third part encourages us not to produce a list of books that qualify as world literature but to think about a kind of reading that propels us out of the zones of place and time with which we are most familiar.

All three parts of Damrosch's definition speak to Mahfouz's literary contributions. How Mahfouz's texts negotiate the national is the subject of much critical attention. Reading texts beyond a canon easily applies to Mahfouz, though his works are often appropriated as examples of a canon. But it is in the second part of Damrosch's definition where Mahfouz's works truly excel: they have taken on new lives outside their culture of origin. *The Cairo Trilogy*, for example, epitomizes a work that began locally, first published serially in the Egyptian newspaper *Al-Ahram*; gained regional popularity; and achieved global fame after Mahfouz won the Nobel Prize (Beard and Haydar, "Mapping" 1–2).

Gaining in translation or traveling well from Arabic to English is not a neutral matter, however. Damrosch recognizes that a translation is not simply a mirror of the original text: "To use translations means to accept the reality that texts come to us mediated by existing frameworks of reception and interpretation" (295). But his articulation of world literature remains limited and limiting without the additional, explicit contextualization of global inequalities that affect literature as much as other forms of production. Resistant translation is a productive way to tackle this problem.

Resistant translation can mean many different things when applied to Arabic literature translated into English. Here I draw on Lawrence Venuti's use of the concept as a dissident cultural politics (20, 306), which speaks directly to some of the most problematic issues involved when texts move from Arabic into English, where global inequalities affect the translation process. A translation can resist assimilation into a target culture in many ways, and a translator's or reader's explicit work of creating or locating this resistance can help the process. To Venuti, this resistance "seeks to restrain the ethnocentric violence of translation"; he proposes that translation of literary texts can be used as a cultural intervention in unequal exchange (20), such as that between center and periphery. Understanding resistant translation can help make world literature a useful framework of analysis for reading Mahfouz.

Building on Venuti's work, Issa J. Boullata uses the specific history of colonialism and orientalism in the region, showing how they have influenced translation from Arabic to English. Taking Venuti's argument in a different direction, Marilyn Booth, a critic and literary translator, asks if it is ethical to focus on difference and resistance when the mainstream political-cultural milieu of the twenty-first-century United States demonizes Arab and Muslim peoples and cultures, showing them as irreconcilably different (50). Booth's question is pertinent to teaching practice: concrete realities should not be sacrificed to an appealing theoretical approach. Even so, there is a place in the classroom for resistance as a cultural intervention. A world literature approach easily incorporates the fiction of Mahfouz, but resistance prompts us to question how and why some of his works are so easily assimilated. A discussion about assimilation and resistance sheds valuable light on the texts themselves and also on the traffic of literary works between the Arab world and North America. If North American parameters set the agenda for world literature, adding resistance to that agenda as a term of analysis will aid us in developing useful new approaches to Mahfouz and elucidate some of the inequalities that, despite our efforts, are often reproduced in our classrooms.

What does it means when a work gains or loses in translation? To evaluate gaining and losing, we must think about the relation between a translation and the text on which it is based. A translation should be read as a work of literature connected to the original text but should also have a life outside it. The challenge is to discuss a translated novel by Mahfouz as an artistic creation in its own right while also giving some idea about how the original text works in Mahfouz's oeuvre as well as in Arabic literary traditions and cultures more generally. We must think not merely about the accuracy of translations but also about the ways in which they convey language, style, form, and voice.

The notion of a literary work's gaining or losing in translation cannot be separated from the global inequalities between center and periphery. Poetry, for example, is a genre deemed more important in the Arabic literary tradition than the novel, which is usually seen as imported into the Arab world from Europe. Arabic literature courses in the Arab world place poetry at the center. But as Mahfouz's popularity attests, the works that have traveled most successfully from Arabic into English are novels. This raises the questions, Are Arabic novels world literature whereas Arabic poetry is not? Is there such a thing as a world genre? Does Arabic poetry's not gaining in translation make it merely national or local? How do we judge a gain or loss in translation?

A similar process is at work in how some of Mahfouz's works are privileged over others in English translation. *The Cairo Trilogy* has received much more attention than his other works, and *Midaq Alley* is taught in courses every year across North America (Leeke). This is because prose that falls into the category of realistic fiction (Hassan sees this category as problematic ["'Littérature mondiale'"]) is taught more consistently and is better received in English. Works most appreciated in English that "gain in translation," to use Damrosch's formulation, are those that match most easily and assimilate to certain North American norms and expectations about literary production.

Texts that "gain in translation" and are deemed accessible to a North American readership more easily meet the definition of world literature. I am expressing Damsrosch's formulation rather sharply here to link it to the history of how the question of accessibility has affected Arabic literature in North America. Phrasing the issue in these terms recalls Edward Said's experience of being told that Arabic was too controversial a language to translate into English in the 1980s—as a response to his suggestion that Mahfouz's works be published in English ("Embargoed Literature" 97). Too controversial, too different, too inaccessible—these are the ways in which Arabic literature has been marginalized in the global circulation of literary works, largely centered in the North American marketplace.

Because of his extensive and varied oeuvre, Mahfouz exemplifies this issue well. Though he is primarily a novelist, many of his works are formally and stylistically experimental. He experimented with the genre particularly after 1967. رحلة ابن فطومة (Rihlat ibn Fattouma; *The Journey of Ibn Fattouma*) and *Arabian Nights and Days*, for example, cross generic lines through their intertextual links to classical Arabic travel literature: Ibn Battuta's travels in the former and the oral storytelling tradition of the *One Thousand and One Nights* in the latter. A text like المرايا (Al-maraya; *Mirrors*) is experimental in that chronology is altered through the arrangement of chapters. أحلام فترة النقاهة (2004; Ahlam fatrat al-naqahah; *The Dreams*) consists of a series of short narrative vignettes describing real or fantastic flights of the imagination that are only loosely connected. Another example of experimentation is Mahfouz's recent autobiographical work, أصداء السيرة الذاتية (Asda' al-sira al-dhatiyya; *Echoes of an Autobiography*).

World literature as a framework of analysis also prompts us to evaluate Mahfouz's status as a world author in relation to his individual works as world texts. We should not focus simply on those novels that are most accessible to a North American audience or that allow a non-Arab reader to relate to them immediately on familiar terms. When deciding if a work like *The Journey of Ibn Fattouma* or *Arabian Nights and Days* gains in translation, therefore, we should keep in mind the principles of resistant translation. These two texts play off earlier Arabic forms in creating modern novels; they do not shape themselves according to a European or international model of the novel. That a work consciously resists certain literary norms of the center should not remove it from consideration as a world text.

Damrosch's articulation of world literature unintentionally reproduces the major problems with traditional comparative literature approaches to Arabic literary texts. The underlying logic of the world literature framework once again places Western literary values at its center. "The world" here is North America and Europe; texts considered world literature are expected to assimilate their unspoken literary norms.

Damrosch does attempt to address this paradox by adding a third term of analysis, stating that world literature should not be a set group of texts but a mode of reading that demands a detached engagement with works "beyond our own place and time" (281). Unfortunately he puts the responsibility for this engagement less on readers and more on texts. He sees readers filling in gaps in literary texts "imaginatively and productively," because "literary meaning gains its full resonance when it is completed according to the reader's individual imagination and circumstances" (292–93). Readers are allowed the freedom of interpretation but not challenged to expand their imaginations and circumstances: they must use their preexistent ideas to fill in missing elements of a text.

Damrosch does suggest that some cultural knowledge is useful for reading world texts but states that world literature will need relatively little of this, compared with literature that "remains national." Rather, he sees world literature interacting "in a charged field defined by a fluid and multiple set of possibilities of juxtaposition and combination: 'intercourse in every direction,' in Marx and Engels's apt phrase" (300). His description is indeed useful for engaging Mahfouz's texts outside the narrow parochialism of Arabic literary studies. Reading Mahfouz in these "charged fields" is an enriching exercise: his works open themselves up in multiple ways to such suggestive frames of analysis. For example, *The Thief and the Dogs* could be taught in relation to its Egyptian historical background, to social relations inflected by class and gender, to crime fiction, to surrealistic works, to other texts that deal with modern underground cultures, and so on. *Arabian Nights and Days* not only is an allegory for contemporary Egypt, including the rise of Islamist movements and government repression, but also retells the *One Thousand and One Nights* in compelling ways, recasting many of its most famous stories. Note that Damrosch called the original *Nights* one of the world's few "irreducibly multinational" works (283). The possible intertextual referents span time, place, and language. The charged fields this text engages allow us to gain from Mahfouz's works—and not only from the most famous of them—in ways that reach well beyond a national categorization.

But Arabic fiction in North America interacts in problematic ways with these charged fields. Twenty-first-century configurations of power are such that the United States wields not only economic and political power in the Middle East but also has established a linguistic and cultural presence not easily ignored. These "zones of translation" between the United States and the Middle East are potent and loaded today as much as ever (Apter 3–4). North American university students do not exist outside this global inequality of power. Suggesting that they should bring works into their frame of reference rather than adopt a new frame reproduces a system of analysis where the terms of the discussion are set by the dominant. Advocating that readers develop their own individual imaginative frameworks of literary analysis for Arabic fiction, therefore, is less appealing in practice than in theory. When Damrosch suggests that some works are not limited to national concerns and are able to become world literature, his intention is to free works from their traditional categories. But because North America, particularly the United States, is a global power, this vision of world literature is difficult to implement in practice. Works that travel most easily into a center of power tend to be those that are familiar in some way—generically, stylistically, or in terms of content. They will therefore represent only part of the "rest of the world" in "world literature," as Mahfouz is only a part of Arabic literature.

Female Characters and Gendered Readings of Naguib Mahfouz as World Literature

The charged fields in which Arabic literature circulates in North America are especially evident in issues related to women and gender in the Arab world. Teaching Mahfouz's fiction while privileging gender as a category of analysis works well in a modified world literature framework. His *Palace Walk* is one place to begin, as the roles of women in it offer interesting points to contemplate: there are many female characters, relationships between men and women are complex, and numerous passages lend themselves readily to a gendered analysis.

Palace Walk opens and closes with Amina Abd al-Jawad's perspective. The cloistered wife of the authoritarian Ahmad Abd al-Jawad, Amina is long-suffering and stifled though not completely unhappy in this role—she can imagine no other. Discussing Amina as a character will inevitably lead to a conversation about women's oppression in Arab society. She is the stereotype of a passive Arab Muslim woman trapped by her traditional society. Many other female characters in the novel, however, are less submissive than Amina and provide a counterbalance to her. The diversity of experiences of women in *Palace Walk* points to their different situations, classes, and educational backgrounds. How female and male characters build their relationships in gendered ways is crucial to understanding the dynamics of social life in the novel. The novel may also be considered the portrait of a bourgeois world in decline at the end of the war, a world not representative of all Arab Muslim men and women or of life in today's Cairo. How the characters perform their genders changes with the passage of time, and people of different class backgrounds have more or less freedom in expressing themselves in gendered ways. The text's omniscient third-person narrator can reinforce stereotypes about Arab women who lack agency, are confined at home, and are victims of their male relatives, just as it tends to underline the fact that men have control over public life, over the flow of information, and over the very lives of these women.

A persistent question in teaching this novel in relation to gender roles is whether Mahfouz wrote it as a critique or an implicit sanctioning of the hierarchy embedded in the patriarchal family structure. An analysis of how the expression of gender allows characters more or less mobility in the family or society and how they navigate gendered hierarchies can challenge simplistic readings of the novel as men oppressing women. Students in my classes have engaged in heated debates over this issue, bringing in textual evidence from the work's style, narrative, and characterization to support their arguments. In my experience, however, students have their preconceived ideas about patriarchy and gender-based oppression in the Arab world reinforced rather than challenged after reading *Palace Walk*.

Palace Walk has certainly gained in English translation. Typical reader comments show that people from many different backgrounds feel that they can make sense of it or relate to it in some way. Responses to the novel in my classes prove it to be the kind of work that Damrosch has in mind in his definition of world texts. Its realism is no doubt one reason. *The Cairo Trilogy* is often labeled realistic, particularly when Mahfouz's works are grouped by category (Colla, "Multiplying"; el-Enany, *Naguib Mahfouz: The Pursuit* 71; Hassan, "Littérature"). The omniscient narrator leads the reader through a series of quotidian events in the lives of the Abd al-Jawad family, told in straightforward chronology. The feelings, actions, and emotions of the main characters mirror historical events. If we label *Palace Walk* a realistic work in the classroom, however, we are then also implying a great deal more about life in Egypt. Works about the Middle East, even imaginative fiction, tend to be read as documentary ethnography, and treating a novel as realistic reinforces this tendency. Students will think that the relationships between the female and male characters represent how real Arab, Muslim, or Egyptian women and men live and interact. Students may find that the novel supports the stereotyped images of women and men from the region that fill mainstream media and culture.

This does not mean that we should not teach *Palace Walk* or other Arabic literary texts that have passive and submissive female characters and domineering and oppressive male characters. But we might try to think about how Arabic literary texts also resist dominant, gendered stereotypes. We might not label certain novels realistic but consider other ways of presenting them to students—for example, *Palace Walk* as allegorical. Though it is not allegorical in the same way that أولاد حارتنا (Awlad haritna; *Children of the Alley*) is, this comparison could provide another avenue of discussion.

Another strategy is to turn the discussion of gender in a different direction. The practice of translation could be considered, examples of the use of language in the original text and how certain elements have or have not been preserved in the translation. The speech of different characters could be analyzed: how Amina and the servant Umm Hanafi speak differently, how Amina and Ahmad speak differently. Bringing gender and class together to discuss language can lead to discussion of Mahfouz's complex engagement with these issues. Classroom discussions about the register or level of Arabic employed for different characters of different genders, class, and status can be very successful, whether or not students have any Arabic-language background. The translation of *Palace Walk* does not offer many points of entry for this approach, but those of us who know Arabic can provide examples from the original as a way of resisting this text's tendency to assimilate easily into a novel that presents a domesticated translation to the North American reader.

Yet another possibility is to add another text by Mahfouz to a class in which *Palace Walk* is taught. *Children of the Alley* is an obvious suggestion, as it speaks to many of the same issues. *Arabian Nights and Days* is a very different kind of allegorical tale but also takes on issues that affect Egyptian society and has a number of female characters who are represented in different ways. Its frame story makes particularly interesting intertextual use of the character Shahrazad from *One Thousand and One Nights*. The novel constructs a frame story that begins where the frame story of the *Nights* ends: Shahrazad learns that she is to be saved and not put to death by Shahriyar—he has reformed and changed his ways because of her storytelling. Despite her father's joyful announcing of the news to her, Shahrazad is depressed because she realizes that she is married to a serial murderer and is not sure what her life will be like with this man, now the father of her children. This example is just one of the interesting twists on typical female roles that can be taken up in teaching the text. It certainly provides a contrast with Amina. *Arabian Nights and Days* allows for discussion of very different kinds of narrative style and form and of how expectations of characters based on gender roles can be both reinforced and subverted.

The novel is also useful because it is not modeled on the European genre. It breaks the mold of realism. The clear intertextual reference to *One Thousand and One Nights*, a work drawn from oral storytelling traditions, opens up different avenues of discussion. Situating Mahfouz in Arabic narrative traditions, however, need not mean that we must emphasize the national in this text. Rather, the text further suggests his world literature status. Many "charged fields of analysis" are open to *Arabian Nights and Days*. At the same time, it resists some obvious stereotypes about the Arab world, particularly in the roles for women and men and the gendered meanings of these roles. It compels the North American reader to think differently about its characters, as it is a fantastic tale and not one that simply describes customs and traditions, gender roles, or the political situation of Egypt. Together with *Palace Walk*, it can provide a challenging portrait of Mahfouz's art.

World Literature and Implications for Pedagogy

It is easier to point to pedagogical difficulties in teaching Mahfouz as world literature in the North American university classroom than it is to suggest practical solutions to them. My responses to this challenge focus on teaching Mahfouz's texts in English translation, though the general principles will also hold in the Arabic-language classroom. Indeed, it would be a mistake to conceive of ways to think about Mahfouz's works as world literature only when Mahfouz is taught in English translation.

One suggestion outlined here is that we contextualize how Mahfouz has become an exemplary figure of Arabic literature globally and that we offer the reasons for this success. It is particularly important to question what it means to us that his work travels well or gains in translation. It can be a useful pedagogical practice for students to articulate the elements of his work that they find travel well, that speak to them, or that make his work unique. Their observations can be put in the world literature framework, keeping resistance in mind. Students can be asked to think about why Mahfouz works well in translation—both for them as readers and in the larger context of the North American university environment. To put the Mahfouz canonized in North America in dialogue with the Mahfouz of Egypt and the Arab world is another way of employing a world literature approach. It prompts a discussion of how canons are built and maintained across cultures, an issue current in Arabic literary scholarship today. It also bridges the gap between theoretical debate and pedagogical practice.

We should expand the range of works by Mahfouz that we teach in our English-language classrooms, paying particular attention to his shorter and more formally challenging works. This does not mean that we should never teach his realistic fiction or that *Palace Walk* and the other works in *The Cairo Trilogy* are not outstanding teaching texts. Rather, in choosing which works to teach, we should think carefully about applying the label of realism and also about the danger that certain novels can become exemplary of Mahfouz's output. Even though we may challenge the ways in which Mahfouz is lionized as a literary figure, we often then reproduce this pattern with our use of certain works and models that reinforce this type of thinking. We might make a greater effort to teach texts like *Arabian Nights and Days*, *The Journey of Ibn Fattouma*, *The Thief and the Dogs*, and even more adventurous departures from the novel, like the compact narratives contained in *The Dreams*.

If we include some of Mahfouz's shorter and more formally experimental texts in class, we might be better able to explore his literary contributions. In any case, using his extensive oeuvre to contextualize the work or works being taught would be a major step in this direction. It would enable students to see different Mahfouz novels as world literature in different ways. Students could then also ponder what resistancy and assimilation mean in relation to success in literary reception.

A world literature approach to Mahfouz allows students to add their own meanings to the texts and to place other works in dialogue with his novels. It also will encourage them to fill in gaps in their own knowledge. Hopefully, it will push them beyond an appreciation of the difference of works that can appear somewhat exotic to them. Resistance comes into play here—whether in questioning Mahfouz's exemplary status, prompting the reading of different works, or comparing his works with each other. Students reading Mahfouz's fiction are challenged to remove themselves from the center and work from within the textual world or even the author's world. Placing the text at the center is a first step in taking global inequality into account when approaching Arabic fiction in a world literature framework. Thinking beyond our own worlds and narrow national parameters while questioning how we define *global*, particularly when we are reading and teaching at the center, will help us develop new approaches to teaching Mahfouz's fiction in our North American classrooms.

Mahfouz's Novels and the Nation

Terri DeYoung

Naguib Mahfouz consistently characterized himself as a child of the revolution (al-Ghitani, "Naguib Mahfouz Remembers" 52; al-Naqqash, "Naguib Mahfouz" 171)—in his case, the 1919 Egyptian revolution, which began in March when he was seven (he was born in early December, 1911). This event, which led to Egypt's nominal independence from British colonial tutelage in 1922, has been seen by most historians, Egyptian and non-Egyptian, as a watershed in the development of a modern Egyptian national identity. It was certainly the starting point for a new state formation for Egypt, in which the leaders of political parties, the king, and the British competed with one another until 1952 (and the advent of a second, more thoroughgoing revolution) for influence, power, and authority over the resources of the country, through a series of short-lived, shifting tactical alliances that did little to address the nation's needs.

Although the 1919 revolution cannot be defined as a success in conventional terms, its impact on the imagination of Egyptians, especially intellectuals, was lasting. As Mahfouz himself has said (al-Naqqash, "Naguib Mahfouz" 178), it was for his generation the model of a genuinely popular revolution. It was seen as involving all classes, high and low, bringing together the major religious groups in Egypt—Christian and Jewish along with Muslim (Gershoni and Jankowski 43)—as well as women and even schoolchildren in a spontaneous outpouring of support for the small group of political leaders who had been deported as a consequence of their request to go to the Versailles Peace Conference to present Egypt's case for self-determination and independence after World War I.

At the beginning of that war, Britain had unilaterally declared Egypt a protectorate, legally formalizing the occupation of the country it had undertaken in 1882—ostensibly at the invitation of the ruler of Egypt at that time, Khedive Tawfiq—to restore order and protect the financial investments of its nationals, especially those in the Suez Canal, which provided a lifeline between England and its colonies in India. Despite this occupation, Egypt remained juridically a province of the Turkish Ottoman Empire through the last two decades of the nineteenth century and the first of the twentieth. But in 1914, Turkey, as an ally of the Germans, declared war on Britain, and the khedive of the time—ʿAbbas Hilmi II—was known as a Turkophile (in fact, he was visiting Istanbul when hostilities broke out). So the British deposed ʿAbbas, replaced him on the throne with his more compliant uncle, Hussayn Kamil, and took over direct rule of Egypt for the duration of the war.

Two days after the armistice was signed, on 13 November 1918, a delegation (in Arabic, الوفد [*wafd*]) led by Saʿd Zaghlul, who had headed the opposition party in the Legislative Assembly, a largely appointed advisory body to the khedive that had functioned briefly before World War I, visited the British high commissioner to discuss in general terms "the future of Egypt" (al-Sayyid-Marsot 48–49). Commissioner Reginald Wingate put them off, and they in response formed an organization known as al-Wafd al-Misri (the Egyptian Delegation), dedicated to promoting their goals. In the ensuing months, the members of the *wafd* fanned out throughout Egypt, speaking publicly to increasingly large crowds about their cause, which gradually evolved into a demand for "complete independence" (الاستقلال التام; *al-istiqlal al-tamm*). On 9 March 1919, Zaghlul and two other members of the *wafd* were arrested for their activities and deported to Malta. The next day massive public demonstrations began.

The British reaction was an immediate show of force. Demonstrators, including students and women, were fired on. Some were killed and many arrested. British censorship during the period makes it difficult to reconstruct events from contemporary Egyptian sources, although it is possible to assemble both photographic and written documentation (filtered, of course, through the colonizer's perspective) from foreign mass-market periodicals, like the *Illustrated London News*. Perhaps the best description of ensuing developments is by the historian Afaf Lutfi al-Sayyid-Marsot, drawing on reminiscences by her father and uncle, who were leaders in the formation of the *wafd*:

> Students carried the news of the uprising all around the country and strikes and demonstrations broke out in the cities, towns and villages. Railway lines were cut and carriages destroyed to prevent the British forces from putting down the uprising so that in desperation General Bulfin, the acting commander in chief of the Army, issued a warning that any further damage to the railways would cause the nearest villages to be burned in retaliation. But the warning did not stop the population, and railway communications came to a standstill. British army personnel and officials were massacred in the rural areas. (51)

By 6 April, Zaghlul and his comrades were set free and allowed to proceed to the Paris Peace Conference, to make their case for Egyptian independence before the victorious allies.

For Mahfouz, the 1919 revolution was the first revolution that emerged at the instigation of the Egyptian masses in millennia, since pharaonic times. It advocated far-reaching social change, stressing equality of opportunity and democratic rule (which he aligns with the traditional Islamic concept of *shura*, or "consultation," with the governed in the selection of the ruler). This broad popular support—and the spontaneity with which it spread throughout Egypt—differentiated it, in his view, from the 1952 Free Officers' Revolution and even the ʿUrabi Revolution (or Revolt) of 1882, both of which he saw as orchestrated by the military and not, at least not initially, reflective of the aspirations of ordinary Egyptians (al-Ghitani, "Naguib Mahfouz Remembers" 115–16; al-Naqqash, "Naguib Mahfouz" 178). This version of 1919, as consistently enshrined in Mahfouz's interviews and reminiscences, projects an idealized narrative of unity and commitment in the "imagined community"—to use Benedict Anderson's famous phrase—of Egyptians. As Anderson notes, such a strategy would be consistent with modernization in the sense that it deemphasizes hierarchical (God-given) and centripetal notions of social stratification and replaces them with a more horizontal, egalitarian model of society (15). Thus it is no surprise that this Mahfouzian master narrative also depicts the traditionally dispossessed (the poor, whether urban or rural; women; and children) as primary actors and agents on the public stage, yet without the necessity of supplanting or diminishing the role of more traditional authority figures (metonymically represented by Zaghlul, as the father of the nation) who initiated the challenge to British hegemony over the political life of Egypt. The united action of all these groups, and their solidarity, eventually forced the foreign, oppressive outsiders (the British other) to back down and listen to their demands, thus leading to at least a significant moral victory, even if it did not achieve its goal of complete independence.

In addition to his personal reminiscences of 1919 (where he foregrounds his role as an eyewitness), Mahfouz used the events of 1919 as a backdrop in several of his most influential novels, especially those of his realist phase, stretching roughly between the end of World War II and 1957, or between the publication of خان الخليلي (Khan al-Khalili; *Khan al-Khalili*) in 1945 and السكرية (Sukkariyah; *Sugar Street*), the last volume of his trilogy الثلاثية (al-Thulathiyya). In fact, this trilogy can be seen as something of a *locus classicus* for explorations of 1919 in Mahfouz's work. Volume 1, بين القصرين (Bayn al-qasrayn; *Palace Walk*), is most notable in this regard, since it deals directly with the prelude to the revolution, as perceived through the eyes of the ʿAbd al-Jawad family, whose middle son, Fahmy, is killed in one of the 1919 demonstrations. The remaining two volumes deal with the aftermath of the revolution, again through the experiences of the same family.

Other important Mahfouz novels of this period reverberate with echoes of 1919. Although the action of زقاق المدق (Zuqaq al-midaqq; *Midaq Alley*)—probably Mahfouz's most accomplished novel before the trilogy and one that has found its way into several national school curricula throughout the Arab world over the years—takes place during World War II, it includes crucial references to 1919. For example, chapter 19—which sets in motion the train of events that will result in the seduction of the main female character, Hamidah, away from the alley by the pimp Ibrahim Farraj—centers on a political rally that contains many references to events from that period. Most notably, the villain of the work, the café owner Kirsha, is described in this chapter as having "taken an active part in the rebellion of 1919" (129)[1] and as having a picture of the deposed khedive ʿAbbas Hilmi prominently displayed in his place of business (127). These details identify Kirsha as a figure representative of the revolution, but not in the heroic vein one might expect from the mythology of 1919—a fact worth keeping in mind when one considers how Mahfouz treats the subject, so dear to his heart, when he speaks in the first person.

I began teaching Mahfouz's novels in 1988, the year Mahfouz won the Nobel Prize and thus became immediately the most canonical of twentieth-century

Arab literary figures. It was also shortly after Fredric Jameson's famous (or infamous) article "Third-World Literature in the Era of Multinational Capitalism" appeared and was soon followed by Aijaz Ahmad's vigorous and pointed refutation of some of Jameson's central arguments. Throughout the time I have presented Mahfouz's work to students—the course I taught in several iterations is called Nationalism and Colonialism in the Modern Arabic Novel—I found both articles useful as a starting point for discussion about the impact and nature of Mahfouz's work.

Early in his article, Jameson made this provocative statement:

> All third-world texts are necessarily . . . allegorical and in a very specific way: they are to be read as what I will call *national allegories* even when . . . their forms develop out of profoundly western machineries of representation, such as the novel. . . . *[T]he story of the private individual destiny is always an allegory of the embattled situation of the public third-world culture and society.* (69)

Most students react as much to the tone of Jameson's remarks as to their overt content, saying (as Ahmad does in his response) that Jameson's categorization appears to hide an evaluative agenda. His use of the term *allegory* nowadays has an overwhelmingly negative overtone, even among those not versed in literary study. Students also generally agree with Ahmad that Jameson is arbitrary in his supposition that there are only a small number of works—none of which are Third World—making up the proper reservoir of the canon (conflated with another problematic term, "the Western tradition") and therefore being worthy of literary study (9). Jameson draws an analogy between Third World novels and subcanonical (what he also calls pulp format) forms found in the Western tradition. He concludes that neither category offers the same "satisfactions" (65) as acknowledged classics like the novels of Fyodor Dostoevsky or Marcel Proust. Both these assertions arouse objections and sometimes statements of support, equally strident, among some students as they try to come to terms with the differences between Arabic novels and the works with which they are more familiar.

I draw attention to what Jameson also says when he draws such a devastatingly limited view of the non-Western novel:

> We [meaning Western literary critics] have been trained in a deep cultural conviction that the lived experience of our private existences is somehow incommensurable with the abstractions of economic science and political dynamics. Politics in our novels therefore is, according to Stendhal's canonical formulation, a "pistol shot in the middle of a concert." (69)

As he stresses in his answer to Ahmad, Jameson to his credit is trying to problematize and point out the limitations of the American (Western) literary establishment's response to novels from other parts of the world, especially as that response is determined by a modernist aesthetic that claims that politics and social concerns have no part in great literature ("Brief Response" 26). If politics and social concerns intrude, they should be considered as unimportant or extraneous to the work's artistic value. Since this principle of modernism has become increasingly less familiar to my students in the two decades I have been teaching the Arabic novel, my observation now usually generates a rather intense discussion about the cultural determinism and ideological underpinnings of any so-called objective aesthetic criterion for greatness.

While the Jameson-Ahmad articles provide a useful and productive introduction to the debate over politics and Third World literature, I refocus discussion on Mahfouz's novels. I point out to students that his work demonstrably enacts a version of political events—the 1919 revolution—that would seem to qualify for candidacy in Jameson's category of "national allegory." (In the course I now teach, I use *Midaq Alley* for this exercise, because it is both shorter and covers a wider range of topics than the trilogy, but the trilogy could also be employed here.) Obviously, numerous references in Mahfouz's novels—like Jameson's own examples taken from Chinese and Senegalese literatures—cannot be processed and understood without some prior acquaintance with the outlines of the 1919 revolution.

I then draw attention to the fact that in Mahfouz's narratives the revolution is not idealized in the way Mahfouz idealizes it when he speaks in his own voice. Instead, it is deconstructed and depicted in problematic ways, which does not fit Jameson's definition of a national allegory. This aspect of Mahfouz goes with his brilliance in creating complex, nuanced characters and should warn students not to be naive readers, not to assume that the author and his characters have identical viewpoints.

A striking example of Mahfouz's technique can be found in chapter 19 of *Midaq Alley*. Kirsha, the novel's least sympathetic and most hypocritical character, is identified as a participant in the 1919 revolution, but his activities during and after the demonstrations are suspect:

> Kirsha really came to life during political campaigns. In his youth he had distinguished himself in the field of politics. He had taken an active part in the rebellion of 1919 and was reputed to have planned the great fire which destroyed the Jewish Cigarette Trading Co. in Hussain Square. He was one of the heroes in the fierce fighting between the revolutionaries on one side and the Armenians and Jews on the other. When the bloody revolt subsided he had found a new, though restricted outlet for his energies in the subsequent election battles. In the elections of 1924 his work was much appreciated even though it was rumoured that he accepted bribes from the government candidate while supporting the Wafd party. . . . His last contact with politics was in 1936; it was then he decided to divorce politics and wed commerce. Since then he merely observed politics as he

> watched other lucrative markets, and he became the supporter of whoever "paid most." (129–30)

To an uninitiated reader, this passage may indicate only Kirsha's tendency toward violence and corruption. In the universe of the mythology of 1919, however, it signals a reference to the "embattled situation" of a society whose most cherished ideals are enshrined in the narrative of the revolution. Kirsha's activities (and the consistency of them) undermine that narrative, showing it to be built on elisions if not outright lies. Nowhere is this clearer than in his reference to the fighting between the revolutionaries on one side and the Armenians and Jews on the other, which refers to an unprovoked attack in Cairo on these minorities by an unruly crowd that had little allegiance to the ideals of Egyptian unity in pursuing independence. This incident is usually cited as an exception to the remarkable solidarity displayed by all the groups participating in the demonstrations (Gershoni and Jankowski 43). That Mahfouz shows Kirsha's relation to 1919 with such a detail surely means that he wishes us to scrutinize not only the character's tie to those events but also the truthfulness of the master narrative itself. This negative view of the revolution, this questioning of its basic assumptions, is reinforced by the fact that all the characters appearing in the chapter—Hamida, Uncle Kamil, even Sheikh Darwish—disapprove of the political rally, which is a metonym for the revolution as electoral process.

A similar point is made toward the end of *Palace Walk*, when the ʿAbd al-Jawad family's youngest son, Kamal (through whose eyes most of the action in the novel is portrayed), is surrounded by a squad of English soldiers stationed in his neighborhood to keep order during the March demonstrations. Kamal has been happily singing songs to get chocolate. Later, his oldest brother criticizes him:

> Yasin laughed loudly. He remarked, "What a daring boy you are. . . . Weren't you afraid when you were surrounded by their legs?"
>
> "Not at all," Kamal boasted. Then he said with feeling, "How handsome they are! I've never seen anyone more handsome before. Blue eyes . . . golden hair . . . gleaming white skin. They look like Aisha [his older sister]."
>
> He suddenly ran off to the study, where he raised his head to see the picture of Saʿd Zaghlul on the wall next to those of the Khedive Abbas II, Mustafa Kamil, and Muhammad Farid. When he returned he said, "They're a lot better looking than Saʿd Pasha."
>
> Fahmy [Kamal's second brother] shook his head sadly and remarked, "What a traitor you are. . . . They bought you with a piece of chocolate. You're not so young you can be excused for saying that. Pupils in your school are dying as martyrs every day. May God grant you failure. . . ."
>
> Kamal went off by himself and took the chocolate out of his pocket. He began to remove its gleaming red wrapper. Fahmy's attempt to make him feel bad seemed to have been in vain, for in his heart there was nothing but contentment and love. (402–03)

Kamal is a more sympathetic character than Kirsha in *Midaq Alley*. He is a sensitive boy who only wants everyone to be happy and is achingly aware when others are not. Earlier, he tried to please Fahmy, a revolutionary activist, by joining a demonstration and declaring his support for Zaghlul (364). Now his comparison of the English soldiers' appearance with Zaghlul's portrait, which finds Zaghlul wanting, is a dramatic rejection of 1919, whose heroic narrative is recalled by Fahmy's reference to the schoolboys dying as martyrs for the cause. That Kamal is never punished in the novel for his association with the English soldiers suggests again that Mahfouz is not interested in supporting the public, accepted version of these events.[2] Although leaving the principles fundamentally intact, he criticizes their implemenation, problematizes them, holds them up to critical scrutiny, in contrast to what a casual reading of Jameson's article would suggest us to expect. In other words, Mahfouz tends not to portray personal experience as commensurate with the national allegory. He dramatizes the contradictions between personal experience and the idealized vision of human nature found in the story of how the nation came to be. In this, his novels seem to go beyond being the "objectif[ication] of the nation's *composite* nature" that must be resolved into a new collectivity (Brennan 51); in fact, they assert that no such resolution can be accomplished.

I have taught several of Mahfouz's novels in various kinds of courses but now teach them mainly in an upper-division survey course that explores the development of the Arabic novel through two major themes that are of interest to students with majors outside the traditional bounds of literature: nationalism and colonialism. Since students come from a variety of backgrounds, I concentrate on the texts and give extensive citation of background reading in the syllabus. Otherwise the class may devolve into a history lesson. Emphasizing background can interfere with developing fresh perspectives on the material. Often students in the classroom offer new readings of a text that are insightful precisely because the students were not given the blinders imposed by conventional historical narrative.

Because the class I now teach is more focused on the development of the novel as a whole in Arabic, I have found it useful to see Mahfouz's work, especially the early realist novels like *Midaq Alley*, as an intervention in the development of the genre. I move beyond the view that he is simply lamenting the nation's inability to live up to the ideals enshrined in its national allegory; I suggest instead that he is using the novel form to subvert the dominant elements of this allegorical discourse. I discuss the influence of *Midaq Alley* on other novels in Arabic: Ghassan Kanafani's رجال في الشمس (Rijal fi al-shams; *Men in the Sun*) and Al-Tayyib Salih's موسم الهجرة إلى الشمال (Mawsim al-hijrah ila al-shimal; *Season of Migration to the North*), each of which exists in dialectic interdependence with this idea. This more generic view also permits me to place the novel—and Mahfouz's development of it—in juxtaposition with poetry, the indigenous and more historically rooted Arabic literary form. The novel has vigorously competed with poetry for ascendancy in Arabic literature during the last half of the twentieth century.

Mahfouz was the first writer in the Arab world to devote himself to the novel, and his choice has had an incalculable impact on the direction of modern Arabic literature, "engineer[ing] the novel's inception . . . as a major art form and establish[ing] it as an ever-thriving continuity" (Jayyusi 13). It is tempting to see this choice, furthermore, as a rejection of poetry. Poetry in Arabic has always been an overwhelmingly lyric genre, expressive of the point of view of an individual, conveyed by a single voice—a mode that has both advantages and limitations. Lyric poetry can explore a personal voice in great depth, but it is limited to that one voice.

The novel, in contrast, developed historically (and was imported into Arabic) as a genre for interweaving multiple voices, expressing multiple viewpoints in ways that did not necessarily harmonize them in the end into a unified vision of the national experience (despite Jameson's assertion to the contrary regarding Third World novels).

Mahfouz indicated the importance of this aspect of the novel as a form when he explained his choice of fiction over historical writing: "The novel represents [better than a historical work] a panorama of daily life with all its problems and questions and characters. This is a part of history the historians do not write" (al-Naqqash, "Naguib Mahfouz" 57). *Midaq Alley* gives important early evidence of how Mahfouz will pursue this strategy and exploit this possibility in the novel. In this work, little attempt is made to align the various viewpoints expressed by the characters or to privilege one over the other. They simply coexist, bound together only in the spatial plane, the setting of Midaq Alley, anticipating the techniques of the more *Rashomon*-like later works, like ميرامار (1967; Miramar; *Miramar*), أفراح القبة (1981; Afrah al-qubbah; *Wedding Song*), or العائش في الحقيقة (1985; Al-ʿa'ish fi al-haqiqah; *Akhenaten: Dweller in Truth*), which take this trend even farther, "emphasizing the gaps between the perceptions of various observers" (Beard 104).

The importance of Mahfouz's innovation here, how he departed from what was commonly found in Arabic intellectual discourse before, is best illustrated for students by providing a representation that portrays the lineaments of Egyptian national identity in a more integrative fashion. The obvious first choice would be a historical work that treats the period, but unfortunately all such works I've read are problematic. Many accounts of modern Egyptian history are either too brief and schematic or too long. The historian provides either a summary of events acceptable to all readers or a balanced presentation that includes all the actors' points of view—Egyptian, British, contemporary, retrospective—in great detail and with lengthy qualification (e.g., al-Sayyid-Marsot; Gershoni and Jankowski).

When time is a factor in planning a course, I resort to using for the purpose of dramatizing the heroic narrative of 1919 the film version of *Palace Walk* (*Between Two Palaces* [1964]). In its last third or so, this film devotes about half an hour to the March demonstrations, giving in a concentrated montage virtually the entire inventory of popular symbols associated with those events: the collaboration of the students with members of the urban proletariat in leadership roles during the protests, the submersion of difference in a grand scene of religious reconciliation, the indiscriminate slaughter of women and children by the British soldiers. Using this version of *Palace Walk* also allows me to contrast it with the novel's telling of these events, which in places is significantly different.

If time allows, I prefer to contrast Mahfouz's version of 1919 (either in *Midaq Alley* or *Palace Walk*) with an earlier Egyptian novel by a good friend of his, Tawfiq al-Hakim. This novel, عودة الروح (ʿAwdat al-ruh; *Return of the Spirit*), both treats of 1919 and has its own special role in the narrative of the development of Egyptian identity. It was published in 1933 to generally favorable notice, but its fame was firmly consolidated in the Egyptian literary firmament only by the revelation, after 1952, that it had been the favorite book, in his youth, of the new leader of the nation, Jamal ʿAbd al-Nasir (Nasser). Mahfouz too read this novel soon after publication, and it is likely that the novel's themes and ideas had as strong an influence on him at the time as they did on the young Nasser.

Hakim's work is in many ways a classic bildungsroman as well as the first serious literary treatment in Arabic of themes that later become staples of the mythology of 1919. It concerns the maturation during the year preceding 1919 of a wealthy young man from a rural background, Muhsin, who has been sent by his parents to Cairo for his final schooling. In the city, he stays with his Aunt Zanubah and her brothers, who are related to Muhsin's father but of modest means (Muhsin's wealth comes from his mother's side). Muhsin is keenly aware that his money sets him apart from all around him, including his fellow students, though he tries to conceal it (44). Further, all the young men in Zanubah's household have fallen in love with Saniyah, daughter of their next-door neighbor, and Muhsin quickly follows suit. As he falls increasingly under her spell, the rivalry he feels with his uncles and the other members of their social circle increases.

This sense of competition and the resulting social isolation is temporarily moderated at the beginning of the second half of the book, when Muhsin returns to his parents' estate for the mid-year school vacation. In the second-class train compartment on the journey there, he sits with a group of fellow passengers that includes a prosperous gentleman (effendi) who has traveled extensively in Europe. When they all hospitably move over to make room for a new arrival, the gentleman remarks that such courtesy would not be extended on a European train. In the ensuing conversation, the group agrees that Egyptians, while perhaps not so materially prosperous as those from other parts of the world, nevertheless have a way of life superior to Europeans. While most of the group initially attributes this to the fact that they are all Muslims, one of the group, "an enlightened man," gives a more nuanced explanation:

> He . . . began adroitly to emend the statement until he showed those present that the word "Islam" that was current in common Egyptian usage at all levels of society really had no religious or sectarian stamp. Its meaning and import were, rather, the emotion of mercy, a goodness of heart, a union of hearts. These were emotions to be found in Egypt and not in Europe.

> There . . . a dog-eat-dog strife prevailed with emphasis on the personal welfare of the individual. (156)

Although Muhsin does not immediately react to this statement, its implications should resonate with the reader, who has recently seen Muhsin himself and his friends acting in ways that are similar to those being criticized as European.

Shortly thereafter, Muhsin overhears a similarly philosophical conversation at his parents' house, between an Englishman and Frenchman who are their guests. The Englishman is dismissive of Egyptians, calling them ignorant and backward (179), but the Frenchman, like the man on the train, finds a more deeply rooted sense of civilization in their character that gives them, he says, a "spiritual power" (180), which he believes will allow them eventually to return to the same level of social organization and moral determination that had enabled their ancestors, the ancient Egyptians, to achieve greatness. He concludes:

> "Yes, Mr. Black, don't look down on those poor people today. The force lies buried within them. They lack only one thing . . . "
>
> "What is it?"
>
> "A beloved."
>
> The Englishman gave him a look, but he could not tell whether it showed doubt or agreement.
>
> The Frenchman answered him after a bit. "Yes, what they lack is that man from among them who will manifest all their feelings and hopes and be for them a symbol of the ultimate. At that time, don't be surprised if these people who stand together as one and who relish sacrifice, bring forth another miracle besides the pyramids." (183–84)

Hakim plays on the ambiguous gendering of the word "beloved" (*habib*) in Arabic, a masculine form that can apply to either a male or female. Knowing how destructive Muhsin's love for Saniyah has been, the reader should be alerted to interpret this as a recommendation—especially in the light of the earlier conversation in the train compartment—that Mushin should replace his female beloved with a more idealized, less personal love object. Muhsin in fact already laid the groundwork for such a move in part 1 of the novel, when he described Saniyah as an object of veneration, an avatar of the goddess Isis (86).

But this process is depicted in the novel as slower and more hesitant than might be expected. When Muhsin returns to Cairo at the end of his vacation, he finds that Saniyah has fallen in love with his Uncle Salim's friend, Mustafa Bey. He is at first devastated but gradually transfers his affection to Saʿd Zaghlul and the Wafd movement, which—as the Frenchman said—constitutes a more worthy, disinterested, and productive object for his affections. Supporting and venerating Saʿd will lead, as it does at the end of the book, to support for the goals of the 1919 revolution and the rebirth of the Egyptian spirit:

> In the month of March, at the beginning of spring, the season of creation, resurrection, and life, the trees turned green with new leaves. Their branches conceived and bore fruit.
>
> Egypt too, in the same manner, conceived and bore in her belly an awesome child. The Egypt that had slept for centuries in a single day arose to her feet. She had been waiting, as the Frenchman said, waiting for her beloved son, the symbol of her buried sorrows and hopes, to be born anew. And this beloved was born again from the body of the peasant. (272)

Thus the beloved object (Zaghlul, Egypt) and the revolution are brought metaphorically, if perhaps too simplistically for some tastes, into perfect alignment.

At the end of the story, this commitment to the rebirth of the country[3] rather than a concern for individual happiness motivates all Saniyah's disappointed lovers to join the revolution. They are arrested by the British for antigovernment agitation and thrown in jail together. There they become sick but, fired by their newfound moral strength, quickly recover. While they are convalescing, they are—in a clear allusion to the opening scene in the book, where they all came down with Spanish flu—visited by the family doctor, who is impressed that, unlike before, they are now truly brothers, not a collection of individuals, who have learned to share and share alike.

Clearly Hakim's novel fulfills almost to the letter Jameson's prescriptive assessment of the Third World novel as a national allegory, unlike any of Mahfouz's later creations. This kind of direct evidence about the background against which Mahfouz wrote convinces students of his importance as an innovator, a writer worthy of their attention in studying how the idea of the modern Egyptian nation was constructed.

NOTES

[1] The Arabic word *thawrah*, usually translated as "revolution," can also be rendered as "rebellion." Since *rebellion* in English is often seen as having less legitimacy than *revolution*, how *thawrah* is rendered can have a political motivation, though I do not believe that here politics was behind the choice of words. A good introduction to the nuances of the Arabic term can be found in Scholch. In his introduction and conclusion, Alexander Scholch discusses the applicability of various English translations of *thawrah* to events in English politics. I myself prefer the translation "revolution" in relation to the events of 1919, in following the definition of this English word as "the overthrow of one government and its replacement with another," but in other contexts "rebellion" or even "revolt" may be more descriptive. The English translator of *Midaq Alley*, a product of the British university system, may have, either consciously or unconsciously, absorbed the terminology used by English political writers, who have generally striven to minimize the importance of the 1919 revolution.

[2] In the film version, Kamal is physically punished for fraternizing with the British soldiers. This difference from the novel underscores a tendency for Egyptian films to

reinscribe rather than challenge the values of the national allegory of Egyptian or Arab identity. Mahfouz wrote a number of film scripts but consistently refused to adapt his own novels to film.

[3] This trope, which equates a woman's honor (*ʿird*) with the land (*ard*), is traditional. Part of the power of the equation derives from the fact that *ard* is one of a handful of word in Arabic whose femininity is heightened because they appear masculine while being treated as feminine in terms of agreement.

Enduring Left Melancholia: Mahfouz's *The Beggar* and the Nasserite Intellectual

Nouri Gana

> What lies beyond involves a Leap of Faith, faith in lost Causes, Causes that, from within the space of skeptical wisdom, cannot but appear as crazy.
>
> —Žižek, *In Defense of Lost Causes*

Naguib Mahfouz's الشحاذ (Al-Shahhadh; *The Beggar*) is a wondrous testament to the crisis of the Arab left. Published in 1965, at the height of the socialist experiment in Egypt, this novel tells the story of Omar Al-Hamzawi, a successful lawyer and upper-bourgeois intellectual who succumbs to a devastating psychoaffective crisis when he learns about the approaching release from prison of his old comrade-in-arms, Othman Khalil. Together with Omar and Mustapha Al-Miniyawi, Othman was involved in an underground cell that in the mid-1930s carried out militant operations against the British colonial establishment. In one of these operations, Othman was chosen by lot to throw a bomb at a British target, in the course of which action he was shot in the leg, caught, tortured, and sentenced to more than twenty years behind bars. Unencumbered by their militant past—especially because Othman, despite being tortured, never disclosed their names—Omar and Mustapha went on to enjoy successful careers, the former as a lawyer and the latter as a journalist. Now, with Othman's imminent release, Omar is consumed by a sense of debt, guilt, and regret as well as by an incessant and involuntary recall of a revolutionary past he can neither mourn nor ignore.

The narrative follows the unfolding of Omar's psychic disarray, which soon becomes an existential crisis and leads to an indefatigable search for the mystical experience that will fulfill what he calls the "long-sought ecstasy" (52). In this essay, I explore how this novel uses the theme of journey to allegorize the spiritual bankruptcy and political impotence of the Nasserite intellectual. I argue that *The Beggar*, while it encodes Mahfouz's ongoing quarrel with the Nasserite regime, presents Nasserism as both symptom and precipitating cause of the failure of the Arab left to apprehend the character of postrevolutionary Egypt and to create grassroots alternatives. The crisis that Omar undergoes is, in turn, as much a symptom of as a melancholy response to the collapse of the Arab left.

Having taught *The Beggar* several times over the last few years, I tested the validity of this argument each time anew in both my undergraduate and graduate seminars and concluded that this line of thought presented a challenge—particularly for undergraduate students, often unfamiliar with the concept of melancholia, Nasser's Egypt, the Arab world, and the Arab left. It is important therefore to locate the novel in its historical context of postrevolutionary Egypt and to introduce students to the Arab left before invoking melancholia as such or left melancholia in particular. Broadly speaking, the Arab left is a constellation of communist, Marxist, and Islamist-leaning parties and groups that initially adhered to a decolonial and nationalist agenda and advocated in the wake of independence a transformational socialist vision. These groups were to different degrees weakened by, among other things, the lack of an overarching and unified socialist movement across the Arab world. The Egyptian left in particular was marginalized by the emergence of Nasser in the mid-1950s as a popular leader who arguably had socialist and revolutionary credentials.

The question that preoccupies Mahfouz in *The Beggar* and in a number of his other novels, such as اللص والكلاب (1961; Al-liss wa al-kilab; *The Thief and the Dogs*), is apparently a simple one: How has the Arab left dealt, if at all, with its (unfolding) crisis? Of course, such a question is pertinent not only to the Arab left but also to left-wing politics on a global stage, particularly following the dramatic collapse of the Soviet-dominated regimes in Eastern Europe in 1989 and of the Soviet Union itself in 1991—events that led to the consolidation of the capitalist system and the emergence of the United States as the only global superpower. Examining the reactions of the left-wing intelligentsia in West Germany to "the unstoppable exit of 'empirical socialism' from the world stage," the German sociologist Helmut Dubiel suggests that they generally "conform to a pattern that invites psychoanalytical interpretation":

> On the one hand, the postmodern reaction, reflecting a presently erupting trend that sacrifices leftist identity altogether—admittedly the maintenance of which had been a matter of excessive exertion for some time. But in the process, it is not only dead weight that is being thrown overboard, but also the very passenger basket itself. Thus the affair might continue to have the appearance of flight. On the other hand we find those who have been beset by a fear of flying. Instead of pitilessly taking stock of a self-destructing reality, their first concern is preserving their own identity. They too are throwing off dead weight. But what characterizes them is the deliberate conscientiousness with which they are doing it. Scrupulously, they make a list of those political and intellectual stocks in the tradition that they want to know are secure against the downdraft caused by the tailspin of empirical socialism. (241)

Drawing on Freud's well-known essay "Mourning and Melancholia" (1915), Dubiel characterizes the first leftist trend as "manic" and the second as "melancholic"—the former viscerally detaching itself from its leftist identity, the latter narcissistically adhering to it even in the face of (or perhaps because of) its virtual implausibility (242). Dubiel is right in positing that these two psychoaffective dispositions exemplify the failure of the work of mourning (*Trauerarbeit*) on the part of the left-wing intelligentsia. As defined by Freud, the work of mourning entails a rather "piecemeal" and "painful" psychic process at the end of which the mourner has successfully withdrawn all (libidinal) attachments from the lost object and simultaneously reinvested them in a new object (253). Dubiel champions the fulfillment of the task of mourning and urges leftists everywhere to work through their manic or melancholic socialist affiliations. For him, as much as for Claus Offe before him, socialism has become an "operationally empty" concept and cannot therefore pave the way to a "post-capitalist state of affairs" (244).

Dubiel's reading of the psychic apparatuses of left-wing intelligentsia through the lenses of mania and melancholia is reminiscent of Walter Benjamin's 1931 scathing critique of Erich Kästner, a left-wing poet of the Weimar Republic. Benjamin traces in Kästner's poetry "a transposition of revolutionary reflexes into objects of distraction, of amusement, which can be supplied for consumption" ("Left-Wing Melancholy" 424). This "metamorphosis of political struggle from a compulsory decision into an object of pleasure" corresponds, for Benjamin, to a state of "tortured stupidity"—"the latest of two millennia of metamorphoses of melancholy" (425–26). Unlike Dubiel's generic characterization, left-wing melancholy for Benjamin is specifically a vicissitude of melancholia: it represents neither melancholia's full scope (including its productive and empowering potentials) nor its bleak and lethal aspects (such as suicide). Wendy Brown rightly conjectures:

> Benjamin treated melancholia itself as something of a creative well-spring. But "Left melancholia" is Benjamin's unambivalent epithet for the revolutionary hack who is, finally, more attached to a particular political analysis or ideal—even to the failure of that ideal—than to seizing possibilities for radical change in the present. ("Resisting" 458)

In *The Origin of German Tragic Drama*, Benjamin indeed argues, "Melancholy betrays the world for the sake of knowledge. But in its tenacious self-absorption it embraces dead objects in its contemplation, in order to redeem them" (157). For Benjamin, Hamlet is the exemplar of melancholia's contemplative and redemptive forces precisely because the work of melancholia confronts him with his own melancholia, which simultaneously awakens in him "the clear light of self-awareness" and inspires his ultimate course of action (158). Left-wing melancholy, by contrast, enacts a state of political exhaustion in which the involuntary disposition to remember the revolutionary past is unaccompanied by any "corresponding political action" in the present ("Left-Wing Melancholy" 425).

I suggest to my students that they read Mahfouz's *Beggar* not only as a reflection of these global debates about the condition of left-wing politics but also as a creative intervention and reconfiguration, from an Arab perspective, of the stakes involved in these debates. For one thing, socialism in the Arab world has existed in miniaturized and variously experimental forms, and it has constituted more of the promise of a future to come rather than a lived empirical reality. For another, the left-wing Arab intelligentsia was not offered the luxury of embarking on the project of mourning its revolutionary past at a time when the Arab world has been and continues to be the scene of colonial and imperial campaigns and simultaneously of decolonial insurrection and revolt. Mourning here would amount more or less to the surrender of identity, whereas melancholia stakes a claim to what is lost in order to redeem it and protest against those who engineered it, be they colonial and imperial powers or oppressive local regimes. Melancholia in the context of the Arab world is therefore not the preferred choice (over mourning) that can be or has been exercised by, among others, Arab leftists, but is indeed the very condition of choice itself. This is all the more so given that melancholia is also the apt response to what Freud calls "a loss of a more ideal kind" (253). For Omar in *The Beggar*, the loss is socialist utopia, which is not a concrete object whose demise can be objectively verified but is a promise whose fulfillment might be frustrated or deferred but whose force may live on undiminished. Dubiel's socialism may have become "operationally empty," but its promise of a "post-capitalist state of affairs" remains alive. I do not mean to suggest that this promise is fulfillable in a near or foreseeable future, but I argue that Mahfouz's novel holds open the possibility of its fulfillment. Really, what else could this promise signify nowadays other than the precarious materialization of possibility?

Given the ideal nature of the promise of socialist utopia, the promise's object transforms at the very moment of its apprehension into an ambient source of melancholia. As Peter Schwenger propounds, there is something melancholy about the act of perception itself: "through perception, [an object] is simultaneously apprehended and lost." "This perception, always falling short of full possession, gives rise," Schwenger further argues, "to a melancholy that is felt by the subject and is ultimately *for* the subject" (2). Although this melancholy structures the mode of existence of all physical objects, it is even more pertinent to nonphysical objects, objects such as socialist utopia whose mode of existence is in excess of the melancholy that structures the mode of existence of physical objects. In contradistinction to the melancholy that structures physical objects, and holds captive the subject of perception in the process, the melancholy that structures an ideal object is always already a given: the subject is at the outset cognizant of the lack of the ideal object in the world of reality but is wedded to such a cognizance only to the extent that it grounds the pursuit of this ideal object. Melancholia is thus the inaugurational and driving force of any socialist project that aspires to a postcapitalist state of affairs. This is essentially the argument of Mahfouz's *Beggar*. The manic and melancholic reactions of the West German left-wing intelligentsia about which Dubiel speaks are secondary to the melancholia that inaugurates and sustains the socialist project. Similarly, Benjamin's left-wing melancholy is but a detour or deviation from the vital role of melancholia in the formation and consolidation of leftist politics. Not infrequently, leftist intellectuals, failing to acknowledge this foundational melancholia, experience the nonfulfillment of the socialist promise as a loss of a concrete object, a loss that necessitates the adoption of reactionary or prophylactic strategies of damage control—the kind of manic or melancholic recourses that Dubiel analyses.

The singular venture of Mahfouz's *The Beggar* lies in its attempt to deconstruct and reconfigure these reactionary, manic, and melancholic strategies in light of the foundational and empowering premises of melancholia in relation to the object of socialist promise. Mahfouz's painstaking dramatization of Omar's crisis and reactionary melancholia becomes an occasion to confront Omar with the foundational melancholia that made possible his socialist commitment in the first place. Insofar as it is a promise whose materialization is projected into the future, the object of socialist struggle is neither fully obtainable nor completely losable, yet the leftist intellectual experiences it as a concrete object that is always under the threat of being lost even while it can never be said to have been fully possessed. A melancholic dialectic emerges: the relation between the leftist intellectual and the object of socialist promise generates the melancholia of which it is a product. The actual breakup of such a relation, for one reason or another, engenders what might be called reactionary melancholia—really, a second-degree melancholia whose shadow more often than not falls on foundational melancholia and threatens to empty it out of its empowering capital. The epiphany that Omar experiences at the end of the novel—and that reawakens him to reality—constitutes precisely the condition of his old socialist struggle: foundational melancholia. This epiphany permits the remetamorphosis or conversion of reactionary melancholia into foundational melancholia. While Omar's late awakening to foundational melancholia proves liberating, as I argue toward the end of this essay, his earlier entanglement with reactionary melancholia has proved impoverishing *yet* necessary for his ultimate transformative reckoning. Rather than simply *resisting* left melancholia, as Brown seems to suggest in her essay of the same title, Mahfouz's novel calls for the necessity of enduring it so that its reactionary direction can be put into the service of the inaugurational melancholia from which the left derives its enduring political potential. What else could be more melancholically empowering for leftist intellectuals at this historical juncture than to reclaim and reactivate their originary melancholia?

In this essay, I trace the genealogy of left melancholia in postrevolutionary Egypt, then examine its configuration in *The Beggar*. Left melancholia functions in Mahfouz's novel as a psychodynamic of disavowal and fetishism: disavowal of an insistent revolutionary past that can neither be overcome nor disregarded and fetishism of whatever object that might help cancel or deflect its impact. I read Omar's detour into Sufism—his indefatigable search for ecstasy, whether through whimsical sex or through abstinence from pleasure and devotion to inward contemplation of the heart, the spiritual organ by means of which divine essence is revealed—as an apotheosis of the psychodynamics of disavowal and fetishism. Sufism here can be seen as a form of escapism similar to opium in ثرثرة فوق النيل (1966; Tharthara fawq al-Nil; *Adrift on the Nile*), but Mahfouz is critical not so much of Sufism as of a condition of complicity toward which we might all—not just (Arab) leftist intellectuals—be moving. In this condition, we abdicate our political choices and responsibilities in the name of soul-searching or any other such alibi that serves to defuse our consciousness of and commitment to our human, historical, and sociopolitical vocation.

With Omar, Mahfouz cautions us that we are all becoming beggars, preoccupied with our own particular needs and pursuits, leaving the task of change in the sociopolitical sphere to the politicians or the powers that be. "I wonder, with the state so intent on applying its progressive ideals, isn't it better for us to be concerned with our own private affairs?" Mustapha asks Omar rhetorically (85). Far from being a "novel of compliance" with the Nasserite regime, as Halim Barakat hastily concludes (218), *The Beggar*, I contend, contests the postrevolutionary conditions of which compliance is a product. It is not its advocate. What is more, by gradually and steadily deconstructing the affective economies and figures of compliance—such as left melancholia, Sufism, disavowal, and fetishism—Mahfouz's novel fleshes out the promise of transforming Omar's escapism, complicity, and compliance into critical and political defiance.

Genealogies of Left Melancholia

The Arab left refers not to a homogeneous or pan-Arab entity but to a spectrum of political movements, alliances, and factions whose common roots lie in nationalist struggles against colonial Zionism and Western imperialism rather than in the ideology of empirical socialism as such. I point out to my students that the ethos of social equality, for instance, has not always been a pressing priority on Arab leftist agendas compared to national liberation, especially during the 1930s and 1940s. As the well-known Egyptian socialist Salama Moussa used to say, "Independence is our first goal and socialism is our second" (Yusuf 14). Not surprisingly, the Egyptian left embraced the Free Officers' revolutionary coup of 1952 and contributed productively to the Revolutionary Command Council's immediate policy measures, especially the land reform program inaugurated in September 1952. This otherwise sanguine collaborative prospect proved no more than a temporary appeasement: the military regime started a clampdown on leftist media by the end of 1952 and went on to abolish all political parties by January 1953, which resulted in arrests, detentions, trials, and demonstrations. The Democratic Movement for National Liberation, the main branch of the Egyptian left, lost no time in denouncing and dismissing the new military regime as "fascistic" (Jankowski 21).

Let us not forget here that the Egyptian left was disenchanted with the revolutionary government as early as August 1952, when the government violently repressed a riot by the textile workers at Kafr al-Dawar (near Alexandria), killing eight and executing the ringleaders (Goldschmidt 106). Since then Egyptian politics leaned toward the right, partly because the right wing was never completely neutralized and partly because Nasser "never permitted the left to reorganize" (Johnson 4). The later leftward and pan-Arabist drift of Nasserite Egypt between 1956 and 1967, in which Nasser encouraged the creation of an

Arab socialist union, further co-opted the oppositional valence of the Egyptian left. Nasser maintained his margin for maneuver even at the height of the socialist experiment. Unlike empirical socialism in China or Cuba, Egyptian socialism was, like its cognates across the Arab world, more a reaction to Euro-American and Zionist interests than a strategy for democratizing and modernizing the postrevolutionary state. Much to the Arab left's chagrin, Arab socialism boiled down to state ownership and management of the means of production, which resulted in the nationalization of key sectors of industry, finance, and commerce. The nationalization of the British and French companies in Egypt, which led to the Suez War of 1956, set a precedent for many later seizures and sequestrations of private property by the Nasserite government.

The disunity and disarray of the Egyptian left were partially due to its intellectual dependency on Soviet-style socialism and international Marxism, which resulted in plural and at times conflicting interpretations, Cold War conspiratorial visions, and divisive organizational stratagems. But the main factor that led to the collapse of the Egyptian left was the emergence of Nasser as a populist leader and prime architect of the 1952 revolutionary coup, as illustrated by his فلسفة الثورة (Falsafat al-thawrah; *The Philosophy of the Revolution*), a tiny book published in September 1954. Nasser's embodiment of a revolutionary leader diverted attention from the Egyptian left and cast doubt over its revolutionary credentials. The tendency to collapse the differences between communism and socialism by the detractors of the Egyptian left undermined the credibility of its noncommunist adherents and practitioners. What further isolated and diminished the legitimacy of the Egyptian left was the oppositional vitality and mass appeal of the anticommunist Muslim Brotherhood, which was not banned until January 1954. Ironically, even the Brothers' targeting of Nasser for assassination—and Nasser's impromptu assertion "If Gamal Abdel Nasser shall die, each of you shall be Gamal Abdel Nasser"—only added to his revolutionary legitimacy and esteem (Jankowski 25). In fact, his popularity became overwhelming in the aftermath of the 1955 Bandung Conference and the 1956 Suez War, both of which brought him worldwide acclaim and conferred on him a leadership role in the Third World and the Non-aligned Movement.

Given that it neither enlisted mass support nor developed a pan-Arab party—and given that Islamist groups in Egypt and throughout the Arab world professed anticommunism while most pan-Arabist movements and Arab regimes felt threatened and delegitimized by the encroachments of international Marxism and Leninism alike—the Arab left was practically meted out a death certificate in the mix. As one commentator suggests:

> The crisis of the Arab left is no less severe than that of the Arab regimes. For decades, opposition movements—leftists, liberal or fundamentalist—have been marginalized not only by ruthless repression but also because the rise of populist movements to power has rendered such opposition ineffective. The national revolutions which swept the Arab Mashriq [east]

> during the 1950s and '60s, mostly under pan-Arabist slogans, initiated traditions and practices which all revolved around the leviathan state. The main effect of these changes on the opposition movements was that they, too, were "etatized." Even the casual and spontaneous outbursts of the poor in "bread riots" against IMF-imposed austerity plans have manifested despair, not organized action. (al-Khafaji 32–33)

When he wrote *The Beggar*, Mahfouz was fully aware of the mood of despondency that had swept the Arab left and the Egyptian left in particular, which faced the choice of either hitching its wagon to Nasserism (understood as a mishmash of pan-Arabism and noncommunist socialism) or going underground.

The Thief and the Dogs stages the theme of betrayal of leftist and revolutionary thought on the part of some members of the Egyptian intelligentsia. Said Mahran, a thief with some Robin Hood in him, is betrayed not only by his wife and friend but also by Rauf Ilwan, his leftist mentor and comrade. From a scribbler in an obscure magazine, *Al-Nadhir*—and from a socialist who once reassured Said "that what is taken by theft should be retrieved by theft" (232)—Rauf had climbed the social ladder overnight and become an upper-bourgeois and careerist columnist working for a mainstream newspaper, *Al-Zahra*. Not only had he become the beneficiary of a system he once philosophized against, he had also become its agent, one of the dogs that force Said to surrender for his vindictive misfires (which are reminiscent of Hamlet's killing of Polonius instead of Claudius). Mahfouz majestically straddles the conventional divide here between family or social betrayal and leftist or political betrayal. He emphasizes, however, the enormity of leftist betrayal—"a betrayal so vile," in the words of Said, "that if the whole Muqattam hill toppled over and buried it, I still would not be satisfied" (181).

While Omar al-Hamzawi in *The Beggar* shares more or less the past leftist activism and present bourgeois status of Rauf Ilwan, he is not as oblivious as Rauf to the fact that the bourgeois status is a betrayal. Moreover, if Rauf typifies opportunistic compliance with the new regime—much as Mustapha al-Minyawi does in *The Beggar*—Omar remains the new regime's tragic conscript. He is a deserter, a renegade, and an escapist of sorts, but only in the sense that he is daily interpellated by a leftist past that he can neither put to rest nor completely disregard. Unlike Said Mahran, whose revolutionary struggle in the name of the poor and powerless morphs into a futile personal vendetta, Omar languishes in a liminal state of melancholy self-impoverishment, oscillating between, on the one hand, disavowals of his past leftist engagement and, on the other, recessive entanglements in the resurrectionary and insurrectionary returns of this very past's unexorcised phantoms. While Said's hopeless struggle matches only the promise of freedom and social egalitarianism that inaugurated it, Omar's melancholy ambivalence symptomizes the demise of this very promise. Insofar as he experiences the nonfulfillment of the promise of socialist utopia as an object loss, Omar wallows under the shadow of reactionary melancholia, oscillating between manic detachment from and narcissistic attachment to his revolutionary past.

In both *The Thief and the Dogs* and *The Beggar*, Mahfouz dramatizes the persistent demand for socialist revolution even while stressing how localized and splintered it has become, being, as it were, contingent upon isolated cases of individual suffering (as in the case of Said Mahran and Othman Khalil) rather than organized around a movement against systematic injustice and inequality. The revolutionary elite (Rauf Ilwan, Mustapha al-Minyawi, Omar Al-Hamzawi), whose task is to educate and mobilize the masses, have gone back on their commitments. Little wonder that Othman Khalil asks Omar during their first encounter after Othman's release from prison, "Be frank with me, my dear friend. Are you a true believer as you once were?" Aware of his betrayal but trying to preserve the appearance of respectability, Omar replies, "I was until the Revolution broke out, then I felt reassured, began losing interest in politics, and turned in another direction" (*Beggar* 115). This argument falters under Othman's probing gaze. Having sacrificed twenty years behind bars for the sake of socialist utopia, Othman holds fast to his principles, pointing out to Omar and Mustapha that it is still absolutely necessary to be a true believer—indeed, never more to be desired than at a time when the Nasserite government has become a defaced simulacrum of the ancien régime (120). Othman rages against Omar and Mustapha: "If you hadn't trusted into hiding, you wouldn't have lost the field" (115), "Just because you have changed doesn't mean truth has changed" (120), "How pathetic . . . I can't believe how degenerate you've both become" (121).

Othman's utopian vision is undiminished and intact, perhaps because of his long experience of "classless" life among prisoners (118). His condemnation of Omar and Mustapha for abdicating their responsibilities as custodians of revolutionary struggle may be seen as leftist critique par excellence. Yet, given its anachronism, it reflects rather what Brown calls a "reproachful moralizing sensibility" (*Politics* 21). The cruelty of Othman's critique may stem not only from the hopelessness of his moralizing exhortation to revolutionary action in the face of the power of the Nasserite regime but also from its being "a strange substitute for action" (40). Othman's fidelity to his principles is genuine, but his complaint reveals the profound disempowerment of the leftist position. Claiming the moral high ground runs the risk of foreclosing rather than keeping open the possibilities for transformative action or radical change in the sociopolitical sphere.

The danger of Othman's moralizing enterprise is that it tends to slip into the rhetoric of the leftist impotence it seeks to contest. Its incitement to action might be read paradoxically as a sign of the broken promise of socialist revolution. Its leftist vision fails to enlist the support of either Omar or Mustapha, notwithstanding their past activism. Clinging to the habits of mind of a prerevolutionary leftist position, Othman experiences his commitment more as an entitlement to than a demand for revolution, mistaking the promise for the object of the promise. He apprehends neither the character of Nasserite Egypt, particularly its preemptive assimilation of socialist rhetoric into its revolutionary apparatus, nor the pervasive crisis of the Arab left of which he is a product and to which his resentment bears witness. In this sense, Othman is no less melancholic than Omar, but while Othman narcissistically denies the demise of the old leftist position, Omar manically denies his attachment to it. In other words, if Othman's undifferentiated identification with his old leftist position is inextricably bound up with the imperative to preserve his leftist identity, Omar's proscribed identification with that position figures forth the identity crisis and the psychoaffective disarray and disorientation of the Arab left in postrevolutionary Egypt.

Formations of Left Melancholia

The Beggar begins with the poignant scene in which Omar sits in a doctor's waiting room, contemplating the painting of a child riding a wooden horse. I point out to students the scene's rhetorical economy, which testifies to Mahfouz's craftsmanship and mastery of the postrealist novel form:

> White clouds floated in the blue expanse overlooking a vast green land where cows grazed serenely. . . . In the foreground a child, mounted on a wooden horse, gazed toward the horizon, a mysterious semi-smile in his eyes . . . he liked the searching child, the tranquil cows. . . . There the child looks at the horizon, and how tightly it grips the earth, closes in upon the earth from any angle you observe it. What an infinite prison. Why the wooden horse, why the cows so full of tranquility? (6–7)

Appropriating a technique commonly used in film, *The Beggar* starts in medias res and then unfolds chronologically. Antedating the beginning of the novel is the scene in which Omar encounters a client who rebukes him for worrying that the government might confiscate the client's land. Omar asked the client, "Suppose you win the case today and possess the land only to have it confiscated tomorrow by the government?" The client responds in a way that would mark Omar's life indelibly: "All that matters is that we win the case. Don't we live our lives knowing full well that it is going to be taken away by God?" (40–41; trans. modified). Omar believes that these words precipitated his disease, which in turn prompted him to see his old friend and doctor, Hamid Sabry. As in *The Thief and the Dogs*, where he originally put it to full use, Mahfouz draws extensively here on the stream of consciousness technique, which was most notoriously brought to perfection by James Joyce in *Ulysses*, a novel that Mahfouz castigated as "terrible" ("I Speak" 94). Although Mahfouz dismissed Joyce and the excessive psychologism that permeates his novel, rendering it nothing more than "licensed chaos" (105), he includes what he calls a "Joycean moment" in the life of his protagonist at certain narrative junctures (95). In this Joycean moment, readers are given access to the thoughts and desires of Omar while he reflects on the painting.

The word *hobbyhorse* may denote "a stick having an imitation [of a] horse's head at one end that a child pretends to ride" or may convey the sense of "a topic to which one constantly reverts" ("Hobbyhorse"). The two meanings overlap here: the insouciant child riding his hobbyhorse adds to Omar's obsession with death, which was triggered by the client's rhetorical question. Before Omar leaves the doctor's office, he examines the painting one more time, as if expecting a change in the child's posture. Alas, "[t]he child was still riding his wooden horse, gazing at the horizon. . . . The horizon still closed in upon the earth" (15). Back at home, his thoughts drift again to the painting: "The child imagines he's riding a real horse. 'He was exasperated, he is exasperated, be exasperated, so he is exasperated, she is exasperated, and the plural is they are exasperated'" (19). The hobbyhorse cannot be forgotten; it will keep intruding at different phases and under different disguises in Omar's unfolding crisis. Mahfouz uses interior monologue to draw attention to what he calls "moments of ill health" in the life of his protagonist ("I Speak" 106). Throughout *The Beggar*, this device acts as an economic stylistic register of Omar's psychoaffective convulsions.

Omar is gripped by what Freud calls "a revolt . . . against mourning" ("On Transience" 288). At first "he [likes] the searching child, the tranquil cows," but he cannot help but color the scene with a lyrical sensibility worthy of the poet still throbbing inside him. Now he perceives only the "infinite prison" that engulfs the child and the earth, in a way reminiscent of Hamlet's similar verdict on Denmark and the world (68). The painting for Omar speaks of the transience of the world of oblivious joy it evokes, a world irrevocably lost to him. But on many occasions he expresses his fascination with this quasi-Nietzschean forgetting (89) or with this "[b]estial oblivion," as Hamlet would put it (Shakespeare 115; 4.4.40), which the grazing cows and the child incarnate. In Alexandria, Omar writes to his friend Mustapha, "Buthayna is happy—how I wish I could read her mind—but the happiest of us all is certainly Jamila, who as yet understands nothing. . . . I met a mad man. . . . I wish I could have read his mind, too" (23–24). Longing for this world of blissful ignorance or exquisite madness, he is troubled by the painting, which bears witness to an object loss he can neither recover nor recover from. Hence, he projects the "infinite prison" within: a heap of broken promises and dead dreams, belatedly conjugated and dispersed into the grammar of exasperation.

The world that the painting conjures up could be cataloged under the same rubric as Omar's past promissory world of love and romance, socialist utopia, committed art, leftist engagement, and organized struggle. In the same letter to Mustapha, he writes:

> By chance I overheard a conversation between two lovers in the dark. . . . God, what a long time has passed without love! All that is left are *mummified memories*. How I would like to sneak into the heart of a lover. As you know, Zeinab has been my only love; but that was more than twenty years ago. . . . However, the memory of insanity is not like insanity itself—the feverish thoughts, volcanic heart, and sleepless nights. Agony lifted me to poetic ecstasies. Tears streamed from my eyes and I approached heaven.

> But these are no more than *mummified memories*. . . . Honestly, I've lost interest in everything. Let them take the three apartment buildings and the revenues. I won't claim that the principles which once nearly landed us in jail along with Othman make it easy to accept, for those days of strife are themselves no more than *mummified memories*.
>
> (25–26; trans. modified, italics mine)

This letter has proleptic force, conveying Omar's unfolding ambivalence toward the past and anticipating his detour into Sufism. His mental condition may invite psychoanalytic interpretation, but it defies any analytic pattern, running the spectrum of affects from mourning and manic detachment to nostalgia and melancholic attachment. No sooner do we get the sense that Omar is nostalgic than he declares that the past is no more than "mummified memories," an accumulated weight whose burden he has cast off. This magic release from the past is undercut by his repetition or overfiguration of the expression "mummified memories," which suggests that the release is incomplete. Far from exemplifying his complete detachment from the past, Omar's letter to Mustapha is suggestive of an unfolding affective response to this very detachment. This response unravels Omar's ungrieved and ungrievable alienation from the ideal objects of his mummified memories—objects that embed not only his love for Zeinab and his dreams of socialist utopia but also his passion for writing poetry and his commitment to socialist struggle. While these same objects can be said to have precipitated the formation of his new identity as a lawyer in postrevolutionary Egypt, they have become quite inaccessible to him beyond their haunting insistence on his psyche and their simultaneous withdrawal into the fractured horizon of loss and longing. How does Omar then sustain a sense of belonging in the wake of this ache of longing?

Omar's longing is at two removes from the foundational melancholia that began and sustained his youthful pursuit of socialist utopia, a pursuit that nearly landed him and Mustapha in jail along with Othman. First, Omar does not take into account the persistence of this originary melancholia in his longing for the cluster of ecstatic effects the "mummified objects" used to generate. Benjamin asks, "What . . . does the 'intellectual elite' discover as it begins to take stock of its feelings? Those feelings themselves? They have long since been remaindered" ("Left-Wing Melancholy" 424–25). Omar has not yet taken stock of the "feelings" that went hand in hand with his former commitment to socialist struggle, a struggle whose object was lacking from the outset, and has thereafter continually fallen short of full possession. The socialist project is clearly inaugurated by a melancholic longing for the possible materialization of a postcapitalist state of affairs that has proved necessary yet elusive, neither fully possessed nor completely lost. For another, Omar experiences his alienation from the objects whose effects he cherishes as an alibi to construct them as lost. Omar's longing does not follow the normal process of mourning, whereby libidinal investment is withdrawn from lost objects and lavished on fresh ones. Nor does it follow Freud's conceptualization of melancholia, whereby lost objects are recuperated through an economy of identification mounted by the ego of the bereaved subject. Given the incomplete loss of the objects whose effects he seeks, Omar constructs them as lost. Yet constructing these objects as lost does not result in mourning since in order for mourning to occur and be accomplished the loss has to be complete (which is neither the case with, for instance, Zeinab who is still around nor with socialist utopia which, while apparently lost, continues to exist by other means, namely as a force of leftist critique and of social justice, et cetera, and cannot therefore be fully mourned). What transpires instead is a twisted process of manic detachment or reactionary melancholia whereby melancholia mediates Omar's "capacity," in the words of Giorgio Agamben, "to make an unobtainable object appear as if lost" (20). Indeed, socialist utopia, as an object of his former leftist commitment, could not be said to have been obtained in order to be then declared lost; what is more, even the construction of socialist utopia as lost does not warrant its abandonment, since the initial pursuit of the utopia was conditioned and set in motion by the acknowledgment of its very lack; finally, socialist utopia is not prior to the inaugurational melancholia of which it is a product and, simultaneously, a driving force.

Whether in his manic detachment from the object of his former leftist commitment or in his narcissistic attachment to the ecstasies it once produced, Omar bathes in reactionary melancholia, which is at two removes from the productive melancholia that must have grounded and enabled his old socialist struggle. Unlike Freud's melancholic subject who simulates the continued existence of an irrecoverably lost object, Omar's brand of left melancholia feigns the loss of his unmasterable objects but longs for the effects they used to generate. What Omar longs for is not Zeinab, who once defied her family and converted to Islam in order to marry him, but the experience of love she evokes in him; nor is poetry writing, which he considers a thing of the past, the locus of his longing but the upheavals of emotion that the writing experience generates in him. He yearns no longer for direct socialist engagement but misses the transcendental dreams and altruistic pursuits to which that engagement gave rise. Yet, what would break the hold of longing except the cultivation of the objects that Omar holds at bay against the incessant returns of the leftist past by which he is held at bay?

Sufi Detours

Omar's longing for foregone ecstasies bespeaks a brand of left melancholia that disavows the very objects whose significance it fetishizes. Perhaps nothing more attests to the psychodynamics of disavowal and fetishism than Omar's tireless search for what he initially calls in his letter to Mustapha ثرثرة لا نهائيّة (325; tharthara la-nihaʾiya; "endless chatter" [23; trans. modified]). His search, prompted by his client's words "Don't we live our lives knowing full well that it is going to be taken away by God?," soon finds utterance in a rich battery of Sufi metaphors such as نشوة (*nashwa*; "ecstasy") and يقين (*yaqin*; "intuitive certainty") or variations on both. Being too unpregnant of his past revolutionary cause, Omar wants to experience the ecstasy of revelation it used to mediate without investing enough stamina in the accomplishment—that is, without subscribing to the tenets of socialist struggle on which Othman insists still. Hence his detour into Sufism: an attempt on Omar's part to experience revelation directly, without any concern for or involvement with sociopolitical reality. Benjamin's terse dismissal of what he calls the "flight into theosophy" is relevant here: "Never have such comfortable arrangements been made in such an uncomfortable situation" ("Left-Wing Melancholy" 425). *The Beggar* suggests a counterintuitive connection between the crisis of the Arab left and the resurgence of Sufism in postrevolutionary Egypt.

By no means am I saying that Mahfouz empties Sufism of its spiritual and sociocultural valences, its vital challenge to orthodoxy, and its long political history—including its resistance to European conquest. Sufism played an important role in the 1881 Mahdist revolt against Anglo-Egyptian influence in Sudan. When Emir ʿAbd al-Qadir, who fought the French for years in Algeria, was defeated in 1847, imprisoned, and eventually exiled in Syria, he wrote extensively on Sufism. Rather, Mahfouz mainly registers some reservations about the potential slide of the political under the spiritual in Omar's flight into Sufism. It is not for nothing that *The Beggar* ends with a scene that stages Omar's emergence from an ecstatic trance into the frying pan of sociopolitical reality. Before it reaches this denouement, the novel charts the trajectory of his Sufi journey, which has three interrelated phases. First, the awakening, which is provoked by Omar's encounter with his client. The search follows, in which Omar pursues the pleasures of the flesh as a mediator of ecstasy. When that fails, he resorts to the heart as a mirror of divine omnipotence, to abstinence, to meditative exercises and autohypnosis, and to total retirement from society and disengagement of the mind from all worldly concerns and responsibilities. Finally there is the phase of arrival, which coincides, much to Omar's surprise, with his reawakening to the exigencies of sociopolitical reality instead of to knowledge of the secret of creation and the ecstasy of direct communication and unity with the divine (فناء *fanaʾ*).

Mahfouz makes use here not of exact Sufi concepts but of a chain of metonymic signifiers that charts a poetics of Sufism. The first part of Omar's search revolves around the hunt for love as a means to ecstasy. Omar longs for "the pleasure of madness," the "strange intoxication," "the long-sought ecstasy," "the first ecstasy of creation," "the raptures of love," and the "fire-brand of sex" (24, 50, 52, 56, 61, 63). His extramarital pursuits with such other women as Margaret and Warda do not result in *nashwa*, given the irreducibility of love to sex, as in Jacques Lacan's well-known formulation of desire in terms of a continual split between demand (love) and need (sex). Mahfouz's language here is performative of the fullness and futility of Omar's search—fullness because, like the constant slide of desire along the metonymic chain of signifiers, the search can never be fulfilled; futility because the void that fuels the search is greater than the capacity to fill it. Omar concludes the first part of his search by a cri de coeur: "The ecstasy of love fades and the frenzy of sex is too ephemeral to have any effect" (96). Erotic pleasure cannot provide *nashwa*, and the new love objects are transient and lure Omar away from his metaphysical destiny. By repudiating the body's pleasures, Omar repudiates all forms of sociality in search of the pure, unmediated, and eternal *nashwa* that the soul's transcendentalizing impulse is finally deemed capable of generating.

Omar's detour into Sufism intensifies both his longing for ecstasy and his alienation from all the objects, old and new, that are deemed no longer capable of producing the rapturous effects associated with the experience of ecstasy. Insofar as it has confronted him with the necessity of deserting all worldly matters to devote himself to the rapt contemplation of the soul, Sufism can be seen to accommodate and aggravate Omar's reactionary melancholia and its psychodynamics of disavowal and fetishism. Sufism is, after all, a license to suffering on the path to divine ecstasy, yet Omar suffers not only because he has not suffered enough (as a Sufi wayfarer would) but also because he can never suffer what Othman must have suffered in prison. Omar wears his illness like a badge of honor: it draws him close to divine ecstasy and gnosis (معرفة [*maʿrifa*]) and allows him to make up for his failure to suffer as Othman suffered. Omar gradually disengages from society in an attempt to find in solitary life "the ecstasy which gives assurance without proof," "to listen to the silence" (122, 127), "to be cured from the call of life" in order "to see His face" (133, 135; trans. modified). This part also ends with a cri de coeur: "When would he see His face? Hadn't he deserted the world for its sake?" (143; trans. modified). His failure to find Sufi ecstasy expresses Mahfouz's unequivocal indictment not of Sufism as such but of the banality with which it is perceived as the "magic key of escape" (41) from the iron grip of history and sociopolitical reality. In fact, Mahfouz insists that he "loves Sufism," provided that it does not become a rejection of life: "Sufism is like a mirage in the desert. It says to you, come and sit, relax and enjoy yourself for a while. I reject any path that rejects life" ("Naguib Mahfouz" 17).

The title of the novel acquires a concrete yet tragically ironic dimension as it encapsulates Omar's narcissistic regression into an infantile stage in which he becomes a mere beggar for ecstasy, as if ecstasy could be bestowed from a benevolent outside rather than achieved from within. Omar has taken literally Mustapha's statement, "And since there is no revelation in our age, people like you can only go begging" (76). Begging for revelation is a far cry from the old activist struggle in which Omar was one of the agents of a revelation in the making—that is, a socialist utopia. Ironically, on the night that he first glimpses divine revelation, his wife is in the delivery room giving birth to their first boy. He laments, "Here she is, able to create, while all [my] efforts have failed" (106). Although Omar is fixated on creation as a means to ecstasy, he is incognizant of the extent to which the rightful path toward it has been transposed by the Sufi ideal that places not creation but the heart at the center of all knowledge. For Othman, whose penchant for secular and leftist critique is perhaps without equal in Mahfouz's oeuvre, "[t]he heart is a pump operating through the arteries and veins. To see it as a means of apprehending the truth is sheer fantasy. . . . You will not attain any truth worth speaking of except through reason, science, and work" (122). When Mustapha tells Othman that Omar is going through a crisis, as if he's "searching for his soul," Othman responds laconically, "Wasn't he who lost it?" (121).

Georges Tarabishi rightly suggests that Omar's search for ecstasy is but a search for "the ecstasy of being free of all ties" ("Allah" 61). Omar's journey into Sufism is as much a break of all ties with the world for the sake of ecstasy as it is a psychoaffective response to his already broken ties with the world. Given that the inaccessible objects of his longing—objects he deliberately constructed as lost—return with the force of the repressed to weigh heavily on his psyche, there lies underneath his leap into Sufism the contours of fetishism. The fetishism of ecstasy enables him to avoid (as in a-void-dance, or Sufi whirling trance) the unbearable truth of the vitality and viability of transformative sociopolitical action in the present. This truth insists, after Othman's release from prison, that their old cell be resurrected and their socialist struggle renewed. It asserts itself in the wake of Zeinab's ability to create a newborn, in the wake of the burgeoning of Bouthayna's poetic talents and her scientific pursuits, and finally in the wake of the engagement of Othman and Bouthayna whose marriage may unite seamlessly science, poetry, and socialism. Throughout the novel, Omar fetishizes events and scenes—his obsession with the painting, his client's words, his illness, the secret of creation, the meaning of life, his search for ecstasy and divine revelation—"to cancel the full impact of reality" and deny the continued existence of the objects whose loss he manufactured (Žižek, *Enjoy* x). Joined-up disavowal and fetishism prolong Omar's detour into Sufism. Yet, what would break the hold of Sufism except the melancholic cultivation of the objects whose endurance Omar holds at bay against the ecstatic longings by which he is held at bay?

Enduring Left Melancholia

If Mahfouz begins *The Beggar* with a Joycean moment, he ends it with a sequence of surreal moments in which Omar taxies toward the Sufi experience of ecstasy but never quite reaches takeoff speed. In the penultimate chapter, he is in a state between sleep and waking, close to divine revelation, but the world of reality encroaches: Bouthayna's reproachful queries, Mustapha's derisive repartees, Othman's menacing incitements. He is also distracted by the history of humankind, from primitive battles to modern warfare. Just at the moment when Omar's heart throbs with expectation, on the verge of revelation, Omar sees not the divine face but the faces of Zeinab, Bouthayna, Samir, Jamila, Othman, Mustapha, and Warda. They exchange heads and assume hybrid shapes. The newborn Samir puts on Othman's head and chases Omar until he falls on the ground, admitting to himself that "ecstasy has become a curse, and paradise a stage of fools" (137). The last installment in this sequence portrays Omar communicating with insects, reptiles, and animals in a scene that collapses Sufism and surrealism. By blending the two, Mahfouz intensifies Omar's failure to achieve ecstasy. Mahfouz wants to stress that Omar's Sufi journey is as unrealistic as a cow's giving up the milk business in order to study chemistry (137). It might not be impossible for the fox to become the guardian of the chicken and for the scorpion to wear a nurse's uniform, but "it is utterly impossible for Man to absent himself from the world" (Tarabishi, "Allah" 62).

While this penultimate chapter may seem to suggest Omar's failure to reach the long-sought ecstasy, its proleptic thrust paints in broad strokes Omar's eventual awakening to reality. The last chapter of *The Beggar* shows how his disavowal of the call of life is rerouted—in the very process of its unfolding—into a poetic reckoning with reality and, ultimately, with the call of life itself. While in his Sufi shack, Omar is visited by Othman, who, true to his socialist ideals, got involved in a new underground operation and comes to Omar looking for a place to hide from the police:

> [Othman:] "Listen, Omar, I'm in a bad situation. They are looking for me everywhere. If they catch me I'll die."
> [Omar:] "So it's you who is running away this time." (139)

Omar refers to the operation undertaken by Othman, Omar, and Mustapha together in the mid-1930s, in which Othman was chosen by lot to throw a bomb on the "pigs" (the British colonial powers) who "sucked our blood long enough" (112). This operation, in which Othman was shot in the leg, captured, and incarcerated while Omar and Mustapha escaped unscathed, is reversed in the last chapter of the novel. Now Omar bears the brunt of Othman's actions and is shot in the shoulder. Given the overdetermined history between the two men, this reversal is a key to understanding Omar's melancholic disavowals and fetishistic Sufi detours.

Throughout the narrative, Omar has been unhinged by an overwhelming sense of guilt. The closer Othman's release from prison approaches, the deeper Omar sinks into illness, as if illness were a prophylactic measure that enables him to cope with his inexpiable debt to Othman. When Omar finally meets Othman after Othman's release from prison, Omar wonders, "He doesn't want to budge. How strange, it's as though you'd never wanted this meeting at all. You share nothing but a dead history, and he arouses in you only feelings of guilt, fear and self-contempt" (113). This unremitting guilt precipitated Omar's "flight into illness," to use Freud's expression—a flight that makes it possible for Omar "to evade a situation of conflict which is generating tension, and to achieve a reduction of this tension through the formation of symptoms" (Laplanche and Pontalis 164). Time and again, Omar tells his doctor and himself that he is "not ill in the usual sense" or that he is an "invalid without illness" (38). His harping on illness provokes Othman's rebuke: "It's unfortunate that the ill only think of disease" (115).

An unsettling emotional constellation of guilt, debt, and self-contempt as well as of empathy with and envy of the ethical enormity of Othman's sacrifice prompts Omar's flight into illness and from there into Sufism. It is as if the fetishistic mode of his illness enables Omar to stake a claim to victimhood and to balance the unquantifiable suffering that Othman has incurred and that Omar can only vicariously—and through illness—approximate. If he is equally a victim, then his loss of what Othman calls "the healthy and sound part" of his self might be a price willingly paid to expiate the debt (121; trans. modified). Illness affords Omar the reversal of fortune necessary to compensate for the better life he led while his old comrade in arms was in jail. Not surprisingly, Omar constantly belittles his achievement as a lawyer. Comparing himself with his doctor in the opening scene of the novel, he reflects, "[A] distinguished physician is widely known; who hears of the lawyer other than those with legal cases?" (7). Omar's self-berating revels in self-engineered symptoms. Yet the sudden reversal of roles in the final chapter of the novel—and the fact that Omar is literally shot back into life—can be seen to achieve just that, that is, to fulfill what vicarious victimhood could *only* approximate.

The bullet that fractures his collarbone pays, albeit belatedly, Omar's share of the implacable debt or just enough of it to supplement the consolatory vistas already operative not only through his flight into illness and vicarious victimhood but also through his detour into Sufism, which becomes, ironically, the midwife of a concrete reckoning with the world of reality. Hence his poetic epiphany at the end of the novel:

> He had the feeling that his heart was beating in reality, not in a dream, and that he was returning to the world.
>
> He found himself trying to remember a line of poetry. When has he read it? Who was the poet?
>
> The line reverberated in his consciousness with a strange clarity: "If you really wanted me, why did you desert me?" (143)

Melancholy disavowal gives way to poetic acknowledgment. Omar awakens to life, to reality, rather than to divine revelation when he impulsively reclaims a long-foreclosed *nashwa*: the ecstasy of poetry. Poetry for him conjures up the world of leftist engagement, socialist struggle, and all the objective coordinates of his past. It comes back at a fitting time, when he is caught in this world's gripping actuality: he is taken in a police car with Othman after having become a suspect whose family is in danger and whose office has been searched by the authorities. Omar's line of poetry is a reversal of Jesus's "My God, my God, why hast thou forsaken me?" (Ps. 22.1). Instead of pointing to a future crucifixion, it stakes a claim to an abandoned life, a claim that has endured the cruelty of reactionary melancholia and Sufi detours. In fact, Omar's very Sufi detour or diversion could be seen as a condition for his later reversion to reality—really, for his "return to the point of entanglement from which [he was] forcefully turned away" (Glissant 26). In other words, Omar returns to the point of inaugurational melancholia, the driving force of his past socialist struggle, equipped with cognizance rather than disavowal, with the energy to *create* rather than to *search* for the meaning of existence, and with the impulse to confront the actuality of the past rather than to transcend or evade it in the name of a metaphysical or a spiritual truth that is somewhat irreducible to sociopolitical reality.

The political force of *The Beggar* comes from its unapologetic assertion that the spirit of revolutionary change cannot be reduced to the failures of the Arab left or empirical socialism on the world stage. The novel's painstaking dramatization of the crisis of the Arab left and of the Egyptian left in particular becomes an acknowledgment of the ways in which the past continues to impinge on the present, wreaking havoc in the psychic apparatuses of former fervent socialists such as Omar Al-Hamzawi. It forces a reckoning with the consequences of living in a state of disillusionment and disenchantment with a utopian past that never comes to pass. While it stages the trajectory of the Arab left's melancholia (as in Omar's vertiginous progress through disavowal, fetishism, and Sufism), *The Beggar* wagers on the enabling potentiality of inaugurational melancholia, its power to ground and reactivate the pursuit of the object of socialist promise. "If you really wanted me, why did you desert me?"—a vague line of poetry, indeed; yet it conveys a sense of reckoning and reconciliation with what Omar deserted to pursue an elusive ecstasy. Omar has become cognizant of an uncannily familiar love object he has so far abandoned but cannot afford to do so any longer—not after having lived through, witnessed, and survived the drama of its concealment and repression.

Because reactionary melancholia is the symptom rather than the cause of the collapse of the Arab left, it becomes in the process of its unfolding a segue into the originary melancholia that constitutes not only the condition of possibility of the promise of socialist utopia but also the condition of its renewal and reinstatement as a political and critical force in the sociopolitical sphere. Unencumbered by the therapeutic rhetoric it reproduces, *The Beggar* is not unmindful of the potential slide of the political predicament of the Arab left into a psychoaffective discourse of pathological overtones as long as the former should find interwoven in the latter a concrete itinerary for the contemplation and elaboration of transformative visions and counterintuitive tactics. Omar endures reactionary left melancholia despite its compromised political potential. Afflicted with all the tensions of which human beings are capable, reactionary melancholia sustains Omar's endurance and leads to his final reawakening to his and every leftist's originary melancholia.

Seizing left melancholia away from the psychodynamics of disavowal and fetishism, *The Beggar* is an empowering novel. Not only does it stage left melancholia while enduring it, it also confronts Omar and the (leftist) reader alike with the foundational melancholia from which the socialist project continues to derive its enormous sociocultural, critical, and political power—especially at a time when empirical socialism has exited the world stage. Socialist critique is never more to be desired than at the current historical juncture of runaway capitalism. Yet "it remains for the person whose cause it is to make the final determination, to keep the initiative, retain the prerogative" (Said, "*Reflections*" 529). By subtly underscoring the viability of *enduring* rather than *resisting* left melancholia, Mahfouz's novel has unraveled one crucial condition of its own possibility, and, I should add, of ours—really, of the indispensability yet fragility of our demand for and endurance in proximity to the object of socialist promise, the promise of a postcapitalist world.

Mahfouz's Posts

Shaden M. Tageldin

When I first conceived this essay on Naguib Mahfouz, the Nobel Prize–winning Egyptian novelist was still alive. Yet I was tempted, even before Mahfouz had passed, to title it "Mahfouz's Ghosts." After all, no one in modern Egyptian literary history has inspired so acute an anxiety of influence in his contemporaries and in his successors. During Mahfouz's long lifetime, to write a novel in Egypt meant to write with him or against him—but always, effectively, for him. Witness the reactions of Egyptian novelists to Mahfouz's legacy in the online special edition of *Al-Ahram Weekly* that ran just after his death on 30 August 2006. Arguing—wrongly—that Mahfouz had "founded the Arabic novel from scratch," indeed "in a vacuum," Mahmoud El-Wardani suggests that the Mahfouzian novel quickly attained iconic—even hegemonic—stature and thus came to define the genre. So deeply was the modern Arabic novel identified with Mahfouz, El-Wardani implies, that it became impossible to write beyond him. Modern Arabic readers, he contends, "associated the form with Mahfouz, seeing the novel as the Mahfouz novel, and this placed an obstacle in the way of the development of the genre." Salwa Bakr, an important writer of the 1960s generation, concurs. Yet she sees in Mahfouz's dominion the condition—not the limit—of creative possibility. "Of course Naguib Mahfouz is a monument," she writes, "and monuments in the history of creativity are always a hindrance; though in the case of Mahfouz he is a positive hindrance." Citing the attempts of the 1990s generation to rebel against Mahfouzian form, Miral El-Tahawi echoes Bakr: "[O]f course this attempt at rebellion is proof of the extent of his influence on us." Alaa El-Aswani, whose bestseller عمارة يعقوبيان (ʿImarat Yaʿqubyan; *The Yacoubian Building*) has been compared with Mahfouz's work, sums up the relational paradox nicely: "His relationship with the generations that succeeded him is that of a father towards his children. . . . Many of those that followed him did so rebelliously, seeking to emerge from beneath his mantle." What emerges from these pronouncements is a portrait of the artist as a hegemonic "old man," one whose narrative techniques pressed with all the weight of tradition on new generations of writers and provoked them to formal rebellion. Mahfouz played the "dead" yet haunting father-ghost to their Hamlet.

But Mahfouz was no ghost, really—not before his death, and not after it. Bakr may dub him a monument, styling him strangely like the unforgettable character of Shaykh Darwish in his 1947 novel زقاق المدق (Zuqaq al-midaqq; *Midaq Alley*): an oracle of Egypt's Westernized future who is nonetheless a throwback to its traditional past, a disjointed amalgam of European and indigenous dress who seems poised to fly apart at the seams of his self-contradiction yet remains oddly inert, immobile as a statue—or sepulchral as a monument. Yet even Bakr hints at this monument's movement: "For the cursory reader his style might seem old-fashioned and repetitive; he did, though, develop important techniques on which new trends were founded, as seen in the writings of the 1960s generation and their successors." Thus, while Bakr problematically confines Mahfouz's generation of "new modes of literary writing" to "the realistic and the historical," she also intimates that the careful reader (the opposite of the cursory reader) will detect elements of the more experimental in his techniques. El-Tahawi says that Mahfouz incarnated the spirit of change that her rebellious generation would emulate: "A lesson we learned from him was changing the mode of writing every few years; he never settled for a single mode." Hardly the picture of a writer immured in unchanging tradition.

The novelist Hala El-Badri confirms Bakr's and El-Tahawi's intuitions with a more daring assessment of Mahfouz's impact: "He seems always to have been in the vanguard, though he is often described as a classical writer. . . . It seems to me that much that we would term modernist comes from the sudden changes of direction in his writing." El-Badri's analysis highlights the fallacy of dubbing Mahfouz a classical or (as Bakr does) an old-fashioned writer. If the Egyptian literary sphere can claim to have abandoned realism for modernism (and beyond), it has done so largely in the spaces of rupture that Mahfouz himself produced as he broke with one form and took up another over the course of his long and extraordinarily prolific literary career.

Mahfouz was alive to me from the moment I first read him. Where some saw only a virtuosic reportage of local color, I saw a kaleidoscopic shattering and recoloring of the local. Thus the notion that Mahfouz had ever been dead or could ever die for the Egyptian writers who struggled, as El-Aswani says, "to emerge from beneath his mantle"—the notion that he was ever as passé as both the 1960s and the 1990s generations of Egyptian novelists occasionally made him out to be—had, for me, long been suspect (see Tageldin, "African Novel" 87–88). But it was teaching Mahfouz's بين القصرين (Bayn al-qasrayn; *Palace Walk*; literally, "Between the Two Palaces") that taught me to question the grave to which his successors so prematurely consigned him and the literary-historical periodizations to which scholars and critics of Arabic and world literature too regularly assigned him. That experience of teaching Mahfouz is in fact the subject of my essay. Thus I chose to title it not "Mahfouz's Ghosts" but "Mahfouz's Posts," to speak of the uncanny ability of his work to see literary and historical beginnings before they begin.

Rethinking Palace Walk*: A Case of the Teacher Taught*

Samah Selim argues that Mahfouz's early realism clinched his success in the Arabic-speaking world because it squared neatly with Arab critics' insistence on "national reality" as the proper subject of the novel. Mahfouz's novelistic craft is perceived as the flowering of the national literature project in Egypt because it traffics in a realism that "has to construct the basic elements of narrative fiction—time, place, character, plot—in a way that 'mirrors' the particular social, cultural, and political reality (*waqi*ʿ) of the national collectivity" ("Narrative Craft" 110). Further, since realism "claims to be simultaneously a universal and a particular form of representation"—heir to a tacitly European "universal" tradition yet capable of capturing a particularly Egyptian reality—Mahfouz's work in that literary mode also guaranteed European approval and won him the 1988 Nobel Prize in Literature (110). Selim's is a trenchant and much-needed intervention into literary historiographies that to this day try to force the evolution of the Arabic novel through the explanatory sieve of European teleology. Still, in assimilating Mahfouz to a national realist project, Selim joins the very critical tendencies she opposes.

I contest these tendencies by reassessing *Palace Walk*, the first novel in Mahfouz's Cairo Trilogy (1956–57), through the lens of pedagogical experience. While the trilogy as we know it today includes two subsequent novels, قصر الشوق (Qasr al-shawq; *Palace of Desire*) and السكرية (al-Sukkariyya; *Sugar Street*), according to Rasheed El-Enany the three novels originally were one, all sharing the title بين القصرين (Bayn al-qasrayn). When Mahfouz's publisher rejected that mammoth volume, only the first third was serialized under the original title in the periodical *Al-Risala al-Jadida* (Apr. 1954–Apr. 1956), and its success encouraged the reluctant book publisher to divide and issue the text as three novels, each bearing a distinct title (El-Enany, *Naguib Mahfouz: The Pursuit* 225–26n4). Written between 1945 and April 1952, just before the Free Officers Revolution of July 1952 brought both British Empire and Turco-Egyptian puppet monarchy in Egypt to an end, *Palace Walk* harks back to the First World War to represent a would-be Egyptian nation trapped between the Ottoman and the British Empires.

In 1914 Britain declared Egypt a protectorate; deposed its last Ottoman khedive, ʿAbbas Hilmi II; and anointed a succession of client rulers, among these Sultan Husayn Kamil and Sultan Ahmad Fu'ad (later King Fu'ad). Thus the novel unfolds, as its Arabic title suggests, between two palaces: the crumbling edifice of the Ottoman Empire and the thickening stronghold of the British. It also unfolds between two other "palaces," especially important to our discussion here. The first is the house of the merchant, bon vivant, patriarch, and philanderer Ahmad ʿAbd al-Jawwad (rendered by the translator, following standard Arabic usage rather than the popular Egyptian form, as Abd al-Jawad); his long-suffering wife, Amina; and the couple's children, Yasin (ʿAbd al-Jawwad's son from a first marriage and thus Amina's stepson), Fahmy, Khadija, Aisha, and Kamal. This family house is situated in the medieval quarter of Cairo for which the novel is named: "Palace Walk." The other palace is the more distant House of the Nation (Bayt al-Umma) of the Egyptian nationalist leader Saʿd Zaghlul, exiled to Malta in 1918 after his delegation (وفد [*wafd*]) requested permission from British authorities in Cairo to travel to London and seek independence for Egypt. In juxtaposing the timeless rhythms of everyday life in Palace Walk with the geopolitical upheavals of both British colonization and the Egyptian anticolonial revolution of 1919, which at first simmer just beyond the street but eventually come home to roost in it, Mahfouz makes Palace Walk a metonym for the social and political fortunes of all Cairo and, by extension, all Egypt.

Certainly, then, the novel is at least partly wedded to the imperatives of national literature. Still, as tempted as one might be, following Benedict Anderson's correlation of novel and nation in *Imagined Communities*, to assume that *Palace Walk* charts the space-time, or Bakhtinian chronotope, of the emerging Egyptian national collectivity, I would argue that Mahfouz's early masterwork is in fact a postnational text, precisely because its sensibility is pre- and thus extranational (Anderson 24–26; Bakhtin, "Forms" 84–85). The chronotope of Palace Walk—this space between two palaces—exceeds the space-time of the modern nation for which the Egyptians of 1919 struggle.

The novel draws its title from its setting in one of the most deeply historic quarters of old Cairo. In 969 CE the Fatimids, the ruling Shiʿite Muslim dynasty in Tunisia, invaded Egypt and established Cairo (القاهرة [al-Qahira; literally, "the vanquisher" or "the city victorious"]) as their seat, banishing Sunni Muslim, Coptic Christian, and Jewish commoners to the nearby city of al-Fustat, which Egypt's first Arab Muslim conquerors had founded in 642 CE. The original Palace Walk—a vast square that bisected the royal precinct of the Fatimids—separated the Eastern Palace, a luxurious complex of buildings that included the residence of Caliph al-Muʿizz bi Din Allah, from the smaller Western Palace, which his son and successor, al-ʿAziz, built for his own daughter, Sitt al-Mulk (Raymond 49–53). By the early twentieth century, when this novel is set, both palaces had long since vanished. Palace Walk survived only as an ancient street. But the division of male space and female space that marks the original two palaces of Palace Walk survives in microcosm in the household of ʿAbd al-Jawwad. And when a regiment of British soldiers sets up camp in Palace Walk itself, the tenth century and the twentieth meet: Cairo's long-ago beginnings in Fatimid occupation coincide and collide with its condition in the age of British occupation, such that its claim to the epithet "the city victorious" is savagely undercut by both past history and present reality (when hasn't Cairo been the city colonized?) *and* held out as a potential, if unlikely, future. Thus the chronotope of *Palace Walk* is continually preoccupied and reoccupied. Multiple pasts and presents, as well as multiple states of being and value, continue to coexist and conflict in pivotal spaces and at pivotal moments.

Indeed, if the novel defines the nation at all, it does so anti- or extranationally. From its very first line, "She woke at midnight," the text wakes to the rhythms not of the nation but of the nation's margins: its eyes flutter open with those of the matriarch Amina, a woman who lives her life almost entirely secluded in the shadows of the home. Amina's gaze confounds the dominant historical narrative of the Egyptian revolution of 1919, which (as Beth Baron's *Egypt as a Woman* has shown) took woman as its icon. She cannot see the nation well enough to tell its time; its chronotope is not hers. Yet her seclusion from history proper—and thus from the nation writ large—is precisely what enables her to see the epistemological continuum between colonialism and nationalism that bourgeois nationalist men of the period, immersed in history, so often miss. Amina's second major awakening in the text, this time at daybreak, finds her vaguely sighting "Egypt" in the shadow of the colony: the clustered rifles and tents of British soldiers occupying her street appear to her "things shaped like small pyramids" (369), things that evoke the pharaonic symbols of a dominant strain of early-twentieth-century Egyptian territorial nationalism (Colla, *Conflicted Antiquities* 155–65, 211–45; Gershoni and Jankowski 164–90). By exposing the lingering attachments of Egyptians to their colonizers through the peripheral vision of Amina as she wakes at midnight or daybreak and by setting the death of her nationalist son, Fahmy, not to the clock of the national chronotope but to the intuitive clock hand of the failing national heart, Mahfouz challenges the notion of "awakening" (النهضة; *al-nahda*) so central to the cultural ideology of Egyptian nationalism. He offers his readers less a picture of national reality than a postrealism that is at once also post-*nahda*, postcolonial, postnational, and perhaps even postpostmodern.

I came to this counterintuitive realization when I taught *Palace Walk* in an upper-division undergraduate course at the University of Minnesota in the fall of 2005 and again in the fall of 2007. The course, Reading Literary Movements, fulfills a core requirement in the undergraduate major in Cultural Studies and Comparative Literature. My version explored the travels of post-1800 literary movements such as Romanticism, realism, and postmodernism across Europe, Africa, and Asia. It focused on Egypt and India, two regions whose experiences of modern European colonialism during the nineteenth and twentieth centuries engendered surprisingly similar debates about the idea of literature and the forms that literature should take. In my syllabus, I put pressure on the very notion of literary movement. I informed my students that we would read not just literary movements but also the movements of literature—or literatures moving. For despite the dynamism that a literary movement implies (or should), too often the phenomenon it describes is construed as static and self-contained.

Movements move across times and geographies, across cultures and continents, and very often definitions (or redefinitions) of literature and the literary travel also with the movements of power and thus acquire considerable political and ideological baggage along the way. Movements entail their own fixations and engender new idées fixes. What happens, for example, when the notion of literary realism travels with empire to places like Egypt and India? One result is that Egyptian and Indian literary traditions fall under the compulsion of the real: they become "insufficient" traditions because they are insufficiently realistic. Some writers call on themselves and on others to submit precolonial literary modes to the demands of the real, which are also the demands of the new. Only in embracing literary realism, these writers argue, can Egypt or India fall in step with the reality of their present, with the space-time of the (colonial) modern. Realism thus moved—transported and translated—becomes a literary analogue of modernization, indistinguishable from modernism at its least resistant to the pressures of modernity.

For all my desire to explode the assumed borders between literary movements, my initial logic in assigning *Palace Walk* followed the conventional literary-critical periodization of Mahfouz's early novels. I classified *Palace Walk* as a realist text and placed it in a tacit progression from the protonovelistic to the postmodern. I did not quite call Mahfouz's text a national one (I had some suspicions about doing so from the get-go), but I suggested as much by counterpoising Salman Rushdie's postmodern, fragmentary treatment of the nation in *Midnight's Children* with Mahfouz's text. With that juxtaposition, I implied that Mahfouz's realism renders his treatment of the nation unitary and representational in a way that Rushdie's postmodernism cannot.

Teaching *Palace Walk* for the first time changed the way I read the text. I divided my class into groups of four and asked each to do a close reading of the novel's opening chapter, focusing on Mahfouz's treatment of space, time, and gender. One student's reaction captivated me. "I can't believe this novel was written by a man," she said. "The opening just seems to be written from a woman's perspective. It's the way a woman sees space: in terms of confinement. I could really relate to that." Her group consisted almost entirely of women: perceptive young women who, in their previous approaches to Arabic literature, had struggled at times to abandon Western presumptions about Arab and Muslim men and women. The sympathy with which Mahfouz represents Amina made these women realize that while they may be free (unlike the cloistered early-twentieth-century matriarch of Mahfouz's narrative) to circulate in public without a father's or partner's permission, the fact remained that their lives as women in the twenty-first-century United States were governed by less visible but no less insidious forms of male control. To my surprise, other women in the group corroborated the first woman's reaction. "Why do you think so?" I asked. Another student replied, "Well, the way the novel opens, you almost think it sees the world through [Amina's] eyes."

When our class reconvened as a whole, I asked this group to share its insight. I then asked others in the class what they thought the novel's narrative point of view might be. Is Amina, the matriarch in whose voice this group had imagined *Palace Walk* to be speaking, really the text's narrator? I asked. No, they replied, not quite. But several agreed that the novel saw through her eyes and spoke with her voice. I took the opportunity to observe that they had just unraveled one of the tricks of narrative art. Mahfouz was using, I explained, third-person omniscient narration to tell his story. We know that the narration is third-person because the novel's English translation begins, "*She* woke at midnight" (1; emphasis added). The original Arabic, I pointed out, begins not with this pronoun but with an expression of time: عند منتصف الليل استيقظت "ʿInda muntasafi al-layli istayqazat" (*Palace Walk* 5; "At midnight she awoke"). Yet the sentence ends with the verb "awoke" conjugated in the third-person feminine singular, rendering feminine the condition of the novel's awakening and perhaps also that of the Egyptian nation. In either case, Amina does not address us directly; Mahfouz's narrator tells us what she does, using the third person. The narrator also tells us what she thinks, and that capacity to penetrate the interiority of Amina's character (and later of other characters in the text) makes the narrator omniscient. The opening of *Palace Walk*—if one reads carefully in English or in Arabic—focalizes that omniscient narration through Amina's perspective. Quite literally: the narrator sees only as and insofar as she sees, and so too do we. That is why we come away with the impression that the novel is hers.

Post-nahda, *-national*, *-postmodern* "Realism"

What would it mean, I wondered, to read *Palace Walk* as a woman's narrative of the *nahda* and the nation? Would such a reading make it a national text at all—the usual study in national realism or national allegory that it is said to be? One of the richest outcomes of teaching Mahfouz's novel in comparative perspective, and also in long historical perspective, is the discovery that such approaches challenge conventional reasoning about Mahfouz's work and its periodization. The notions that Mahfouz developed the Arabic novel ex nihilo or that, as Fatma Moussa contends, he "condensed the development of the novel in Europe—which took more than a hundred and fifty years in the case of the English novel, for example—in the course of his work" ("Master") presuppose that the Arabic novel must follow the developmental trajectory of the European novel. In so doing, such notions partake directly of the dominant literary-historical ideologies of the *nahda*, or Arab literary renaissance. By the late 1920s, Arabic literature was said to be in a state of chaos, crying out to be tamed into teleological step with Europe (Tageldin, *Disarming Words* 224–26). Ideologues of the *nahda* clung stubbornly to the idea that Arabic literature—particularly prose fiction—was immature and asynchronous with the modern. Drawing on Hippolyte Taine's understanding of literature as a reflection of the *race*, *milieu*, and *moment* of its author (xxii–xxxi), intellectuals such as Muhammad Husayn Haykal—author of another novel (زينب; 1913; "Zaynab") wrongly said to be the first in Arabic—saw a need to bring the Egyptian novel in line with the European by transforming it into a literature of national reality (Gershoni and Jankowski 35–39, 131). The realization of the Egyptian nation depended on the realism of its representation in fiction. Because I taught Mahfouz comparatively and in historical context, my students did not take the *nahda*—or its peculiar assumptions about realism—for granted.

Take, for instance, the concept of awakening so central to the *nahda*, to which Mahfouz obliquely alludes when he opens *Palace Walk* with the line "She woke at midnight." Analyzing the first chapter, my students paid close attention to the many different ways in which he ambiguates the idea of awakening, to the turns of phrase that evoke liminality. "Midnight" suggests the cusp not just between the end of one day and the beginning of the next but also—as both the English "midnight" and the Arabic "muntasaf al-layl" suggest—the cusp between the two halves of night. Is Amina awakening to the light that the *nahda* wishes to usher into Egypt—the light of تنوير (*tanwir*; "enlightenment"), so often identified with the West? Or is she awakening to the night, to an alternate modernity that challenges that of the *nahda*? The remainder of the first paragraph suggests a world of indeterminate awakening and indeterminate time. As my students underlined each token of indeterminacy in the passage, they observed that "For a few moments she was not sure she was awake"; that "There was no clue by which to judge the time," since the street noise Amina hears belongs equally to "early evening, midnight, or just before daybreak"; and that "She had no evidence to rely on except her intuition, like a conscious clock hand . . . which revealed that her husband had not yet rapped at the door and that the tip of his stick had not yet struck against the steps of the staircase" (1). Only at the end of the chapter does realist time return, with the clocklike tick of Ahmad ʿAbd al-Jawwad's stick on the stairs of the family home.

But if the ticktock of ʿAbd al-Jawwad's stick marks the arrival of the real in the hazy nightscape of Amina's world, that real is not necessarily a national real. Although ʿAbd al-Jawwad, we later learn, is an ardent supporter of the revolution, he does not wish it to encroach on the rhythms of his everyday life. Nor does the awakening to measured time unfold in the natural daylight of national *tanwir*. Rather, it unfolds in the artificial light of a lamp that Amina, the most extranational or antinational character imaginable, holds up to guide its way: "Hearing the tip of his walking stick strike the steps of the stairway, she held the lamp out over the banister to light his way" (7). So ends the beginning of the first chapter of Mahfouz's novel, and so begins the *nahda* of Egypt—its renaissance, its awakening or reawakening—in the ambivalent time of Amina's darkness and in the artificial daybreak whose birth Amina induces, traditional lamp (مصباح; *misbah*) in hand. The novel's first point of view is Amina's. Her clock hand of intuition anticipates real time in the fantastic indeterminacy of darkness. And her own hand, holding the lamp, lights the nightscape in which the novel opens and transmutes that night into false day—the *misbah*, after all, is literally an instrument that makes morning. Amina's awakening is asynchronous with realist and national time. Yet her time is the novel's.

Nothing makes a point more concrete than comparison. To help my students better understand how Mahfouz's *Palace Walk* rewrites the truisms of national realism from a women's perspective and to model a transregional and intermedia approach to comparative literary studies, I turned to a filmic translation of the dynamics of female vision and invisibility that govern the narrative logic of *Palace Walk*. I asked my students to compare the opening scene of *Palace Walk* to that of *Charulata* (1964), a film by the celebrated Indian director Satyajit Ray. Based on Rabindranath Tagore's 1901 Bengali novella *Nastanirh* ("The Broken Nest"), the film is set in late-nineteenth-century Calcutta at the height of British colonial rule and the Bengal renaissance. At first glance Charulata, the title character, is no Amina: given to reading the novels of one of the leading figures of the Bengal renaissance, Bankim Chandra Chattopadhyay, the young Bengali woman is more connected to the phenomenon of national awakening than her older Egyptian counterpart. Yet for all her immersion in the cultural sphere of Bengali literary awakening, Charu is, like Amina, confined to the home and isolated from the public sphere of the nation. Her husband, Bhupati, the publisher of a Bengali nationalist newspaper, gives much of his ardor to the cause of freedom and little attention to her. In an exquisite reading of the visual metaphors of Ray's film, one of my students observed that the limits of Charu's lonely gaze—circumscribed first by the slats of the blinds that shadow her windows, then by the lenses of the lorgnette she uses to take a closer look at the distant street (and distant husband!)—frame the film's first shots. The student's insight is important. Like Amina, who peers from the tiny interstices of her latticed windows at Palace Walk below, Charu inhabits the margin from which we witness and interrogate the limits of both the Bengal renaissance—after all, her awakening to modern literature has not succeeded in liberating her from the traditional home—and Bengali nationalism, which is not prepared to admit her to the scope of its vision. As in Mahfouz's novel, in Ray's film it is through female eyes that we see the nation and its awakening and envision a postnational reality that opposes and exceeds both.

The architecture of space, time, and awakening in the opening scene of Mahfouz's *Palace Walk* becomes a structural leitmotif of the novel. To demonstrate this point, I asked my students to compare the first chapter of *Palace Walk* with three later chapters, 3, 54, and 56, in which its architecture reappears. Chapters 3 and 54 explicitly pit national time against Amina's time. In chapter 3, day breaks in the ʿAbd al-Jawwad household to the "sound of dough being kneaded rhythmically, like the beating of a drum" (14)—that is, to the sound of Amina and Umm Hanafi, the family's servant, baking bread in the oven room. From the outset, Mahfouz marks the oven room as Amina's sovereign realm, spatially marginal yet socially central to the life of the household.

At the beginning of chapter 54, it is precisely to the beat of Amina's drum that Fahmy, the middle son of the family, wakes to memories of the previous day's general strike and demonstration against British colonial rule, from which he had escaped within an inch of his life when the British fired indiscriminately on the protestors. The drumbeat measures the dissonance between his nationalist preoccupations and the chronotope of everyday life, the space-time that his mother, Amina, regulates and rules:

> Fahmy opened his eyes when he heard the sound of dough being pounded in the oven room. The shutters were closed, and the room was almost dark except for the pale light coming through the openings between the slats. . . .
>
> How amazing! Here was his mother making bread as always. . . . Here was the morning light, both splendid and shy. Its first rays were gently seeking entry. Everything was proceeding as usual, as though nothing had happened, as though Egypt had not been turned upside down, as though bullets were not searching for chests and heads. . . . (356)

What is fascinating about Fahmy's perspective as he awakens to visions of the national struggle is the uncanny resemblance that his perspective bears to Amina's. Fahmy's view of the street is as circumscribed as his mother's; his only connection to the public sphere is the faint light of dawn streaming in between the slats of his shuttered windows. Since the nation is all but invisible to his housebound seeing eye, he struggles to realize it with his unbound mind's eye. By the end of the chapter, his recollections of the demonstration climax in a powerful generalization, from his awakening to that of the nation. His interior monologue concludes, "A self-conscious awakening had rocked the Nile Valley" (360) (لقد زلزلت اليقظة الواعية أرض وادي النيل; Laqad zalzalat al-yaqazatu al-waʿiyatu arda wadi al-Nil [342]). Yet again Amina's quotidian time interrupts national time, its "beats of the dough" and "closed shutters"—its sound-and-light show of awakening—bringing Fahmy's earth-shattering vision rudely down to earth:

> He turned his mind away from the deluge of memories and began to follow the beats of the dough once more. He looked around the room, slowly becoming visible as the sun rose outside the closed shutters. His mother was making bread! She would continue to knead the dough morning after morning. . . . Great activities would not interfere with minor ones. . . . But not so fast. . . . Was a mother not part of life? She had given birth to him, and sons fueled the revolution. She fed him, and nourishment fueled the sons.
>
> (360–61; the suspension points after "not so fast" are in the trans.)

The laws of the domestic world of women—to which men are subject in the family home—obstruct, enable, and obstruct again Fahmy's access to the home for which he yearns: the House of the Nation, the public sphere of nationalist struggle. In his conception, the mother both abets and averts revolution. She births and nourishes the sons (and daughters) who revolt, yet she insists that life as usual continue in her household: no matter how fierce the bloodshed beyond her doors, she continues to make children and loaves. Clocked to the rhythms of the womblike oven room that births him, of the maternal hand that feeds him, and thus to the beat of Amina's alternative reality and alternative temporality (which competes with both the ticktock of ʿAbd al-Jawwad's stick and Fahmy's inaudible national time), the daybreak and sunrise of Fahmy's awakening and the nation's *nahda* become time zones as precarious and ambivalent as midnight in their illumination of the real, and national reality becomes barely distinguishable from dream.

Chapter 56 echoes the spatial and temporal dynamics of the novel's opening scene, yet with a difference. The opening scene establishes the "precolonial" or extracolonial routines of the ʿAbd al-Jawwad household: precolonial in the sense that British occupation has not yet touched Palace Walk directly, has not yet palpably altered the rhythms of native routine—the timed yet timeless awakening of Amina to her wayward husband's return, midnight after midnight. Now we find Amina, stirred once again by the clock hand of her intuition, awakening at the other end of night, daybreak. This time her eyes open not on routine but on its rupture—a rupture she re-visions *as* routine. Peering, like Ray's Charu, through the peephole of her sitting-room window, Amina makes out the first glimmerings of British presence in Palace Walk. But when she sees the colony for the first time, she also sees the nation for the first time: she intuits the colony in the shadow of the nation, the nation in the shadow of the colony. What is arresting about her first apprehension of the British encampment in Palace Walk is its echo of Egyptian national space. The clock hand of her intuition collapses time and therefore space in ways that confound any distinction between colony and nation. The "indistinct human figures" she sees could be Egyptian (although, of course, they are British soldiers), and the "things shaped like small pyramids" and "objects like short trees" she sees, which turn out to be the clustered rifles and tents of the colonizers, evoke the pyramids of Giza and the local natural environment (369). Those pyramids would join other pharaonic symbols as visual shorthand for Egypt in post-1919 nationalist, *nahda* iconography. Amina, then, sees the nation proleptically; she anticipates the future (the Egyptian nation-state) in the still-present past (the British colonial protectorate). In her re-vision, colony and nation both become foreign to Egypt. The only Egypt that should exist, in her view, is an extracolonial, extranational continuity that precedes, eludes, and transcends the ruptures of time, space, and community that both the colonial and the national would impose on it. Palace Walk embodies that continuity.

By spying the hidden shape of nationalist Egypt in the very geometry of the colonial forces gathering in Palace Walk, Amina exposes the underlying structural homologies between colonialism and nationalism and suggests that the Egyptian nation looks much like the British colonizer. Thus she dissolves the notions of Egyptian national authenticity and realism to which nationalist politics and literature aspire. This rejection of the dream of authenticity marks her gesture—and Mahfouz's novel—as not just postnational but also postpostmodern.

Consider that Amina's antinational vision of the nation in *Palace Walk* continually contests the mainstream nationalist and *nahda* imaginary of Fahmy. A student of secular law at the new Egyptian University (established in 1908) and thus a modern educated national subject (effendi) in the making, the aptly named Fahmy—*fahm* (فهم) means "understanding" in Arabic—is the only truly committed nationalist in his household. Throughout the novel, Fahmy distributes handbills that speak with the voice of a unitary nation. Declaring, in ringing tones, that "there is no one . . . , from one end of the country to the other, who does not seek independence" (346), one such handbill tucks neatly away all wisps of possible indifference to the nationalist project, insisting that no individual and no geography can exist or speak outside the boundaries of the nation. Even in translation, the totalizing force of the handbill's rhetoric—its ability to swallow individuals and communities into a single corporate person who speaks on their behalf—was not lost on my students. They offered astute readings of the fault lines separating the claims of the personified nation from the attitudes of inassimilable persons: men like ʿAbd al-Jawwad and Yasin (for whom pleasure trumps politics), children like Kamal, women like Amina.

Building on their readings, I went on to underscore important differences between English translation and Arabic original. Significantly, the Arabic term that the handbill uses to describe the emerging nation—أمّة (*umma*)—is one traditionally applied not to bounded secular polities but to the transnational mother community of Muslim believers. It is a word derived from أم (*umm*; "mother"). Yet Amina, the flesh-and-blood mother of *Palace Walk*, sees no part for the *umm* or the *umma* in Fahmy's nationalism. As Fahmy's exchanges with his mother make clear, the *umma* as nation holds no currency with her; it is "not worth the clippings from his fingernail" (347). Further, responding to his nationalist charge that "[a] people ruled by foreigners has no life," she counters with both the commonsensical chronotope of life in its most quotidian, antinational sense—"But we're still alive. . . . I bore all of you under their rule"—and the historical chronotope of the precolonial, prenational Islamic *umma*, the mother "community of Muhammad," which, she notes, flourishes despite colonization (347). Amina's invocation of this community may seem an appeal to precolonial authenticity (and thus a gesture distinctly at odds with postmodernism proper, which contests any notion of authenticity), but it is not. To Amina, there is no break between the precolonial and the colonial, only continuity, and therefore no need for the fiction of return to an uncontaminated past.

In fact, as my students and I discovered, Amina uses the concept of motherhood to envelop the colonial power in the national fold, abolishing the distinction between colonizers and colonized and thus at a stroke canceling both the colonial and the nationalist projects. "Why do you despise them, son? . . . Aren't [the British] people like us with sons and mothers?" she wonders, drawing on her own relationship with Fahmy to humanize a colonizer that—historical truth be told—so often did not extend the same humanity to her people (347; the suspension points are in the trans.). She is "overcome by astonishment" when Fahmy tells her that a وفد (*wafd*; "delegation") led by the Egyptian nationalist leader Saʿd Zaghlul has sought permission from the British colonial authorities in Cairo to travel to London and argue for Egyptian independence. "They're going to the land of the English to ask them to get out of Egypt?" wonders Amina. "This is in very bad taste. How could you visit me in my house if you're wanting to throw me out of yours?" (324). She pursues this line of questioning throughout the scene:

> How can [Zaghlul's *wafd*] ask [the British] to leave our lands after they have been here all this long period. When we were born and you as well, they were already in our country. Is it humane for us to oppose them after this time we've spent living together as neighbors and to tell them bluntly, and in their country at that, to get out? (324)

Ignorant of the facts of world geography ("Where in God's world is this London?" she asks) and choosing to ignore the facts of world history, she reimagines

London and Cairo as one, eliding both the physical and the political boundaries that separate colonizer from colonized (324). Although the British and the Egyptians each have their own houses and countries, history for Amina has brought the British into Egypt not as occupiers but as guests in Egyptian homes and increasingly, as their presence in Egypt becomes naturalized, as neighbors whose claims to a home in Egypt are virtually equal to those of Egyptians. While she intends England by the phrase "in their country," her words are deliciously (and dangerously) ambiguous. They suggest that Egypt might be every bit the land of the English that England is.

To be sure, Amina is not altogether innocent of the political history of British imperialism in Egypt. She notes that after the 1882 British occupation, it was Queen Victoria "who ordered Urabi [the Egyptian nationalist Ahmad ʿUrabi] banished, although according to what was said she admired his courage" (325). In suggesting that the queen's admiration for ʿUrabi trumped her injustice toward him, Amina selectively appropriates the history of empire to support her contention that colonizing Britain and colonized Egypt could live in harmony with each other. Amina provokes Fahmy's derision when she expresses the hope that Zaghlul and his fellow nationalists might appeal to the womanly—indeed, maternal—instincts of Queen Victoria to win Egypt's freedom. "[S]he's a woman and no doubt still bears in her chest a sensitive heart," Amina insists. "If they speak to her the right way and know how to win her affection, she'll be sympathetic to their views" (325). The statement represents a historical counterfactual on many levels. As Fahmy points out, Queen Victoria is long dead—reinforcing our suspicion that Amina thinks entirely outside the temporal logic of colonialism and its obverse, nationalism. Also, history tells us that the queen was generally no friend of the aspirations of the colonized for independence. Victoria's lifetime, after all, saw her 1877 coronation as empress of India and the expansion of British imperial dominion over much of the globe. Woman Victoria may have been, but her maternalism toward the subjects of empire matched the paternalism of her male counterparts.

Still, Amina insists that a fundamental humanity binds the British to the Egyptians. Even as the revolution of 1919 begins to gather force in Egypt, she prays, "God, I ask you to watch over my husband and children, my mother and Yasin, and all the people: Muslims and Christians, even the English, my Lord, but drive them from our land as a favor to Fahmy, who does not like them" (35). I asked my students to compare her stance toward the British with that of a mother figure in another text we had read. They realized that Amina recalled Anandamoyi in Tagore's *Gora*, a mother whose ecumenical vision of humankind similarly refuses to countenance difference between even the *krishtan* (Christian) colonizer and the Bengali colonized and who insists on raising the Anglo-Irish orphan Gora as her own child. Both Amina and Anandamoyi anticipate the too-humanist mother who must be overcome by the nationalist rebel in Aimé Césaire's *Et les chiens se taisaient* (68–70; "And the Dogs Were Silent"), cited by Frantz Fanon in his theorization of nationalist violence (86–88).

Why so much attention to the ethos of the postnational mother in *Palace Walk*? Certainly Mahfouz was no friend of British colonialism in Egypt; on the contrary, he was a lifelong sympathizer with the Wafd Party, the nationalist party that Zaghlul founded. But Mahfouz never actually joined the Wafd; he cherished his freedom as a writer too deeply (Mahfouz, "Naguib Mahfouz" 5). Ever interested in the psychology of his characters, he was not content to represent reality as nationalist discourse wishes to imagine it. More astutely than any other Egyptian novelist of his time, he exposes the psychological paradox that wedded the imperatives of nationalism, a political awakening intent on making Egypt independent from Europe, to those of the *nahda*: the literary and cultural awakening predicated on making Egypt modern like Europe. Probing the mentalities of Amina and her heirs, he undermines the myth of the uniformly resistant colonized subject.

Throughout the novel, Yasin and Kamal—the oldest and the youngest of the family's three sons—are powerfully attracted to their British colonizers; they love the British as much as they fear them. I called on my students to decode the psychodynamics of both sons' interactions with the British. When an English soldier smiles at Yasin and asks him for matches, I asked them, why does that smile so disarm Yasin that he forgets his fear and becomes "transported by delight," then hastens "with all the energy he could muster" to buy a box of matches for "the mighty, smiling soldier"? Why does he exult when the soldier says, "in English, 'Thank you'" (395)? How does Mahfouz's representation of the encounter complicate our understanding of the relationship between colonizers and colonized?

I asked my students to read the following passage closely:

> Yasin had not yet recovered from the impact of that magical smile. Now here was "thank you." It was like a glass of beer a person drinks to refresh himself when he has had enough whiskey. It filled Yasin with gratitude and pride. . . . As soon as the soldier gave the first sign of moving away, Yasin told him in a friendly manner that came straight from his heart, "Good luck, sir."
>
> Yasin proceeded to the house almost reeling with joy. What good luck he had had. . . . An Englishman—not an Australian or an Indian—had smiled at him and thanked him. . . . An Englishman—in other words, the kind of man he imagined to embody all the perfections of the human race. Yasin probably detested the English as all Egyptians did, but deep inside he respected and venerated them so much that he frequently imagined they were made from a different stuff than the rest of mankind. This man had smiled at him and thanked him. . . . Yasin had answered him correctly, imitating English pronunciation so far as his mouth would allow. He had succeeded splendidly and had merited the man's thanks.
>
> How could he believe the brutal acts attributed to them? Why had they exiled Saʿd Zaghlul if they were so gracious?
>
> (395; only the first suspension points indicate ellipsis)

Notice how the colonizing Englishman, by masking his power with love, effectively seduces the colonized Egyptian into submission to his power. For Mahfouz surely associates Yasin's response to the English soldier with the hedonistic pleasure that Yasin—like his father—takes in wine and women. Given the Islamic prohibition on the consumption of alcohol and the indulgence in illicit sex, both pleasures have the spice of taboo. Yasin's surrender to English charms is couched in metaphors of erotic-alcoholic intoxication: the beer of the soldier's "thank you" intensifies the effect of the whiskey of his "magical smile."

One of my students recognized the fact that the soldier's Englishness makes his smile and thanks "count more" for Yasin. I agreed. Why is this so, I asked? Why are Yasin's comparisons of the Englishman with the Australian or the Indian important in a colonial context? Another student noted that Australians and Indians were, like Egyptians, British subjects in one form or another. But the Australians perplexed her. They were white; as such, wouldn't an Egyptian read them as surrogates of British imperial power? I suggested that even the Australians' whiteness cannot trump their subject status in Yasin's eyes. What Yasin craves is recognition from the imperial master himself, from "the kind of man he imagined to embody all the perfections of the human race." The effect of that recognition? Yasin surrenders whatever shred of hatred for the English that he may have harbored. He can no longer believe the English capable of "the brutal acts attributed to them." More than that: his remarkable "Good luck, sir" wishes empire all the best in his country—and thus converts him into the closest possible ideological and linguistic approximation to Englishness. Yasin himself remarks how "splendidly" he succeeded in "imitating English pronunciation so far as his mouth would allow" (395).

Putting the scene in historical perspective, I explained to the class that its dynamics recall Napoléon's first proclamation to the people of Egypt of 2 July 1798, which circulated in Arabic and assured Muslims, the land's dominant religious group, that the French were not just friends of their interests but sincere Muslims like them. Napoléon's self-translation into equivalence with Egyptians piqued suspicion but also the curiosity of some Egyptian intellectuals and catalyzed their efforts, long after his occupation ended, to master French, to translate French texts into Arabic, and to translate Egyptian culture into Frenchness (Tageldin, *Disarming Words* 14–15, 33–65).

At first glance, the seduction of Yasin by colonial power would seem to separate him from Fahmy's Egyptian nationalism. Yet that separation is illusory, for the logic of Egyptian national awakening is the love child of the logic of colonial power. Amina's is not the only margin from which Mahfouz's *Palace Walk* interrogates the suspect kinship of colony and nation and imagines the possibilities of a postnational and postcolonial future. From an even more marginal position than Amina's speaks a black woman, Nur. A maid who serves Zaynab, Yasin's wife, and who lives on the roof of the ʿAbd al-Jawwad family home, Nur inhabits an insider-outsider position both to that house and to the House of the Nation. Although free, Nur lives at the pleasure of her lighter-skinned Egyptian employers. When, on the very night that the British encamp in Palace Walk, a trapped and bored Yasin approaches her for sex, she can only rebuff him with a repeated "Shame on you, master," uttered (according to Yasin) in a tone that conveys no real resistance (382). Still, the content of Nur's response and her pointed reference to the master-slave dichotomy that conditions her relationship to Yasin make their consensual sex verge on rape. Discovered by Yasin's angry wife, Nur flees. Amina retreats to the oven room; she will have nothing to do with the "incident" on the roof (391). Yet that incident has everything to do with Egypt's relationship to England, its de facto master, during this period.

In Mahfouz's text, Nur's seduction-rape by Yasin immediately precedes and thus prefigures Yasin's seduction-coercion by the "mighty, smiling soldier" who charms him not only into serving British empire but also into forgetting empire's brutality. Like Nur, Yasin and Egypt confront the colonizer with ambiguous shame-on-yous tinged with submission. Like Nur's relationship to Yasin, Yasin's relationship to the English soldier and Egypt's relationship to England are relations of coercion disguised as consent. Yasin's delight in English recognition tells us as much. Thus, as relieved as the ʿAbd al-Jawwad household might be to see Nur banished from even the marginal position she occupied in the family home, her words and actions illuminate the discomfiting posture of Egyptian nationalists like Zaghlul, who forget the truth of coercion and embrace the seduction of consent when they seek Egypt's freedom through gentlemen's agreements with London. Recalling Egyptian nationalist iconography of the Sudan, which sometimes represented the Sudan as a (sensual) black woman subordinated to a (modest) whiter Egypt, she also evokes the precarious sovereignty of the Sudan, then ruled by the Anglo-Egyptian Condominium and thus colonized not only by the British but also by an Egypt under British dominion—what Eve Troutt Powell has called a "colonized colonizer" (22). In any case, Nur's blackness and intimated slave origins exclude her from Egypt's increasingly European-identified national self-racialization and self-stylization. But her name means "light" in Arabic, and her persona sheds light on those faces of itself Egypt wishes to hide, questioning both the limits of national inclusion and Egyptian nationalism's illusory pretensions to equal footing with European colonialism. She is an agent of counter-*tanwir*, or counter-enlightenment.

Like Nur's encounter with Yasin and Yasin's exchange with the English soldier, Kamal's confrontation with the British encamped in Palace Walk smacks of colonial seduction. In this scene, Amina, Fahmy, and Yasin look on, with varying degrees of trepidation, from the window of the family home as a group of English soldiers circle little Kamal and ask him to sing. The anxious family notices that "[t]he fact that [Kamal] and the soldiers seemed to understand each other indicated that they could use the Cairo dialect of Arabic to some extent" (398). Again we find the British ingratiating themselves with the Egyptians they rule, this time by speaking the local colloquial language. Kamal's response, the equally colloquial Arabic song he sings to the British, strikes an ambiguous chord of terror, supplication, and love:

I want to go home,
Darling.
They've taken my boy,
Darling.

> He sang it all the way through in his pleasing voice while the soldiers watched, their mouths open and smiling. They clapped their hands in appreciation at the end of each phrase. One of them was touched when he understood part of the meaning of the song and began to shout, "I'm going home. . . . I'm going home."
>
> (399; the suspension points are in the trans.)

The English translation of Kamal's song neutralizes the force of Mahfouz's original Arabic, which reads, يا عزيز عيني \\ بدي أروح بلدي \ يا عزيز عيني \\ السلطة خدت ولدي (Ya ʿaziz ʿayni // Biddi arawwah baladi / Ya ʿaziz ʿayni // Al-sulta khadit waladi [*Palace Walk* 378]; "O dear to my eye // I want to return to my country / O dear to my eye // The authorities have taken my son"). The Arabic hints that so long as the British occupy Egypt, Kamal is not in his country even though he stands on a Cairene street. Where the translation refuses to name Kamal's captors, referring only to an unspecified "They," the Arabic tells us outright that power (read: empire) has spirited him away. Finally, what the English renders as "darling" the Arabic renders more ambivalently as عزيز عيني (*ʿaziz ʿayni*), where the more obvious denotation of *ʿaziz* in this context (عزيز; "dear") also carries a whiff of a less common denotation of the word, "ruler, overlord." As in Yasin's encounter with the British, attraction and coercion mix uncomfortably here. Even in English translation, Kamal's song remains evocative—it expresses both his own deepest wishes ("I want to go home") and his mother's deepest fears ("They've taken my boy")—and ironic, given the response it elicits from one of the English soldiers, who starts to cry, "I'm going home. . . . I'm going home" (أروح بلدي. . . . أروح بلدي; Arawwah baladi. . . . Arawwah baladi).

Kamal and Amina, I pointed out to my students, speak the same language in this song; the lines associated with son and mother both appeal to English humanity for Kamal's release. But what is the difference, I asked, between Kamal's "I want to go home" and the Englishman's echo "I'm going home"? One of my students noted that the shift from "I want" to "I'm going" across the two lines underscores the power difference between the Egyptian boy and the English soldier: Kamal can only wish to go home; the yearning soldier assumes he will. Lest we read the soldier's cry as testimony to Kamal's victory over the English, an acknowledgment that the soldier will have to leave Egypt and leave it to the Egyptians, the remainder of the scene insists on the asymmetry of English and Egyptian power and shows us how cleverly the English woo Kamal into submission. When Kamal finally returns unscathed to his family, we learn that the soldiers have not only elicited information about the women in his home—to seduce them? to rape them?—but also diverted his allegiance from the Egyptian nationalist struggle to English rule. They have accomplished these ends by proffering a piece of chocolate in a "gleaming red wrapper" (403). "It's a Valentine!" one of my students exclaimed. And she was right, I think—a valentine calculated to buy Kamal's love for the British. Witness the boy's conclusion that the British, with their "[b]lue eyes . . . golden hair . . . gleaming white skin," are "a lot better looking than Saʿd Pasha." Indeed, he cries, "They look like Aisha!" (402–03; the suspension points are in the trans.). Ultimately, Kamal's attachment to the British supersedes not just his loyalty to Egyptian nationalism (incarnated in Saʿd Zaghlul Pasha) but also his loyalty to his family. With their red valentine, the British have managed to replace even Kamal's beloved sister Aisha as his prime love object. Fahmy's accusations of treachery fall on deaf ears, "for in [Kamal's] heart there was nothing but contentment and love" (403).

That two of the family's three sons, Yasin and Kamal, embrace Amina's ethos and survive while Fahmy, diametrically opposed to her worldview, dies in an anticlimactic moment of nationalist struggle suggests that the so-called naive politics of women might take a more accurate temperature of Egyptian attitudes toward the nation than the more historically informed politics of men. It is quite literally on his mother's watch that the most revolutionary character in the novel, Fahmy, can imagine the nation at all. As ardently as Mahfouz supported many of the aspirations of Egyptian nationalism, he always represents those aspirations as fully realizable only in metaphoric darkness—in Fahmy's hallucinatory moments between sleep and wakefulness or in his equally confused daydreams of national glory, which revise his daily flights from colonial danger as brave confrontations in which, if he falls short of actual martyrdom, he at least sustains wounds for the sake of the nation. When British bullets finally find Fahmy, the confident nation of the handbills rapidly slips away. All that is left is his inner voice: "How loud the clamor is. But what are they screaming about? Do you remember? . . . There's nothing. Nothing. Darkness and more darkness. A gentle motion's pushing with the regularity of the ticking of a clock. The heart is flowing with it" (492–93). What remains, in death, is nothing more than the darkness of Amina's midnight and daybreak: a darkness in which the Egyptian subject must grope to see the colony, the nation, and the future of both imperialism and the nationalist project—not by the clock of the national chronotope but by the intuitive clock hand of the failing national heart.

If Mahfouz's *Palace Walk* is the first major postcolonial Egyptian novel, the *post-* of its postcolonial might better be described as the *post-* of the postpostmodern. Fredric Jameson has argued that the schizophrenic is the paradigmatic postmodern subject (*Postmodernism* 25–27). But the colonized subject is by definition a schizophrenic: a divided subject forced to inhabit the colonizer's lifeworld as much as the colonized subject's own native lifeworld, which itself is divided from whatever *native* meant before colonialism redefined that term. Thus it stands to reason that a Eurocentric periodization of the postmodern should fall apart in transit to a colonial context. Western literary theory locates postmodernism after modernism and modernism after realism, but the colonial condition telescopes time and space: its postmodernism, realism, and modernism coincide, refusing to march in single-file succession. The colonial epistemology of Westernization couples realism with modernism, calling on the non-European to eschew the "irrationality" of the mythological, the marvelous, and the unseen for the "rationality" of the historical-material *Geist*: to embrace the hypervisibility of the modern as the only real there is.

The world into which that coupling forces colonized subjects at once divides them from a native world understood otherwise and plunges them into the chronotope of postmodern schizophrenia. Thus postmodernism for colonial subjects is not a postcolonial movement at all but a movement tethered to the *post-* of the colonial. If the postmodern is the colonial (hence the realist and the modernist too), then the task of the postcolonial novelist is to transcend it, to imagine a postpostmodernist world. To speak the language of Kwame Anthony Appiah with the tongue of Homi Bhabha, Mahfouz's *post-* is almost the same as the *post-* of postmodernism, but not quite. It is not a *post-* indifferent to history or authenticity, as Jameson suggests the *post-* of postmodernism is (*Postmodernism* 6; "Regarding Postmodernism" 12, 18–19), but a *post-* that imagines history and authenticity before, against, and beyond the claims that colony and nation make on them. It sees with Amina's pre-, anti-, and extracolonial-national eyes.

My argument here draws on Appiah's rethinking of the relation of the *post-* in postcolonial to the *post-* in postmodern. According to Appiah, the novels of "the postcolonial stage" of African novelistic production are "novels of delegitimation: rejecting the Western imperium, it is true; but also rejecting the nationalist project of the postcolonial national bourgeoisie." He dubs such novels not only "postcolonially postnationalist as well as anti- (and thus, of course, post-) nativist" ("Is the 'Post-'" 435) but also "postrealist" (438): they delegitimate both "the form of realism" and the "content of nationalism" (435), challenging these in "the name of the ethical universal; in the name of *humanism*," a "postcolonial writers' humanism" that he aligns with "the concern for human suffering" (438). Appiah suggests that the experience of Western neoimperialism and local neocolonialism—the postindependence repetition and perpetuation of colonial structures of political, economic, and cultural inequality by both ex-colonizers and new African national elites—has left African novelists disenchanted with the nation, with the colonial-national politics of modernization, and thus with the rational modernity (my inference) of the realist form. The homologies between the colony and the nation have led these writers to demand accountability from the neoimperial West and the neocolonial African state for the human sufferings they perpetuate, while also insisting on a "human" that evades and transcends "the postulation of a unitary Africa over against a monolithic West—the binarism of self and other—[that] is the last of the shibboleths of the modernizers that we must learn to live without" (439). These modernizers are not just Western but African too—in Egypt's case, I would add, also Arab. In Mahfouz's economy, they propagate a logic of national awakening, of اليقظة (*al-yaqaza*) or *al-nahda*.

By postrealistically apprehending Egyptian pyramids in the shadow of English guns, Amina's eccentric female eyes—Mahfouz's eyes—foresee a future moment when the nation will kill its own. They foresee the neocolonial future in and from the colonial-national past. Mahfouz does not, of course, delegitimate the national project. He does, however, question its pretenses to purity and totality, its purported freedom from colonial contamination, and its claim to absolute representativeness (and representation): the "*All is true*" of Balzacian realism (Balzac 6). Amina's humanism—and that of Yasin and Kamal, her philosophical heirs—may not be demanding enough: it may not exact the full accountability from the British that Egyptian suffering demands; it may make too easy the leap to equality and love and thus perpetuate the English occupation of Egypt, perpetuate human suffering. Yet surely it does not inhabit the "perpetual present" of Jamesonian postmodernity ("Regarding Postmodernism" 6). If anything, Amina's humanism places the past, the present, and the future on a single continuum of perpetuity. It does not altogether forget the human sufferings of colonial history—at least one Egyptian of 1919, after all, appeals to the imperial dead, to Queen Victoria, for an end to British occupation. It also lights the way to the nonbinaristic understanding of self and other, the nonbounded, nonnational sense of world community, that postcolonial subjects, whether ex-colonizers or ex-colonized, must embrace if they are to defeat for good the fundamental logic of imperialism. For to post a letter in the mail or a text in public space—a wall, a Web site, or any space in which the spoken or the written word circulates—is to relay it, to send the past to the future. Mahfouz's *Palace Walk* does just that. Standing, with Amina, outside history, Mahfouz becomes, in the words of Salwa Bakr, "the historian of what traditional academic histories exclude." In speaking of Mahfouz's posts, then, we might register as afterlives of Mahfouz not just the imitations and insurrections he continues to provoke in novelists across the Arabic-speaking world but also the prescience of his political and aesthetic challenge to the national realism with which he has been so long—and so incorrectly—identified.

NOTE

This essay makes use of part of my "The African Novel in Arabic" (*The Cambridge Companion to the African Novel*, ed. F. Abiola Irele [New York: Cambridge UP, 2009], 85–102).

Mahfouz and the *Arabian Nights* Tradition

Justin St. Clair

> "Last night," he said, in my wanderings I lit upon a story that was like one of yours, Shahrzad."
>
> Despite her hidden sorrow, she said smiling, "The fact that stories repeat themselves is an indication of truth, Your Majesty."
>
> —Naguib Mahfouz, *Arabian Nights and Days*

One of the greatest challenges to teaching Naguib Mahfouz in translation is providing sufficient context to allow students to access the text productively. Immersed in cultural and political matrices that are unfamiliar to the average American student, the fiction of Mahfouz may well "provide a means of capturing the flux of Egypt's history in the twentieth century," but it is precisely this daunting flux that dissuades some instructors from teaching Mahfouz in the first place (Moussa-Mahmoud, "Depth" 155). This need not be the case. While I would never deemphasize the cultural contexts in which Mahfouz wove his fictions, I would nonetheless suggest that, as with any richly textured literary output, productive alternatives do exist. This essay offers an approach to the novel ليالي ألف ليلة (1982; Layali alf layla; *Arabian Nights and Days* [1995]). Instead of presenting the text by way of sociopolitical specifics, it seeks to situate it in two literary traditions: (1) the long, tangled history of the translation, fabrication, and publication of the *Arabian Nights*; and (2) an international corpus of postmodern fiction obsessed with fabulation and metafiction.

Arabian Nights and Days is, nominally speaking, an extension of the *Arabian Nights* tradition. Mahfouz flouts the cycle's governing frame and offers an account (delivered not by Shahrzad but by an omniscient, third-person narrator) of Shahriyar's sultanate from the thousand-and-first night forward. Mahfouz's exploration of the "happily ever after" is devilishly playful: he recycles and recasts a myriad of characters, tales, and details from the *Arabian Nights* and whips the resulting mélange into something at once wholly original and eerily recognizable. The effect is unsettling, and part of the reward of reading the novel becomes an exercise in identification, as readers struggle to situate themselves in Mahfouz's world by matching bits and pieces of the novel with their corresponding origins in the extant narrative tradition. Whether this repetition is an indication of truth as the epigraph to this essay suggests (Mahfouz, *Arabian Nights* 98), remains an open question. In any case, most American students' familiarity with the *Arabian Nights* is limited to a few Disneyfied atrocities and the odd misremembered storybook. Consequently, a successful introduction to the novel requires backstory. On the several occasions that I taught *Arabian*

Nights and Days in general education courses, I laid the groundwork by pairing the opening frame sequence of *The Arabian Nights* with a brief history of the *Nights* tradition.[1]

A Very Brief History of the Nights

Given the extensive and convoluted history of the *Arabian Nights,* an appreciation of the tradition must begin with a brief description of its transmutations, for as Mahfouz assembled *Arabian Night and Days,* he had at his disposal—and made use of—a heterogeneous hodgepodge of genetically diverse material.[2] While the derivation of many stories in the *Nights* canon will never be known, "it is evident that some . . . circulated orally for centuries before they began to be collected and written down" (Haddawy, *Arabian Nights* [1992] xv). As early as the tenth century, a number of these oral folktales had been gathered and transcribed; Haddawy cites the Arab historians al-Masʿudi (896?–956) and ibn al-Nadim (936?–995?), who "speak of the existence of such collections in their time" (xv). Among the various textual precursors to the *Arabian Nights,* a lost Persian collection titled *Hazar Afsana* ("A Thousand Legends") is commonly believed to be a direct antecedent, supplying both "the popular title as well as the general scheme" (xvi). A number of the stories in the *Nights* can be traced back to even earlier collections. The *Jataka,* for example, a fifth-century Pali collection, includes the two stories embedded in the *Nights* frame itself, "The Tale of the Ox and the Donkey" and "The Tale of the Merchant and His Wife" (Irwin, *Arabian Nights* 65).

Centuries of scholarly speculation identified India as the likely source for many of the *Nights* tales, transmitted and transmuted into Arabic from Sanskrit and Persian traditions. As Robert Irwin is careful to note, however, diffusionism—"the notion that aspects of culture start from a single source and spread from there to other civilizations" (68)—has fallen from favor. Not only are there "no conclusive grounds" for establishing India as the unique source of the *Arabian Nights,* but it must also be remembered that pathways of cultural exchange are bidirectional (not to mention multitudinous and tangled) and that India, therefore, "received stories as well as transmitted them" (77, 78). In any event, there is little debate that some of the narrative strands of the *Arabian Nights* tradition circulated independently, both before and after the cycle's codification. Migrating both eastward and westward, these stray snippets have cropped up in a variety of places—from Boccaccio's *Decameron* (c. 1350) to The Squire's Tale in Chaucer's *Canterbury Tales* (1390s), to mention two sites of cross-pollination from the fourteenth century.[3] It was not until the opening decades of the eighteenth century, however, that the *Arabian Nights*—as a collection—would become a known quantity in Europe.

The Frenchman Antoine Galland (1646–1715) is credited with placing the *Nights* before a European audience. In fact, he

> played so large a part in discovering the tales, in popularizing them in Europe and in shaping what would come to be regarded as the canonical collection that, at some risk of hyperbole and paradox, he has been called the real author of the *Nights*. (Irwin, *Arabian Nights* 14)[4]

In the 1690s, Galland worked as an assistant to Barthélemy d'Herbelot assembling the *Bibliothèque orientale* (1697), which he completed and published after d'Herbelot's death in 1695. The *Bibliothèque orientale* was a landmark text in the history of European orientalism—an alphabetized compendium of Eastern curiosities that numbered in excess of eight thousand entries and was, in the words of Edward Said, "more capaciously thorough than any work before it" (*Orientalism* 64). Following the success of the *Bibliothèque orientale* (and capitalizing on a newfound European fascination with an imaginary Orient), Galland published a French translation of the Sinbad story cycle in 1701, then spent the rest of his life assembling the first European version of the *Arabian Nights* (*Les mille et une nuits*), which appeared in twelve volumes between 1704 and 1717.

In assembling his translation, Galland made use—by chance, it would appear—of the oldest extant *Nights* manuscript, a fourteenth-century Syrian copy currently housed at the Bibliothèque Nationale in Paris. Nevertheless, "instead of following the text faithfully, Galland deleted, added, and altered drastically to produce not a translation, but a French adaptation, or rather a work of his own creation" (Haddawy, *Arabian Nights* [1992] xx). He also incorporated tales from other sources into his edition, including a number of stories related to him by a Christian Arab from Aleppo named Hanna Diab. Interestingly, "Aladdin and the Magic Lamp" and "Ali Baba and the Forty Thieves"—two of the best-known tales in the United States—are found in no Arabic source material that predates Galland's version. Whether Galland conjured these tales from the *quatorzienne* ether or adapted them from some lost source is unknown, but the distinct possibility that several of the *Nights* tales most popular in the West may have sprung from the imagination of a Western orientialist has not gone unnoticed by commentators.[5]

With the success of Galland's *Les mille et une nuits*, unauthorized English translations (so-called Grub Street editions) soon appeared in London. It was not until 1811, however, with Jonathan Scott's publication of *Arabian Nights Entertainments*, that "the first literary translation of Galland's work into English" appeared (Irwin, *Arabian Nights* 22). The early 1800s saw an outpouring of *Nights* publications, including the first four Arabic print collections: Calcutta I (1814–18), Breslau (1824–43), Bulaq (1835), and Calcutta II (1839–42).[6] The new accessibility of Arabic print versions in turn led to a host of European language translations, the first of note being Edward Lane's English translation (1839–41). Lane made use of Calcutta I, Breslau, and Bulaq in constructing his version—a version that, to assess it kindly, "tends toward the grandiose and mock biblical." "Where the style is not pompously high-flown," Irwin continues, "it is often painfully and uninspiringly literal" (24). In addition to his stylistic shortcomings,

Lane capriciously censored whatever he found prurient, tedious, or otherwise objectionable. Nevertheless, his erratically edited (if family-friendly) translation remained the English benchmark for nearly half a century.

The late Victorian period saw two additional translations, issued almost simultaneously: John Payne's nine-volume effort (1882–84) and Richard Burton's sixteen-volume edition (1885–86). As Lane had done, Payne and Burton made use of the recently produced Arabic print editions; however, whereas Lane strove to produce "a detailed but expurgated version," Payne and Burton set out to produce versions "as full and complete as possible" (Haddawy, *Arabian Nights* [1992] xix–xx). Such a methodology led to a wide variety of embellishments and questionable inclusions, all to satisfy the completist compulsion. In order to circumvent British obscenity laws, both translators sold their editions through subscriptions, Burton issuing his only after "Payne had resolved to publish no further editions of his work" (Irwin, *Arabian Nights* 29). Receiving Payne's blessing (and making liberal use of Payne's translation), Burton proceeded to publish what arguably has become the most (in)famous and influential English version of the *Arabian Nights*. Burton contributed to the *Nights'* already tangled history, making editorial decisions that sometimes verged on the inscrutable. For example, unable to locate "Arabic originals for some of Galland's 'orphan tales,' he adopted the bizarre procedure of retranslating them from Hindustani translations of Galland" (30). Some critics, such as Irwin, find the result "turgid and obscure,"[7] but Burton has his champions (32). Jorge Luis Borges, for one, asserts that "to peruse Sir Richard's translation is no less incredible than to read it in 'a plain and literal translation with explanatory notes' by Sinbad the Sailor" ("Translators" 98–99).[8] A. S. Byatt calls Burton's efforts "energetic and lively" and notes his "delight in archaisms, alliteration, internal rhyme and decoration" (xvi). Whatever one thinks of the final product, there is no denying that Burton casts a long shadow over both *Nights* scholarship and Western orientalism writ large. Burton's translation, Borges writes, "has a preordained prestige with which no other Arabist has ever been able to compete" (98).

Since then, various other editions and versions have surfaced. Notable among them are J. C. Mardrus's French edition (1899–1904), subsequently rendered into English by Powys Mathers (1937), and an inexpensive Penguin edition translated by N. J. Dawood in the 1950s, remarkable if only for its ubiquity. In 1984, after decades of painstaking work, Muhsin Mahdi published a definitive Arabic edition of the fourteenth-century Syrian manuscript of the *Arabian Nights*. Hussain Haddawy translated the Madhi edition into English, which was published by Norton in 1990. Haddawy's rendition was immediately lauded as a landmark achievement, though some bemoaned the fact that, although an "accurate" representation of the fourteenth-century Syrian text, his translation "left out an entire tradition, both written and oral, spanning the fifteenth through the nineteenth centuries, and comprising hundreds of stories" (Haddawy, *Arabian Nights* [1996] xi). Haddawy addressed this concern—at least in part—by producing a second, well-received collection titled *The Arabian Nights II: "Sindbad" and Other*

Popular Stories, which contained four additional tales: "The Story of Sindbad the Sailor," "The Story of ʿAli Baba and the Forty Thieves," "The Story of ʿAla al-Din and the Magic Lamp," and "The Story of Qamar al-Zaman and His Two Sons."

The Frame

While the assortment of tales known collectively as the *Arabian Nights* has evolved considerably over the past millennium, one thing has remained relatively constant: the collection's governing frame.[9] As conventionally told, the frame relates the story of two brothers: the elder one, Shahrayar, ruler of India and Indochina, and the younger, Shahzaman, king of Samarkand. Shahrayar requests a visit from his younger brother, and Shahzaman, on preparing to leave on his journey, finds his wife in the embrace of a servant. Furious, he slays them both and with a heavy heart quits the province for his brother's kingdom. After a melancholy month moping around Shahrayar's royal quarters, he chances on Shahrayar's wife astride a slave. This discovery immediately lifts Shahzaman's spirits, for, as Shahzaman disparagingly observes, the infidelity of women is man's "common lot" (Haddawy, *Arabian Nights* [1992] 5). Noting the change in his brother's mood, Shahrayar demands to know what has transpired. When he verifies Shahzaman's account, the two brothers embark on a journey, vowing to return only should they find "one whose misfortune is greater" than their own (8).

The trip lasts a single day. On the first night, Shahrayar and Shahzaman encounter a jinni, who, in order to preserve the chastity of his beautiful wife, keeps her locked in a chest. While the jinni sleeps, however, the woman tirelessly cuckolds him, adding Shahrayar and Shahzaman to her list of conquests with the threat that, should they refuse her advances, she would awaken the jinni. After submitting to her demands, the brothers return to their respective kingdoms. Shahrayar, in an attempt to circumvent "the deceit of women," embarks on a bloody campaign: each night he takes a new "wife" from among his subjects and in the morning orders her execution (6). This practice continues until the kingdom is virtually bereft of marriageable women.

Shahrayar's vizier, meanwhile, charged with carrying out the king's gruesome stratagem, has two daughters: Shahrazad, the elder, and Dinarzad. One day Shahrazad approaches her father and demands that she be given to the king in marriage, so that she "may either succeed in saving the people or perish and die like the rest" (Mahfouz, *Arabian Nights* 11). Her father, understandably, is loath to comply, but after the two exchange parables,[10] he consents. Shahrazad then embarks on a stratagem of her own: each night she begins telling the king a tale and just before dawn suspends the story at its climax. This *narratus interruptus* serves to extend her life a night at a time, as Shahrayar issues a daily stay of execution so that he may hear each tale's conclusion. After one thousand and one such nights, tradition holds, what Shahrazad has conceived (both narratologically and in utero) compels Shahrayar to repudiate his agenda.

Arabian Nights and Days *in the Classroom*

In my experience teaching *Arabian Nights and Days*, I have found that students' immediate reaction to the background material is often one of skepticism. Their doubts are directed neither at the historical account nor at the connection between Mahfouz's novel and its antecedents; rather, students have difficulty accepting Mahfouz's liberal appropriations. Our cultural notions of authenticity, it seems, are so deeply ingrained that students tend to distrust anything vaguely derivative. Invariably, they will ask such questions as "Well, isn't he just plagiarizing, then?" and "Can't we just skip Mahfouz and read the real stories?" As a result, I have found it helpful to highlight specific ways in which Mahfouz revises the *Arabian Nights* instead of focusing on how the novel recycles elements of the tradition.

One productive place to begin is to examine the way in which Mahfouz recasts the narrative perspective of the *Arabian Nights*. Although the frame allows the inclusion of a wide variety of tales, this device is limiting: all the tales must be filtered though Scheherazade, and many of them are themselves secondhand accounts. Mahfouz jettisons the frame for an omniscient third-person perspective. Students are quick to note this difference but slow to articulate the import of such a narrative shift. A brief interrogation of the novel's narrative perspective goes a long way toward legitimizing—in the eyes of the students—Mahfouz's literary project. I point out that the third-person narrator has unfettered access both to the human world and to the spirit world in *Arabian Nights and Days* and that this access opens additional space in the narrative for dramatic irony. For example, early in the novel, the narrator's ability to transcend the earthly realm alerts readers to the fact that Sahloul the bric-a-brac merchant is actually "the Angel of Death, Azrael's agent in the quarter" (68). Thus, while all the human characters in the novel proceed in ignorance of Sahloul's otherworldly function, readers can delight in the ghastly knowledge that his appearance signals a character's demise. Moreover, a foreknowledge of Sahloul's role opens a number of opportunities for readers to find humor in the disjuncture between what they know and what the characters know. In one episode, for example, Sahloul exonerates a murder suspect by proving that the alleged victim, who has been taken for a corpse, is still breathing. "[H]ave you any experience of medicine?" the governor asks in amazement. "No, sir," Sahloul replies, "but I have experience of death" (151). Students, able to find a number of other instances of dramatic irony in the novel, come round to the notion that more is occurring here than literary theft.

Another way to engage skeptical students is to examine how *Arabian Nights and Days* internalizes more than a century of psychological realism. Whereas the traditional tales present characters as little more than ciphers, Mahfouz imbues his with complex interiorities, motivations, and desires. This difference provides an excellent opportunity to expose students to the notion that psychological realism is a relatively modern artifice rather than a natural fictive mode, as many of them assume. My purpose is to suggest not that *Arabian Nights and*

Days is a work of realist fiction but only that the novel incorporates the tropes of psychological realism. Nor should Mahfouz's revisions be taken as an indictment of the *Arabian Nights*: the traditional characters are not poorly fashioned but just operate under a different paradigm. The third-person perspective of *Arabian Nights and Days* allows its readers access to the characters' inner lives, and pairing a consideration of that perspective with an investigation into the psychological complexities of the characters can be a constructive and rewarding strategy. Students are easily able to identify places in the text that provide a glimpse into the minds and motivations of the characters—from Fadil Sanaan's consternation on receiving the Cap of Invisibility to Shahriyar's struggles with the concept of justice. In identifying such episodes, moreover, students develop an appreciation for the way Mahfouz's adaptations transcend mere appropriation.

A third point of contact between the *Nights* tradition and Mahfouz's novel that I emphasize in the classroom is the way in which the novel subtly reimagines the ideological underpinnings of the traditional tales. The handling of Sindbad in *Arabian Nights and Days* is an excellent example, and when teaching the novel, I always assign "The Story of Sindbad the Sailor" as a supplemental reading. The traditional tale includes two separate characters named Sindbad: a porter (or landsman, as Burton styles him) and his more famous counterpart, a sailor. The porter is an extremely poor man whose good fortune consists of little more than the opportunity to listen to his wealthy namesake recount tales of adventure. Despite the disparity in their stations, however, the impoverished laborer does not question his lot in life; rather, he praises God's inequitable apportioning of fates:

> Glory be to You, o God, Creator and Provider! You bestow riches on whomever You wish, without reckoning. O Lord, I ask You forgiveness of all sins and repent to You of all faults. O Lord, there is no argument with Your judgment or Your power. You are not to be questioned on what You do, for You are omnipotent in every thing. Glory be to You! You enrich whomever You wish and impoverish whomever You wish. You exalt whomever You wish and humble whomever You wish. There is no God but You. How great is Your majesty, how mighty Your dominion, and how excellent Your government! You have bestowed favors on one you have chosen of your servants, for the owner of this place is in the height of comfort, enjoying all kinds of pleasant perfumes, delicious food, and fine beverages. You have foreordained and apportioned to Your creatures what You wish, so that among them some are weary, some are comfortable, and some enjoy life, while some, like me, suffer extreme toil and misery.
>
> (Haddawy, *Arabian Nights* [1996] 3–4)

The traditional telling serves both as a religious justification for social inequality and a parable that legitimizes and reinforces extant power structures.

Mahfouz drastically revises the tale, collapsing both Sindbad the Landsman and Sindbad the Sailor into a single character: a porter named Sindbad, who, "fed up with lanes and alleys" and "fed up with carrying furniture around, with no hopes of seeing anything new," runs off to sea (9). On his return, well traveled and wealthy, the once lowly porter offers advice even to the king himself. Students, often inclined to focus on the adventures of Sindbad, may initially overlook the implications of Mahfouz's revision, but a directed discussion soon elicits other textual examples where *Arabian Nights and Days* cleverly criticizes the social order. This observation can easily be expanded into a discussion of how the redeployment of an ancient literary tradition can serve to protect a novelist from political repercussions.

My experience teaching *Arabian Nights and Days*—even to students who are merely fulfilling general education requirements—has been quite positive. Students' discomfort with recycled material can be used to great advantage in the classroom by emphasizing Mahfouz's departure from rather than fidelity to the *Arabian Nights* tradition. The points of contact between the *Nights* and Mahfouz's novel that I have outlined, moreover, are easily adaptable and can serve as launching points for class discussion, guidelines for small-group work, or even prompts for writing assignments.

Additional Nights and Days

Situating Mahfouz's *Arabian Nights and Days* vis-à-vis the *Arabian Nights* tradition is only one way to contextualize the novel. For instructors wishing to explore in greater detail some of the tropes and techniques Mahfouz employs, I offer a second contextual framework: a corpus of international postmodern fiction that exhibits a comparable obsession with the *Nights* tradition. Such an approach obviously requires a greater investment of time—in terms of both preparation and course logistics—but it provides a range of rewarding pedagogical possibilities, which include pairing *Arabian Nights and Days* with another novel; constructing a multiweek, modular unit around *Arabian Nights and Days*; or even building an entire world literature course around the literary traditions of the *Arabian Nights*.[11]

For those interested in constructing a unit or course with *Arabian Nights and Days* as the centerpiece, Vilashini Cooppan's concept of "globalized reading" is particularly useful. "Globalized reading," Cooppan asserts,

> does not attempt to create an alternative canon so much as to change the prevalent positioning of the canonical and the non-canonical as one another's opposites, with the election of the one appearing to dictate the disappearance of the other. Taking a text considered world-making and placing it alongside one from another tradition and time, globalized reading changes the way we see. It displaces the hegemonic sense of "world" as

> fictive universality in favor of a vision of many worlds, individually distinct and variously connected. In this model, if Caribbean and African retellings of the *Odyssey* confirm a powerful critical narrative that holds Homer's poem great precisely because it has been so often imitated, the retellings equally invite construction of a different narrative, one that reads in the migratory movements of literary texts a far less unidirectional plot than the simple creeping expansion of a particular Western tradition. (32)

Cooppan's "globalized reading" is tailor-made to our purposes: it is a technique for teaching the "individually distinct and variously connected" versions, visions, and re-visions of the ever diverse *Nights* across centuries and cultures and suggests the utility of juxtaposing ancient literary tradition with a diffuse contemporary response. Of her own experience with globalized reading, Cooppan reports that the

> tracing of individual textual themes and devices, coupled with a pedagogical narrative about the migratory patterns of literary form, produced at least a partial sense that our heterogeneous material might also coalesce at various moments and in various places into something approaching a new literary history of genre. (35)

Teaching *Arabian Nights and Days* in concert with other, like-minded postmodern novels—including John Barth's *Chimera*, Italo Calvino's *If on a Winter's Night a Traveler*, and Salman Rushdie's *Haroun and the Sea of Stories*—will produce precisely the effect Cooppan describes, particularly when emphasis is placed on such postmodern preoccupations as self-referential framing devices and metafictional conceits.

First, Mahfouz's reweaving of the *Arabian Nights* tradition can be represented to students as a postmodern attempt to combat literary exhaustion, which Barth defines as "the used-upness of certain forms or exhaustion of certain possibilities" ("Literature" 29). He refutes the age-old lament that fiction is spent, that narrative has run its course, and that there are no new stories left to be told by invoking the *Arabian Nights* tradition as an exemplum of literary possibility. There is wit in this move—what could be more pertinent to a discussion of literary exhaustion than a narrator who stays up all night telling stories?—but also an acknowledgment that postmodern fiction, for all its playful rejection of some literary techniques and traditions, embraces others. Barth focuses on Borges's fascination with the six-hundred-and-second night:

> One of [Borges's] frequenter allusions, is to the six-hundred-and-second night . . . , when, owing to a copyist's error, Scheherezade begins to tell the King the story of the thousand and one nights, from the beginning. Happily, the King interrupts; if he didn't there'd be no six-hundred-and-third night ever, and while this would solve Scheherezade's problem—which is

> every storyteller's problem: to publish or perish—it would put the "outside" author in a bind.

Barth not only "suspect[s] that Borges dreamed this whole thing up"—("the business he mentions isn't in any edition of *The Thousand and One Nights* I've been able to consult," he declares)—but he even claims to have been accused of inventing Borges (33). I suspect Barth is being willfully disingenuous, muttering under his breath about literary invention even as he articulates the merits of recycling: anyone with access to Burton's *The Book of the Thousand Nights and a Night* can find the episode, as Borges describes it, in the sixth volume (198–201).

Barth highlights "the story-within-the-story turned back upon itself" as one key strategy by which the expanse of literary history can be "slyly employed against itself precisely to make new and original literature." Borges's "interest in such instances," he notes, "is threefold":

> First . . . they disturb us metaphysically: when the characters in a work of fiction become readers or authors of the fiction they're in, we're reminded of the fictitious aspect of our own existence, one of Borges' cardinal themes, as it was of Shakespeare, Calderón, Unamuno, and other folk. Second, the six-hundred-and-second Night is a literary illustration of the *regressus in infinitum*, as are almost all of Borges' principle images and motifs. Third, Scheherezade's accidental gambit, like Borges' other versions of the *regressus in infinitum*, is an image of the exhaustion, or attempted exhaustion, of possibilities. (33)

Barth, then, interrogating Borges's fascination with the *Arabian Nights* tradition, offers a strategy by which postmodernists can follow the modernist dictum to "make it new" without following the modernists, can produce fiction despite an overwhelming sense that its possibilities are exhausted, and can create something new and original out of something old and (at least somewhat) familiar.

This strategy is precisely what Mahfouz has undertaken in *Arabian Nights and Days*. First, as a fictional construction built expressly from preexisting components (characters, plotlines, settings), his novel turns the *Arabian Nights* tradition inward on itself, a gambit that combats exhaustion by making new and original fiction simply by forcing a tradition to swallow its own tail/tale. He short-circuits the tradition, moreover, by subverting its boundaries, escaping the frame both narratologically (shifting the perspective from first to third person) and chronologically (setting the action beyond the close of the traditional cycle). Second, Mahfouz combats literary exhaustion by indulging the postmodern obsession with metafiction. Students, when set to the task, are quick to note the multitude of metafictional moments in the novel, from Shahriyar's self-referential commentary on the nature of the novel (which serves as this essay's epigraph) to the fiction within a fiction that occurs when commoners decide to comment on current affairs by establishing a mock sultanate.[12] Third, Mahfouz includes a unique and engaging version of *regressus in infinitum*, employing the transmigration of souls as a literary technique. Over the course of *Arabian Nights and Days*, we trace the police chief Gamasa al-Bulti, as he becomes, in succession, Abdullah the Porter, Abdullah of the Land, the madman, and finally Abdullah al-Aqil (the Sane), the new chief of police. All but the final transformation are metempsychotic episodes. By allowing a single character multiple lives, each cut off at its climax, Mahfouz not only uses metempsychosis to transcend the limits of mortal exhaustion but also succeeds in mirroring the narrative structure of the *Arabian Nights* itself.

Instructors willing to spend additional nights and days on Mahfouz's novel can amplify its formal and thematic concerns by pairing it with one or more of the aforementioned texts: Barth's *Chimera*, Calvino's *If on a Winter's Night a Traveler*, and Rushdie's *Haroun and the Sea of Stories*. Barth's *Chimera* puts in fictive form many of the ideas and arguments of his essay on the literature of exhaustion; it also mines the same literary terrain that Mahfouz covers. Barth's novel is actually a triptych composed of three separate novellas. The opening "Dunyazadiad" is most useful to someone teaching *Arabian Nights and Days*. Largely from Dunyazade's perspective, the tale is a spirited spoof of authorial inspiration, a metafictional meditation on exhaustion and the limits of literary appropriation. In the novella, Scheherazade receives her stories from a time-traveling genie (one John Barth), stories he retrieves from a modern edition of the *Arabian Nights*. All goes swimmingly until he reaches the book's end and can no longer provide Scheherazade with life-sustaining tales. Much as Mahfouz does in *Arabian Nights and Days*, Barth constructs something wholly new and original from the bones of an extant tradition. The insistently metafictional nature of the tale not only is unsettling (if humorously rendered) but also lends itself well to comparison with Mahfouz's novel.

Calvino's inventive *If on a Winter's Night a Traveler* employs "a stratagem prompted by the literary tradition of the Orient," to borrow the novel's own words. The book alternates between numbered frame chapters and titled tales, each suspended "at the moment of greatest suspense" (125). Unlike the *Arabian Nights*, the interrupted tales are never resumed, and readers (both the protagonist of the frame chapters and the real-life readers) find themselves ever more embroiled in an inexplicable series of literary transmissions, translations, and transmutations. Although *If on a Winter's Night a Traveler* contains multiple allusions and references to the *Arabian Nights*, it is not a reworking of the tradition in the fashion of *Arabian Nights and Days* or *Chimera*. Nevertheless, the novel's formal obsession with the *Nights* and its repeated use of the *regressus in infinitum* trope (including one memorable episode in which a character becomes lost in a fun house of mirrors) make it a rewarding counterpoint to *Arabian Nights and Days*.

Haroun and the Sea of Stories presents another option to an instructor teaching *Arabian Nights and Days*. A fable for children of all ages, Rushdie's novel playfully engages the same salient themes we have been discussing. Haroun and his father, the storyteller Rashid Khalifa, take their names from Harun al-Rashid (763–809), the most famous of the Abbasid caliphs and a recurring character in the *Arabian Nights*. Rushdie's Rashid, also known as the Ocean of Notions, runs out of stories, and the book recounts Haroun's adventures as he attempts to restore his father's gift. As does Mahfouz in *Arabian Nights and Days*, Rushdie cloaks important political and metaphysical considerations in playful fabulation, and the text includes a running metacommentary on the value and efficacy of narrative.

At a remove—by several decades—from Barth's essay on literary exhaustion, it becomes clear that a number of postmodernists have followed his prescription precisely. In addition to turning stories within stories on themselves, highlighting metafictional conceits, and employing *regressus in infinitum* as a trope, a number of these writers have specifically paid homage to the *Arabian Nights* tradition. Reading Mahfouz as a member of this coterie underscores both the formal techniques and the thematic objectives of *Arabian Nights and Days*.

In this essay, I have provided a contextual teaching strategy for Mahfouz's *Arabian Nights and Days*. A brief investigation of the *Arabian Nights* tradition presents students with the raw material to appreciate Mahfouz's revisions and in addition introduces them to a nonlinear alternative to literary realism. Such an approach encourages them to rethink their ideas regarding authenticity and textual authority—especially given that some of the tales with which they are most familiar (e.g., "Aladdin" and "Ali Baba and the Forty Thieves") are, generously speaking, late additions to the narrative cycle. Brief samplings of translations as diverse as Haddawy and Burton reveal, in metareflexive fashion, the importance of context. Reading Mahfouz in concert with other, like-minded postmodern tellers of tales allows for the amplification of both formal and thematic concerns—from framing devices to the utilization of metafictional conceits—and helps students appreciate the manner in which postmodern fiction, to reshuffle Barth's dictum, combats exhaustion by slyly employing literature against itself.

NOTES

[1] If this background material is to be covered using supplemental readings, I suggest assigning the prologue ("The Story of King Shahrayar and Shahrazad, His Vizier's Daughter") and the first two interrelated tales, "The Tale of the Ox and the Donkey" and "The Tale of the Merchant and His Wife"—the first sixteen pages of Haddawy's 1990 translation (Haddawy, *Arabian Nights* [1992]). For a brief overview of the *Arabian Nights* tradition (beyond the one included in this essay), I recommend Robert Irwin's engaging and accessible *The Arabian Nights: A Companion* (1994). Several selections—particularly the opening two chapters, "Beautiful Infidels" and "The Book without Authors"—provide a detailed account of the cross-cultural transmission and dissemination of the *Nights*.

[2] Some scholars might take issue with the descriptor *heterogeneous* as applied to the *Nights*. Haddawy, for one, asserts that as "different as their ethnic origins may be, these

stories reveal a basic homogeneity resulting from the process of dissemination and assimilation under Islamic hegemony, a homogeneity or distinctive synthesis that marks the cultural and artistic history of Islam" ([1992] xv). Nevertheless, many readers are struck by the—pardon the student vernacular—"random" inclusions, which range from bawdy jokes to bucolic fables, from song lyrics to the supernatural.

[3]The Squire's Tale incorporates elements of "The Ebony Horse." See, for example, Pollard vii–xx.

[4]While Galland played a significant role in the dissemination of the tales to a Western audience, to consider him the true author of the *Nights* is certainly hyperbolic. In fact, part of the appeal of the *Nights* to postmodern practitioners is the collection's resistance to authorial attribution.

[5]According to his diaries, Galland first heard the tale "Aladdin and His Magic Lamp" from Hanna Diab in 1709 (Haddawy, *Arabian Nights* [1992] xvii). The source he used in translating "Aladdin" is unknown. The Sinbad cycle—another of the handful of *Nights* tales recognizable to an American lay audience—does have an Arabic source that predates Galland. However, its association with and incorporation into the *Arabian Nights* also occurred as a result of Galland's work.

[6]These four editions have traditionally been designated by the locations of their publication. As Irwin notes, "there are considerable problems regarding the sources and status of all these texts" (*Arabian Nights* 21). The Breslau edition, for example, was collated by Maximilian Habicht, who claimed to have based it on a mysterious Tunisian manuscript. The Tunisian manuscript did not exist.

[7]Irwin also calls Burton's translation "distinctly unattractive," complaining, "I thought I might slit my throat rather than continue with this enterprise" (*Arabian Nights* 1).

[8]While evidently an expression of admiration, this particular remark is also, in fine Borgesian fashion, a playful jab at the fictionality of Burton's translation.

[9]The oldest surviving textual fragment of the *Arabian Nights*, which dates from the ninth century, is a snippet of the frame. For more on this ancient fragment, see Abbott.

[10]"The Tale of the Ox and the Donkey" and "The Tale of the Merchant and His Wife."

[11]Those wishing to construct an entire course around the literary traditions of the *Arabian Nights* have at their disposal many texts beyond the purview of this essay. Two of note are Edgar Allan Poe's "The Thousand-and-Second Tale of Schehrazade" (1845), in which the eponymous heroine relates a series of modern marvels and is condemned for "tak[ing the king] for a fool" (373), and Borges's *Ficciones*, which contains a number of relevant short stories, including the exquisitely rendered "Tlön, Uqbar, Orbis Tertius" and "The Library of Babel." "Tlön, Uqbar, Orbis Tertius" considers a fictional encyclopedia with a publication history as tangled and mysterious as that of the *Arabian Nights*. The narrator, on acquiring the 1001-page eleventh volume, is carried away into the nonce land of Tlön, as the tale interrogates the meaning of authorship, the production of literature, and the possibility of impossible worlds. "The Library of Babel," meanwhile, is an apt complement to *Arabian Nights and Days*.

[12]See the chapter titled "The Sultan" (172–78).

Hamida's Options: Egyptian Futures versus British Interests in Mahfouz's *Midaq Alley*

Barbara Harlow

Hamida's Options

Hamida, one of Midaq Alley's more notorious residents, does not want to spend the rest of her life in this seeming Cairo cul-de-sac. What are her options? And what might be the alley's claims on her, raised as she has been by a foster mother, Umm Hamida? Umm Hamida is a matchmaker of sorts, among whose concerns are the ensuring of the future of her neighbors' marital happiness or sexual satisfaction, the longevity of the entire quarter, and Hamida's opportunities—and taking advantage of what auspices promise.

When teaching زقاق المدق (Zuqaq al-midaqq; *Midaq Alley*), it can be useful to remind students that Hamida, among the many characters in Naguib Mahfouz's 1947 novel, is not only infamous but also the most frustrated of the alley's denizens. Her fight for a better future for herself is in turn symptomatic of the historic fractures in the social structures of Egypt's capital city in the waning years of World War II. On her regular afternoon walks, for example, Hamida encounters other girls returning to the alley from their factory jobs and recalls a "girl from Sanadiqiya Street who was even poorer than she." More important, she remembers that "fortune sent a rich contractor who transported [that girl] from her miserable hovel to a fairy-tale life" (*Midaq Alley* [1992] 40). Factory work and a fairy-tale life are two options that Hamida considers. But during those promenades, when the young woman's "greedy and ambitious mind" speculates on the "power centered around her love for money" (40), she is considered by three men who have other options in mind: Abbas, the alley's barber, who will seek employment with the British army in the hope of increasing his chances with Hamida; Salim Alwan, the company owner who asks Umm Hamida to make him a match and secure Hamida for him as a second wife, only to succumb to a heart attack once the deal has been done; and Ibraham Faraj, the pimp and procurer who succeeds in seducing Hamida into whoring for a clientele both foreign and local—but mostly foreign.

Because Hamida's options can be read as a gendered allegory of Egypt's modern predicament, they need to be grounded in that same historical precariousness. Written in 1947, set during World War II, and anticipating perhaps the 1952 Free Officers Revolution, Mahfouz's *Midaq Alley* recapitulates the bitter and controversial story of the British occupation of Egypt since 1882, the nascent nationalism of 1919, and the debate over the rights of small nations following World War I. The novel also reflects on the possibilities that history offers in the daily lives of the neighbors who congregate in Midaq Alley: Hamida; and her several suitors; the poet Sheikh Darwish, who competes with the radio; Kirsha the café owner with his homosexual proclivities; Zaita the crippler; the electioneering politician Ibrahim Farhat; the widow Mrs. Afifi with her own ambitions; and the wise and devout soothsayer Radwan who listens to them all.

Hamida's options are writ large across the readings of the novel, which, drawing on historical, documentary, and critical sources, follows Hamida through 1940s Cairo, mapping the roads of colonization and occupation that lead there and the paths of decolonization and independence that alternatively open and close myriad speculations on Egypt's new narrative—and on possibilities, in a twenty-first-century context, of globalization and the continued, now neocolonial, contest over the Middle East. In other words, what were—and what are still—Hamida's options?

According to Fouad Ajami, a pundit and historian who concluded his obituary of Mahfouz by reclaiming the author from modern Egyptian history for timelessness, "[r]eaders came to him looking for Egypt and its political condition, its mind and its moods. . . . But there runs through his output—well over fifty works of fiction—a different, and more universal, concern." For Ajami, "at the heart of [Mahfouz's] fiction lay not Egypt's modern history, but something even grander: man's battle with time" ("Humanist" 33). The literary critic Hosam Aboul-Ela, by contrast, has argued:

> In the West, much of the project of turning Naguib Mahfouz into a novelist who is bankable for publishers and consumable for nonspecialist readers has been built upon the construction of an exceptionalist argument that sees him as above the political fray. ("Writer" 341)

Aboul-Ela points out that "Mahfouz has managed to scandalize every Egyptian President since 1952 but without ever crossing the line, without ever pushing far enough to be punished" (342). The inhabitants of Cairo's Midaq Alley, situated in Mahfouz's own neighborhood of "old Cairo" or the al-Gamaliyya district of the burgeoning city in the early 1940s, residents who lived through the blackouts and air raids of World War II, may not have been punished either—although two of them do wind up in prison and another is dead by the novel's end. But their living space and enduring lives, like Mahfouz himself, had to accommodate to the historical and political changes wrought by circumstances beyond their control: the war's end, the unrelenting influence of British occupation, heart attacks, moral setbacks, cultural outlets, personal outcomes, political foreclosures.

Midaq Alley: *Geographic Cul-de-Sac or Historical Thoroughfare?*

Hamida's options are introduced in Mahfouz's novel through a description of Midaq Alley as a blind alley, a dead end, like so many other passageways in the Islamic city. The prefatory setting appears to run counter to the Hegelian narrative of a dominant nineteenth-century philosophy of history that places Egypt rather early on in the grand scheme and historical narrative of advance and progress, culminating as that story does in the occidental setting of the sun over European lands:

> The sun began to set and Midaq Alley was veiled in the brown hues of the glow. The darkness was all the greater because it was enclosed like a trap between three walls. It rose unevenly from Sanadiqiya Street. One of its sides consisted of a shop, a café, and a bakery, the other of another shop and an office. It ends abruptly, just as its ancient glory did, with two adjoining houses, each of three stories. (1)

In the café, owned by Kirsha, who, much to the ire of his wife, has a fondness for young boys, the long-standing position of Sheikh Darwish is challenged by the introduction of a radio, and so the bard laments, "The poet has gone and the radio has come. This is the way of God in His creation. Long ago it was told in *tarikh*, which in English means 'history' and it is spelled h-i-s-t-o-r-y" (9). Meanwhile Hamida is observed on her regular afternoon meanders through and beyond the quarter from that same café and its adjacent structures: "she was aware that four eyes were examining her closely. The eyes belonged to Salim Alwan, the company owner, and to Abbas, the barber" (39). Hamida, as prurient as she is chaste, is no less observant:

> She leaned out of the room's only window, which overlooked the street, and stretched her arms out to the open shutters, drawing them together so that only a couple of inches of space was left between them. She then sat resting on her elbows, placed on the windowsill and gazed out into the street. . . . (28)

Midaq Alley, however, the *zuqaq* with all its lexical resonance in Arabic of "dead end," was "enclosed like a trap between three walls." Or was it not?

The scholarly debates among academic orientalists and other extracurricular European visitors, from Napoléon and his army of scientists and soldiers in the early nineteenth century (referred to by the historian Juan Cole as an "Enlightenment juggernaut" [65]) through such sympathetic imperial and well-traveled bilateral partisans as E. W. Lane (*Manners and Customs of the Modern Egyptians* [1860]) and Lady Duff Gordon (*Letters from Egypt* [1865]), concerning the definition of the Islamic city—its physical layout, political design, religious influences, administrative functions, social mores—have been as rife as the internecine, often lascivious, conflicts among the residents of Mahfouz's Midaq Alley. In her assessment of the "Islamic city," Janet Abu-Lughod, an urban planner and sociologist, suggests that "the blind alley or dead-end court street was such a device for achieving this compromise between the exigencies of life and the directives of female seclusion" (168). According to Abu-Lughod,

> when densities are high [as in Midaq Alley] and houses too small to contain the manifold activities women are supposed to do in them, the spillover space becomes appropriated as semi-private space and co-residents who might inadvertently have visual access are appropriated into a fictive kinship relationship to neutralize danger. (168)

Was it on the basis of such a "fictive kinship relationship," I ask my students, that Abbas, Hamida's unrequited suitor, took his revenge on the unwanted and unwonted intrusions into the social integrity of the dead-end court street that was Midaq Alley?

Renowned for its medieval mosques, madrassas, and markets, al-Gamaliyya was declared a world heritage site by UNESCO in 1979 and has ever since provided the staging for conflicting scenarios, on the part of international foundations, the Egyptian government, and sundry NGOs, for its restoration, renovation, or rehabilitation. What is, as Abu-Lughod has queried, an Islamic city, after all? In their inquiry into the future of old Cairo, the architects and demographers Keith Sutton and Wael Fahmi suggest that the very term should be reexamined:

> Perhaps an alternative nomenclature to "Old Cairo" or "Medieval Cairo" could be "pre-Europeanised Cairo" which delimits its street pattern and layout from the strongly European influenced nineteenth-century layout and buildings of Mohamed Ali's period and later. (78)

Sutton and Fahmi endorse a rehabilitation approach to al-Gamaliyya and its sociological and heritage-influenced urban context. Whereas renovation looks to the preservation of particular monuments or significant buildings for the sake of a "tourist-historic city" (73), and renovation is "associated with demolition" (75), rehabilitation looks to the neighborhood "as the cultural built environment heritage of the city's present population whether living within or outside the medina district itself" (76). But that is now, and *Midaq Alley* was then, in the early 1940s, when the British still occupied wartime Egypt—"the intersection," as Mahmoud Hussein refers to it in his now-classic Marxist study *Class Conflict in Egypt, 1945–1970*, "of a decadent past and an obstructed future" (36).

British suzerainty over Egypt harked back to 1869 and the massive debts that had been incurred by Khedive Ismail in entertaining European royal guests (including building sumptuous palaces for their short-term monarchical housing) on the occasion of the opening of the Suez Canal. That control was further consolidated after the defeat of the nationalist uprising led by ʿUrabi Pasha in 1882, when Britain formally occupied the country. By 1944, as a second world war was winding down, the British were themselves reeling in the maelstrom of managing both national resistance in their colonies—such as Egypt—and the imperative of maintaining the international military fronts appropriate to the waging of a second worldwide conflagration (see Wichhart). It was not until 1952 and the Free Officers Revolution that Egypt would begin to see its way out of the cul-de-sac of colonial control, or perhaps even 1956, when Egypt under President Gamal Abdul Nasser nationalized the Suez Canal in the interest of pan-Arabism and defeated the tripartite aggression of the combined forces of Britain, France, and Israel, who hoped to sustain their foothold (if not a waterway) in and through the Arab Middle East.

At the time of publication of *Midaq Alley*, especially in the context of the setting of the novel several years earlier, the influences of the war were palpable even in the cloistral confines of the close-knit alley. The topical and tropic intersections of demography and topography (i.e., of characters and setting) are ridden and riddled by the tensions between colonial occupation and international conflict, not to mention the blackouts and air raids that regularly shatter the more or less quiescent internal turmoils of the alley's social relations. Midaq Alley's contested cartography is decidedly situated in a conflicted chronology of Egyptian futures and British interests. Midaq Alley—in other words, Hamida's options—could be read, to cite Abu-Lughod, as a contribution to the concerns that have emerged from the question of an Islamic city:

> A city at one point in time is a still photograph of a complex system of building and destroying, of organizing and reorganizing, etc. In short, the intellectual question we need to ask ourselves is: Out of what forces were the prototypical Islamic cities created? (162)

The question of whether or not Midaq Alley is a component of a "prototypical Islamic" city is redrafted in the stories of the suits brought forward by the pretenders to providing for Hamida's future—or her provisioning of their own personal aspirations.

Trysts and Turns

Students should recall that all three of Hamida's suitors, each in his own way, have their own designs on the alley, plans for protecting the enclave or breaching its boundaries. Furthermore, the pretensions of each—Abbas Hilu, the unassuming barber; Salim Alwan, the presuming company owner; Ibrahim Faraj, the presumptuous pimp and procurer—are premised on their respective investments in both a prolonged war and the continued British occupation of Egypt and the benefits these combined conditions might yet hold out for Hamida's options.

Abbas Hilu

Despite her misgivings, or what some in the alley saw as her "greedy ambitions" (40), Hamida was obliged to admit, at least at first, that, given her limited options as an orphan raised by a foster mother, she could not afford to overlook Abbas's overtures. Nonetheless,

> [h]er feelings toward him were strange and complicated. On the one hand, he was the only young man in the alley who would make a suitable husband for her, while she, on the other hand, dreamed of a husband like the rich contractor her neighbor had married.

Who, Hamida asks herself in the course of a first meeting with Abbas, "would satisfy her if this kind young man did not?" (42, 43).

Abbas, that "kind young man," maintains a barber shop in Midaq Alley and wishes for nothing more than to live contentedly to the end of his days in the alley—ideally, of course, with Hamida as his equally contented wife—amidst the reassurance of the neighborly comforts and conversation of their fellow residents, especially Uncle Kamil, who generously shares both his space and the treats from his sweet tray. Abbas's good friend but lurking rival as well, Hussain Kirsha, is less sanguine about the two young men's prospects. Hussain works for the British army and sees that employment as a way out of the restrictions of the alley. In a lengthy exhortation, he advises Abbas to take a similar path:

> Shake off the miserable life, close up your shop, leave this filthy alley behind. Rest your eyes from looking at Uncle Kamil's carcass. Work for the British Army. It's a gold mine that will never be exhausted. Why, it's exactly like the treasure of Hassan al-Basary! This war isn't the disaster that fools say it is. It's a blessing! God sent it to us to rescue us from our poverty and misery. Those air raids are throwing gold down on us. (36)

Abbas, thinking he has won Hamida's assent to marry him, follows Hussain's advice.

Unemployment in Egypt was high. Just a few years later, as Mahmoud Hussein points out, "On the eve of Nasser's takeover [1952, with the Free Officers

Revolution], half of the Egyptian population of working age was partially or totally unemployed" (xvix). Under wartime conditions and with British occupation in full sway and swagger, Abbas abandons his shop and trade as the alley's barber for the opportunity to earn enough for him to secure Hamida's consent to their marriage. The pair's leave-taking is poignant if also pecuniary and penurious:

> He was silent a moment and then added, "I leave you in the name of love. By its strength may I return with lots of money."
> "A great deal of money, I pray to God," she murmured, almost unaware of what she said.
> "With God's permission and by the grace of Hussain. All those other girls will really envy you."
> She smiled happily and agreed. "Ah, how nice that would be!" (109)

The "grace of Hussain," invoked by Abbas on the occasion of his farewell to his betrothed is not that of Hussain Kirsha but that of the holy Sayyidna Hussain, grandson of the Prophet Muhammad and son of Ali. Sayyidna Hussain was killed at the battle of Karbala in AD 680, and the magnificent Cairo mosque, built in AD 1154 to house the imam's head, imposed its—and his—religious influence over the entire neighborhood, which just managed to survive under the shadow of the ever-watchful edifice.

The former barber has other leave-taking to do:

> That night Abbas visited Hamida's mother to say farewell. Then he went to the café, accompanied by his friend Hussain Kirsha, to have their last coffee together before departure. Hussain was happy and triumphant with the success of his suggestion, and he said to Abbas, his voice somewhat challenging, "Say goodbye from now on to this wretched alley life. Now start to enjoy a real life." (110)

That "real life," the life of an employee of the British occupier's war apparatus, will be lived, not insignificantly, in Tell el-Kebir, situated midway between Cairo and Ismailia on the Suez Canal. In Ismailia, more than half a century earlier, in 1882, Ahmed ʿUrabi Pasha was defeated by British forces and sent into exile in Ceylon. He died in exile, but Abbas, who instead of resisting the British occupiers is working for them, will die in Cairo, during a short leave to confirm his commitments with Hamida. But that story comes later, for while Abbas is serving the British and their war efforts in Tell el-Kebir, Hamida's mother, professional matchmaker that she is, arranges another marriage for her foster daughter.

Salim Alwan

Salim Alwan, a company owner and family man with a wife and numerous children, has also had an eye on the alley's most eligible young woman. Hamida herself was well aware of her physical attractions and Alwan's attentions, if not his sensual intentions, as she surveyed her prospects during her afternoon walks. She would not choose Jaada, the husband of Husniya the bakeress; Kirsha the café owner; or Uncle Kamil asleep over his platter of sweets. Even Abbas is spurned. But Salim Alwan is another story. "Well now, Mr. Salim Alwan," Hamida muses capriciously, if with some residual sense of propriety,

> the company owner, has just lifted up his eyes, lowered them, and raised them once again. We'll say the first time was an accident, but the second, Mr. Alwan? Sir? Watch now, he's just started a third time! What do you want, you senile and shameless old man? You want a rendezvous with me every day at this time? If only you weren't a married man and a father, I'd give you look for look and say welcome and welcome again! (28)

Hamida, as it happens, is willing to abandon that scruple when Umm Hamida later approaches her with Salim Alwan's unexpected and untoward proposal. The preening and covetous company owner, after long indecision regarding his commitments to family and business, finally came to the conclusion that "[w]hat good was his fortune if he were to deny himself what he wanted and what he could so easily have. Why should he be consumed with longing for a body that could be his at merely a nod of his head?" (140). He invites Umm Hamida to his office to negotiate the bargaining for the hand—and body—of Hamida. Hamida is willing to conclude the deal. "Here at last," she thought,

> was the stroke of fortune she had always dreamed of. This at last was the man who could give her all the luxury and freedom from drudgery she prayed for. She could think of no cure for her hunger for power other than a great deal of money. She wanted the other things it would bring: dignity, beautiful clothes, jewelry, pride, and a whole new world of secure and happy people. (142)

So Hamida agrees to Salim Alwan's terms, despite the near-universal disapproval to be expected from her neighbors in Midaq Alley, especially the righteous and wise Radwan Hussainy, whose upright stance and mature experience provide consistent social support and reliable spiritual succor for all the alley's residents.

Like Abbas and Hussein, who sought to profit from the British war effort through employment, Salim Alwan seeks to increase his fortune from the British, though his strategy smacks of profiteering. His company had long

> dealt with perfumes, wholesale and retail, and there was no doubt that the wartime cut in imports from India had badly affected trade. However, the company managed to keep both its reputation and its position and, indeed, the war had doubled its activities and profits. The wartime situation convinced Salim Alwan of the wisdom of trading in commodities

> which previously had not interested him—for example, tea. Thus he had become active in the black market and profited heavily from it. (62)

He is no more or less than a bit player in what the political scientist Robert Vitalis has described as a "war within a 'war'" in his analysis of the "role played by . . . local investors in the precipitous collapse of the British neocolonial project" (104). According to Vitalis, "[d]uring World War II, Egypt's business oligarchs escalated their private war over markets, contracts, concessions, subsidies and related state-mediated opportunities for accumulation" (104). Mahfouz's Alwan too has taken advantage of the fact that, as Vitalis notes, the "war had completely disrupted Egypt's normal channels of trade" (113).

Taking the perspective of labor rather than capital, Joel Beinin and Zachary Lockman, historians, concur in the argument that the "main stimulus for the growth of large-scale mass production industry . . . was World War II" (257). *Workers on the Nile*, their study of "nationalism, communism, Islam, and the Egyptian working class" from 1882 to 1954, suggests that the alternative options offered to Hamida by Abbas on the one hand and Salim Alwan on the other were similarly war-related. But both kinds of collaboration were a threat to British postwar control over colonial properties and human resources. Abbas, for all his modest and malleable demeanor, represents the frustrated futures of young Egyptian males available to trade union organizers, and Salim Alwan is symptomatic of the business interests of Egypt's emerging national industrial bourgeoisie or capitalist-investor stratum and its market-driven challenge to British power.

Salim Alwan, however, suffers a heart attack and is obliged to reconsider not only his own life-and-death prospects but also his offer to Hamida. Hamida's hopes have been dashed:

> Salim Alwan had collapsed near death after giving her a day and a half of hope for the life she had always wanted, and now this had happened, after she had banished Abbas from her dreams. Because she now knew there was no hope of marrying Alwan, she renewed her engagement to the barber, even though she felt only scorn for him. (161)

Has Midaq Alley too exhausted its options?

Ibrahim Farraj

Ibrahim Farraj is an outsider to Midaq Alley, and he first appears in the neighborhood at a surprise political rally, the preparations for which awakened the alley's residents one morning to a "tumult of great noise and confusion," caused by men who "were setting up a pavilion in a vacant lot in Sanadiqiya Street, opposite Midaq Alley." Uncle Kamil fears that a funeral pyre might be in the making, but a young passer-by reassures him that the construction is for an "election campaign party" (148). Ibrahim Farhat, independent candidate for the office of deputy representing the district, is coming to canvas for votes and meanwhile has made himself comfortable in Kirsha's café. Because Kirsha was once one of the more politically inclined denizens of the alley, having a history of participation in Egypt's anticolonial campaigns that goes back to the nationalist rebellion of 1919 led by Saad Zaghlul's Wafd forces, he is of especial interest to Farhat. But Kirsha has of late "rejected respectable life and now . . . [cares] only for the pleasures of the flesh" (152). He has redirected his energy from the promises made by national heroes to the attractions of young men. As Joseph Massad argues in his critical reading of *Midaq Alley*, "the central genre that represents modern and contemporary sexual practices is fiction, especially the novel" (269). According to Massad, the "first work of modern Arabic fiction to deal with the question of same-sex desire seriously is Naguib Mahfouz's [*Midaq Alley*]" (272). The turn taken in Hamida's options through her encounter with Ibrahim Farraj, heterosexual though it might be, is still illicit. Honor, as both Hussein and Abbas will eventually argue with each other, is at stake.

When Hamida first sees Ibrahim, he is unnamed and unrecognized, a stranger to the alley, and she is still reeling from the news of Salim Alwan's heart attack. "[Farraj] entered her life at a time when she was overcome with despair" (161). But even in the excitement of the political campaign, she notices the lurking intruder. As happened with Abbas and Salim Alwan, she watches him watch her:

> She turned from the reciter and moved her head until her eyes met those of a man staring at her with insolent intensity. Her eyes rested on his and then quickly turned back to the stage. However, she could no longer recapture her earlier interest. She was overcome by an intense desire to look toward the left once again. Confusion and panic gripped her as his eyes pierced her with that same shameless insolence; at the same time they seemed to smile at her in a curious way. She could not bear to look at him. (156–57)

She wonders, "This man [is] obviously well-to-do and what could he be doing in Midaq Alley?" (157).

Hamida soon discovers what, for, "from that evening on, he came regularly to Midaq Alley" (160), spending late afternoons in Kirsha's café, biding his time perhaps, until one afternoon she tempts him. The seduction is rebuffed but then rewarded the following day, when the man takes the initiative. A series of clandestine rendezvous follows between pursued and pursuer, all within the alley's environs. "What could he want?" Hamida asks herself. "The question seemed idle to her, for she could see only one reason for his continuous pursuit of her. The same thing that Abbas wanted earlier and Salim Alwan too before fate struck him down" (183).

But marriage with him is not to be. Transported in a taxi, Hamida finds herself in Ibrahim Farraj's flat on Sharif Pasha Street, in Cairo's European quarter, well beyond the purview and oversight of her neighbors in Midaq Alley. Ibrahim watches Hamida,

> as she quickly walked away, [with] a sardonic smile on his lips. He told himself, "Delicious, no doubt about it. I'm quite sure I'm not wrong about her. She has got a natural gift for it. . . . She's a whore by instinct. She's going to be a really priceless pearl." (198)

She finds herself under the tutelage of her erstwhile suitor, now mentor—and pimp. She excels in her lessons in oriental and Western dancing and learns the English needed for practicing her new profession. She soon becomes, as she herself admits with pride, "a favorite of the soldiers and her savings were proof of her popularity" (199). That her whereabouts are sought from the "police station at Gamaliya and Kasr al-Aini Hospital" (233) suggests that Midaq Alley's otherwise religious residents are no more averse to enlisting the help of representatives of the state than were the nineteenth-century Cairenes, whose testimony on police and forensic medicine has been examined by Khaled Fahmy in critical essays on criminal law in nineteenth-century Egypt ("Anatomy" and "Police"). Hamida is considered a missing person.

Foreclosures

Abbas discovers that Hamida is missing when he revisits the neighborhood on a short leave from his own version of British employment, eager to bestow on his beloved his wedding present, a "gold necklace with a small dangling heart" (232). Except that it is Abbas's heart that has been left dangling. For want of better company, he takes up again with Hussein, who has lost his job with the British, given the impending end to the war, and returned reluctantly to his father's home with a wife and a brother-in-law in tow. Abbas and Hussein go to Vita's bar to compare and bemoan their respective marital predicaments. Shortly thereafter, Abbas catches up with his beloved, only to find that she is not missing at all but living a life of shame. Seeking solace in the wine that he shares with Hussein, he laments, "There's no hope for Hamida now, she's lost forever, but I am not going to let that filthy gangster escape without punishment." Hussein disagrees: "Hamida is the real culprit." Still Abbas nurses his affection for Hamida. "[D]on't you think," he replies, "this fellow has insulted our honor and therefore must be punished?" (278).

A critical question for students is, Whose honor? Hamida's? Has she any honor anyway? Her husband's? But she still has no husband. Her family's? But she has no family—only a foster mother. Midaq Alley's? In any case, the transgression must be punished. According to Beth Baron, "[m]en are sometimes killed for their role in dishonouring women, particularly when the man [is] an outsider or perceived to be socially inferior, yet women turn out be the victims on most occasions" ("Women" 2). Hussein admonishes Abbas, "Why didn't you murder her?" (279). After all, as Amr Shalakany has summarized, "[e]xtramarital sex, or *zina*, is the paradigmatic *hadd* [crime entailing fixed penalties] with respect to sexual offenses under *fiqh* [jurisprudence] and its rules are often intertwined with those criminalizing sodomy . . . " (16). What now are Abbas's options?

Hussein and Abbas exit Vita's bar to reconnoiter the tavern where Hamida is reputed to consort with her clients, only to find a shocking tableau, reminiscent of scenes of nineteenth-century oriental odalisques:

> From then on things happened so quickly that Hussein was left in a daze. He saw Hamida sitting amidst a crowd of soldiers. One stood behind her pouring wine into a glass in her hand, leaning toward her slightly as she turned her head toward him. Her legs were stretched on the lap of another soldier sitting opposite her, and there were others in uniform crowding around her, drinking boisterously. Abbas stood stunned. . . .

Abbas's "anger foamed within him and blinded his vision, and he quite forgot that he had any enemy other than her. He charged madly into the tavern, roaring out in a thunderous voice, 'Hamida . . . '" (278). In the ensuing scuffle—a conflict that engages men and a woman, a spurned Egyptian lover and British soldiers, Midaq Alley and greater Cairo, Egypt and Europe—Hamida is wounded and Abbas is killed. As for the British soldiers, as Hussein says to his father afterward, "who can expect any justice from them?" (283). Is this sorry and sordid scene to be the dénouement then, in the words of the alley's poet, Sheikh Darwish, who translated *tarikh* into "history" and spelled it "t-a-r-i-k-h" (9), that "everything comes to its *nihaya*?" As the learned sheikh of the alley says, in the final words of *Midaq Alley*, "And the word for this in English is 'end' and it is spelled e-n-d . . . " (286). But perhaps it is not the end.

Exit . . .

Midaq Alley can be read in many ways, according to various interpretative trajectories and following various disciplinary itineraries. In other words, the novel is no more or less a cul-de-sac than is Midaq Alley. Like Hamida, the reader has options, and this essay has endeavored to suggest at least some of those critical opportunities, by referring to multicurricular resources: literary criticism, history, anthropology, sociology, political science, law, urban studies, Arabic studies, women's studies. At the end of the novel, Umm Hamida has renewed "contact with her foster daughter, who was well on her way to convalescence and recovery," and her neighbors in the alley are already "gossip[ing] about how the mother seemed to be hoping to reap some of the profits of this ample treasure" (285). Thus, while Midaq Alley provides the historical intersectional setting for multiple Egyptian futures and conflicting interests, *Midaq Alley* offers itself as an intertextual work of many interests and more than one future.

Teaching Mahfouz: Style in Translation

Maysa Abou-Youssef Hayward

When I teach Naguib Mahfouz's classic novel *Midaq Alley*, students sometimes ask, "What about the translation? Are we getting 'the real thing'?" I tell them yes—and no. Even through the lens of a different language, they experience many elements of Mahfouz's style, although some nuances of language use and cultural reference disappear in translation. But students gain as well. An effective translation, like Trevor LeGassick's, highlights key elements of the original and interprets as well as transmits the text. Moreover, students learn about the complexities of the Arabic language and cultural differences during their reading experience. A teacher aware of these complexities and differences can turn seeming disadvantages into advantages.[1]

Style in translation has seldom been studied. As Jean Boase-Beier points out, translation research has "paid relatively little attention to matters of style," while "insights from translation studies have rarely been brought to bear on stylistics" (9). Yet a look at style and translation in Mahfouz opens windows onto Arab culture and issues of power and domination, gender, social position, religion, and politics. Responding to these issues helps students question the roles culture and language play in their lives. In this essay, I introduce some key elements of translation theory and stylistics. I then look at seven elements that shape Mahfouz's distinctive style in *Midaq Alley*: levels of language use, the narrator's role, dialogue, sequencing of presentation, setting, images and symbols, and humor. Along the way, I suggest several pedagogical exercises.

Theories of Translation

Contemporary translation theory divides into two camps. Domestication, the traditional approach, advocates smoothing over cultural and linguistic differences, thus naturalizing the source text. A domesticated translation tries to re-create the original as if it were first written in the language of the translation. Speaking of translating the *Aeneid*, John Dryden says, "taking all the materials of this divine author, I have endeavoured to make Virgil speak such English as he would himself have spoken, if he had been born in England, and in this present age" (26). Three centuries later, Eugene Nida advocates a similar approach. Translation should find a "dynamic equivalence" for the original in the new culture:

> A translation of dynamic equivalence aims at complete naturalness of expression, and tries to relate the receptor to modes of behavior relevant within the context of his own culture; it does not insist that he understand the cultural patterns of the source-language context in order to comprehend the message. (159)

In a domesticated translation, differences between languages and cultures are erased; the reader may be only slightly aware that the work has been translated.

On the other hand, foreignization validates difference and asks translators to retain the foreign in their renditions. In order to disrupt the target culture, Lawrence Venuti encourages the translator to display the linguistic and cultural differences of the foreign text. For Venuti,

> translators and their readers [will] read translated texts in ways that seek to recognize the linguistic and cultural difference of foreign texts. . . . The foreign text is privileged in a foreignizing translation only insofar as it enables a disruption of target language cultural codes, so that its value is always strategic, depending on the cultural formation into which it is translated. The point is rather to elaborate the theoretical, critical, and textual means by which translation can be studied and practiced as a locus of difference. . . . (41–42)

Domesticated translations assume an underlying, universally accessible message in the text; foreignized translations see the text as located in a particular language and culture, and the foreignizing translator should make those linguistic and cultural roots visible to the reader.

Each of these theories deeply distrusts the other, perhaps because of political and even religious issues. However, a middle ground can be reached. A completely foreignized translation would create an insurmountable wall between the reader and the text. But I would argue that no translation completely domesticates the source text. The original's linguistic and cultural qualities exert a constant gravitational pull on the translator, never freeing him or her completely from the source. Readers of a translation will continually be challenged to respond to difference and in doing so rethink their own cultural assumptions.

In his introduction to *Midaq Alley*, LeGassick claims a domesticating approach:

> Arabic is, of course, a language far different in syntax and sounds from English and gives expression to a highly distinctive people and a complex culture. The translator has, then, an almost limitless range of choices and dilemmas over vocabulary and arrangement when attempting to convey the spirit of a work of fiction. The present translation offers an approximation of how Mahfouz might have expressed himself had English been his native tongue. (xi)

LeGassick echoes Dryden's and Nida's expectation that a novel can be wholly transplanted from one language to another. Yet LeGassick's translation retains many stylistic complexities and a foreignness that resists domestication. The translation is successful, though not, perhaps, in terms of the definition LeGassick provides.

Translation is cultural performance, first enacted by the translator responding to the original and then by the reader in response to the translation. Reading Mahfouz, students actively participate in building meaning through a dialogue with the translation. In understanding the distinctive, undomesticated differences of the translation, students must question their positions in their own culture, opening the possibility for change in response to the translation's style.

Literary Style and Translation of Style

Style is a surprisingly hard concept to characterize. As John Tinker writes, style is "[d]ifficult to define, you know it when you see it. Style identifies the writer. It frames sensibility. . . . Style also, according to several recent studies, is the essential element of language that shapes subjectivity and subcultures." He remarks, "Writing about style seems to encourage aphorisms," perhaps because style involves complex qualities impossible to quantify. If style is unquantifiable, it involves more than word choice and arrangement. In my view, style is a set of traits related to how a writer handles many parts of the writing task. Seymour Chatman takes such an approach:

> Since style has so many senses, let me specify the very ordinary one I mean. It is simply that set of features which individualizes some individual or group. . . . Style [is] the constellation of idiosyncratic practices that distinguish the work of artists. (25–26)

When speaking of Mahfouz's style, I refer both to the narrow definition of style arising from word choice and syntax and to the larger elements that create the distinctive feel of the author.

An Overview of Midaq Alley

Mahfouz first published زقاق المدق (Zuqaq al-midaqq; *Midaq Alley*) in 1947. Translated in 1966 by LeGassick, with a revision in 1975, and frequently republished, *Midaq Alley* demonstrates the main features of Mahfouz's literary style. The setting, a poor alley (حارة; *hara*) in old Cairo in the early 1940s, gives students a sense of the unfamiliar, of something different from both their everyday world and their exotic expectations of ancient Egypt. In the alley, the inhabitants treat one another as family, the members linked by marriage, economic ties, and a shared history. In Midaq Alley live a barber, a sweet seller, a marriage broker, a dervish, a merchant, a store owner, a baker, and other assorted characters, with a focus on Hamida, the foster daughter of the marriage broker Umm Hamida. The novel concludes when Hamida's rejected fiancé, Abbas, finds her working as a prostitute for the British and hurls a glass at her, cutting her face. The British soldiers, in return, beat him to death. Yet at the end, the alley absorbs even this tragedy: "This crisis, . . . like all the others, finally subsided and the alley returned to its usual state of indifference and forgetfulness" (284).

Mahfouz sets the novel in a specific historical context (the British protectorate, economic problems, the rise of fundamentalism, and the spread of technology) that continually intrudes on the traditional world of Midaq Alley. Social problems also intrude, including prostitution and drugs. To help my students organize the various contexts and relationships, I provide a handout that synopsizes them and defines key terms and concepts. In response to the various issues of intrusion, the alley's residents offer mutual support in a hierarchical structure. Mahfouz illustrates their interactions through a literary style that reveals the characters' public and private intentions. The translator's challenge is to incorporate these complex stylistic features into the translation. Teachers of Mahfouz will benefit by an awareness of how to approach his stylistic techniques.

Mahfouz's Style: Levels of Language Use

For a translator, the level of formality in language use is the first stylistic feature to consider. Arabic has three distinct levels. While speakers are aware of and use different registers in different contexts, the multiglossic situation is particularly important for writers. The three levels of style are the high formal, the middle language, and the vernacular.

The high formal style, the فصحى (*fusḥa*), is the most common form of literary writing. Having a sophisticated vocabulary and complex sentence structures, it differs from everyday Egyptian Arabic in word endings, syntax, verbs (particularly irregular verbs), and punctuation. The effect resembles what an English speaker might feel reading the complex and highly structured prose of Henry James. The middle style, Modern Standard Arabic, is less complex in word choice and structure, a simplified, more workable, and more easily understandable version of the high formal. Prose by such writers as Margaret Atwood or John Updike would make a reasonable comparison. Writers generally consider vernacular, the عامية (*ʿamiyyah*), as vulgar and unsuitable for literary expression. The tough street language of Hunter Thompson or Amiri Baraka might be equivalent.

Mahfouz writes in a simplified version of *fusḥa*, though his characters' dialogues show an awareness of the *ʿamiyyah*, and he sometimes even uses language from the vernacular in their dialogues. For Arabic readers, his style excels in fluency and intelligibility; he chooses the simplest vocabulary available in the formal style. In effect, he translates the speech of his lower-class characters into a literary language that retains the sense of its origins in his character's ideologies. In Mahfouz's prose, characters express themselves as if they could write and speak in the simplified formal style. Mahfouz thus preserves both the formal style of the literary novel and the linguistic and cultural origins of his characters in Cairo's alleys.

Related to levels of language use is the distinction between the more formal and guarded public speech and the more colloquial talk that occurs in private. Teachers may wish to address the difference between public and private speech, an important distinction for Mahfouz and for Egyptians generally, and for English speakers as well. In public a sense of formal behavior goes along with conventional language. Egyptians are always aware of their relation to others and seek to express and retain social ties in public. They often use expected, conventional responses, such as proverbs, in social settings to communicate these bonds directly or indirectly. Formal practices reinforce traditional social ties in public speech.

Privately people behave more openly. In private, Mahfouz's characters express themselves freely, monitored only by family and close friends. Shifts in register, however, can give the private a touch of the public (when the colloquial is rewritten in formal language) and vice versa (when the formal is used in informal settings). Because Mahfouz maintains the formal language as his base, it becomes the context to bring these different worlds together.

Mahfouz's own "translation" of these different worlds into a single language might seem to create a monologic text, hiding the interplay of language levels. Paradoxically, however, when the public and private worlds intermingle, differences are accentuated. Because the formal language, usually associated with abstract, highly complex, and intellectual ideas, is used for writing about the concrete, simple, and emotional world of the alley, Arabic readers become aware of differences between these two worlds. The reader of the original recognizes the interplay between the private and public worlds and between hidden and revealed intentions.

Readers of the translation respond to a different kind of interplay. Although the higher level of style translates relatively easily into Standard Written English, the vernacular is difficult to integrate in the text. Proverbs, sayings, puns, wordplay, and curses strike English readers as foreign. The translator may either find near equivalents in English or translate the sayings literally. In the former case, the reader recognizes that the English equivalent could not have been used in the original; in the latter case, the reader is struck by the foreignness of the saying. The foreignized elements of the translation jar the reading process. Students must negotiate a position in relation to the translation and deal with the ruptures caused by the aggressive presence of the foreign.

To show how these different worlds marked by different language levels interact, I examine a scene from early in *Midaq Alley*. The landlady Saniya Afify visits one of her tenants, Umm Hamida. The marriage broker suspects Saniya will ask for a raise in rent but soon realizes that this older widow actually wants to find a husband. This situation is basically public: both women have a type of power that calls for formality and distance. Yet each wants to appear informal and friendly to gain a certain end. Mahfouz constructs a dialogue in which each character negotiates her needs. Because each fears the other (Saniya wants to avoid embarrassment and Umm Hamida worries that the rent may be raised), the dialogue remains cautious and indirect.

After Saniya relates some gossip about the alley, Umm Hamida asks a conventional question,

> "And how are you, Mrs. Afify?"
>
> She frowned a little and replied, "The truth is that I am tired out, Umm Hamida!"
>
> The older woman arched her eyebrows as though really troubled. "Tired? May God lighten your load!"
>
> Mrs. Afify made no reply while Hamida, her tenant's daughter who had just come into the room, placed a tray with coffee on the table and left again. Then she said indignantly, "Yes, I am tired, Umm Hamida. Don't you think it's exhausting collecting the rent from the shops? Imagine a woman like me standing in front of strange men asking for rent . . . "
>
> Umm Hamida's heart had missed a beat at the mention of the rents, but she said sympathetically, "Yes, you are quite right. May God come to your aid." (17)

I direct my students' attention to how the translator reflects Mahfouz's concern with public and private worlds. LeGassick uses the more formal "Mrs. Afify" for the less formal ست سنية (*Sitt Saniya*; "Madame Saniya"—Saniya is her first name) of the original. The issue of names occurs again in the last line, when Umm Hamida says, in the original, صدقتي ياستي (*Sadakty ya sitti*; "True, my lady"), which LeGassick translates as "Yes, you are quite right." The more informal direct address in the original (*ya sitti*) breaks the ice and closes the distance between the ladies. Is there in English a functional equivalent for addressing a person informally yet preserving respect? I ask my students to create situations in which they might have to maintain a similar relationship. A discussion with their own landlord, their boss, an older neighbor, or even their teacher would be good examples. Students quickly become aware of the strategies in English for negotiating social distances—and at this point the world of Mahfouz begins to seem less foreign.

The conventional references to God and religious sayings also help establish distance while showing concern. Umm Hamida's phrases, "May God lighten your load" and "May God come to your aid," establish the register for prayer. The dialogue uses other repetitive devices as well. Not only does Umm Hamida repeat, in similar terms, her prayer for Saniya but also Saniya repeats the statement that she is tired. The foregrounding of tiredness creates a path for more dialogue. As the reader discovers shortly, she is not merely physically tired but also tired of living alone, without a man—a connection she makes in speaking of standing before "strange men" to collect her rents. Mahfouz plants the reader's doubt in her tiredness through repetition and through Umm Hamida's reaction:

the marriage broker raises her eyebrows "as though really troubled," emphasizing her doubts about Saniya's excuse. Although these strategies may at first seem foreign to English speakers, both conventional references to God and repetition are common tactics English speakers use every day. I ask my students to find such correlates to express similar states of mind.

In interpreting the use of conventional religious expressions, the repetition, the physical reaction of Umm Hamida, and the author's comment on that reaction, students actively build meaning in the dialogue. They must imagine or invent the cultural assumptions these strategies display. After discussion I ask them to re-create the scene in their own time and setting. As we progress, the politics of gender and class also become apparent. The dialogue clarifies each woman's intentions. My exercise shows students how similar negotiations may occur in the students' own culture, although the terms of those negotiations are certainly different. The re-created scenes vary in content, yet most preserve the process of developing a dialogue through hints rather than straightforward expressions. As students create dialogues in English, they try to preserve the speech registers appropriate to different statuses between their invented characters.

Style and the Narrator's Role

As in any fictional work, the narrator's position is important in the presentation of dialogues and in establishing a particular style. Mahfouz's omniscient third-person narrator typically plays three different roles in relation to his characters. He starts by objectively describing the events and the setting. Then, when characters interact or when the narrator pauses to describe one character, the narrator becomes a commentator, reporting on the character's inner life. At a certain point, however, he steps into the character, talking as if he were a medium for the character's inner voice, speaking it directly to the reader. He then backs out again.[2] There is a kind of double voicing present in which the narrator seems to be objective, and yet he undercuts this objectivity with a trenchant satire of the Egyptian world.[3]

To look more closely at how the narrator interacts with the characters, their dialogues, and the reader, I use an aspect of pragma-stylistic theory that deals with the narrator's report of characters' speech. Generally this reportage may be direct or indirect. In direct speech the speaker's words are given in the text. The narrator introduces those words by reference to the speaker's name, and the speech is set off in quotation marks (or, in Arabic, preceded by a dash). In the passage above, direct speech is found in the line, "She frowned a little and replied: 'The truth is that I am tired out, Umm Hamida!'"

In free direct speech, the text lacks the name of the speaker or quotation marks (or, in Arabic, a dash) or both. Examples are often found in continuing dialogue, when quoted speeches follow each other without the indication of a speaker. In the following passage, Umm Hamida and Hamida discuss a new engagement for Hamida:

> "But you are engaged to be married!"
> "A girl is free until the marriage agreement is signed. Nothing has passed between us but words and a dish of sweets!" answered Hamida, laughing sarcastically.
> "And the recitation of the Qur'an?"
> "Forgiveness is honorable . . . "
> "Punishment for abusing the Qur'an is harsh, you know." (146)

Four of the five speeches are not identified by speaker, although the context allows the reader to determine who is speaking. In free direct speech, the effect is that the narrator relinquishes control; the characters seem to take over and speak directly to each other without the narrator's intervention or consent.[4]

In indirect speech, the narrator reports in paraphrase what a character thought or said. For example, Salim Alwan, a wealthy older man, tries to decide whether to pursue Hamida:

> The truth was that he did not know whether it was this [his youthful desires] that attracted him to Hamida, or whether it was his passion for her which made him more conscious of his wife's inadequacies. Whatever the reason, he felt an irresistible urge for new blood. He finally said to himself, "What's wrong with me? Why should I deprive myself of something made lawful by God?"
>
> However, he was a respectable man and longed for people's esteem. The thought that he might be the center of gossip horrified him. He agreed with the saying, "Eat what you please, but wear what pleases others." So it was that he ate his bowl of wheat, but as for Hamida . . . ! Good Heavens!
>
> If she had been from a noble family, he would not have hesitated a moment to ask her hand. But how could Hamida become a fellow wife of his present wife, Mrs. Alwan? And how could Umm Hamida become his mother-in-law just as the late Mrs. Alifat had been? How on earth could Hamida become the wife of the father of Muhammad Salim Alwan the judge, Arif Salim Alwan the barrister and Dr. Hassan Salim Alwan?
> (70–71)

In the final paragraph, the narrator reports Salim's thoughts in the form of questions as they might have been framed in Salim's mind, but that they are reported in the third person ("his present wife," for example, rather than "my present wife") shows that the narrator is still in the text. At other points, the text shifts from indirect to direct speech and from indirect to free direct speech. In the first paragraph, the narrator paraphrases Salim's thoughts and reports on his "irresistible urge," then quotes directly what he "said to himself."

In the second paragraph, the narrator's statement that Salim, "agreed with the saying, 'Eat what you please, but wear what pleases others.' So it was that he ate his bowl of wheat," might seem to be an innocent use of a saying followed by an action exemplifying part of the saying. Actually, the statement allows the narrator to comment on Salim, that he is ignoring an important part of the marriage, Hamida's perspective. His inner struggle concerns only how Hamida will affect his image. In the first part of the line, "So it was that he ate his bowl of wheat, but as for Hamida . . . ! Good Heavens!," the narrator objectively reports that Salim eats his wheat. But who is the source of the phrase "Good Heavens!"? By the novel's stylistic conventions, the remark would be the narrator's; there are no quotation marks (or dashes) and no indication, such as "thought Salim," that the phrase comes from Salim. The reader, however, assumes that it does, for such a comment would be uncharacteristic of the narrator. Once again, the narrator has moved almost imperceptibly from indirect to free direct speech.

As an exercise after this scene, I ask students to create a series of hypothetical scenarios of "What would happen if . . . ?" By retaining the cultural codes of behavior, students gain insight into the politics of survival in a highly structured context. I ask them to list what is allowed and what is not in Mahfouz's cultural norms and in their own equivalent cultural norms. Students try to imagine that they live in an alley in which the politics reflects their contemporary interpretations. I ask them to create a character using Mahfouz's style of moving among direct, free direct, and indirect speech. Students are often surprised at the ways that different stylistic perspectives offer different and competing views of a character and a situation.

Dialogue and Style

Readers are not entirely free, of course, to construct their own characters. Characters are created by the author, described by the narrator, and re-created by the translator. The characters reveal themselves in dialogue. As Roger Fowler says, "A character can be criticized within the very language he is made to offer" (120). Mikhail Bakhtin also points out that "*in a human being, there is always something that only he himself can reveal, in a free act of self-consciousness and discourse, something that does not submit to an externalizing secondhand definition*" (*Problems* 58), such as an omniscient narrator's description. Students discovering a character's self-definition will thereby increase their own self-awareness.

Students might sympathize with Hamida because of Salim's selfishness, but she speaks and acts in a similarly selfish way. After Umm Hamida reminds her that violating a religious oath is punishable, Hamida responds angrily:

> "I don't give a damn!" snarled the girl.
>
> Umm Hamida beat her breast and cried, "You serpent's child, you!"
>
> Hamida noticed traces of hidden approval in her foster-mother's eyes and she cried, laughing, "Go and marry him yourself, go on."

> This pleased the woman and she clapped her hands together and snapped, "It's just like you to sell a dish of sweets in exchange for the bowl of spiced green wheat."
>
> "On the contrary, I've refused a young man and chosen an old one."
>
> "There's plenty of fat on an old rooster!" roared her foster mother. (146)

This exchange replicates many features of the scene in which the narrator describes and responds to Salim. Yet, whereas earlier the narrator commented on the scene, here the characters speak for themselves. Mahfouz places readers in the middle of a dialogue that they must interpret to understand the characters. Unlike Salim, Hamida has no concern for what others think of her; the فاتحة (*fathah*; signifying a public announcement of their engagement) that she does not "give a damn" about is a social as well as a religious commitment. Unlike Salim, Hamida will sacrifice love, or at least physical pleasure, for money and position.

There is a double meaning behind Umm Hamida's taunt, "It's just like you to sell a dish of sweets in exchange for the bowl of spiced green wheat." On the one hand, the meaning, which barely survives in the translation, is of trading something sweet (the physical love of the younger man) for something less pleasant. On the other hand, a meaning that is lost is of trading a lower-class dish (in the original, the "dish of sweets" is بسبوسة [*basbousa*], a confection bought on the streets) for an upper-class one (the "spiced green wheat" is فريك [*feriek*], an expensive dish of barley with pigeons, inherited from Turkish cooking). Hamida's answer that she has traded a young man for an old one is her declaration that she is sacrificing herself for money; at the same time, she is challenging her foster mother's hasty response that love should take precedence over money. She and Umm Hamida agree that money is all.

The disagreement emphasizes their agreement. They disagree for the pleasure of arguing, a love of disagreement that asserts mutual loyalty. The mother's conclusion, "There's plenty of fat on an old rooster!," shows that sexual, economic, and social power survive growing old. Umm Hamida thereby admits Hamida's unstated desire for sex, with the image of eating (the fat rooster is tastier and richer) and the reference, lost in the translation, to the pigeons in the *feriek* (pigeons are supposed to be eaten to improve sexual performance). The women see Hamida's suitors as commodities to be eaten, not as human beings. Mahfouz's dialogue reveals the characters' relationships and intentions.

Should the teacher worry that the referentiality of words and phrases may be lost on the students or the teacher? As I see it, the stylistic disruption caused by these references creates a fertile ground for students to become involved in participative thinking. Many issues arise when the interactions of characters are discussed, and gender roles, the politics of economically confined women, and the frustrations of social codes. Students, equating such tensions with their own situations, may find that their problems are similar to those of Mahfouz's characters.

Sequencing, Setting, Images, and Symbols

Just as the translation of dialogue creates disruptions for the reader, the translation of other stylistic features, such as setting, images, symbols, and the narrative's order of events, allows participative thinking. To exemplify these features, I examine Mahfouz's description of Zaita, a maker of beggars:

> In the wall facing the entrance, there is a small, wooden door which opens on to a grimy little outhouse, smelling of dirt and filth, for it has only one tiny window in the opposite wall overlooking the courtyard of an old house. About an arm's length from the window there is a lighted lamp, placed on a shelf, throwing a dim light on the place, with its dirt floor covered with various and indeterminate rubbish; the room looks like a garbage heap. The shelf supporting the lantern is long and stretches the entire wall; on it are bottles, both large and small, various instruments and a great number of bandages, making it look just like a chemist's shelf, were it not so extraordinarily dirty.
>
> On the ground, almost directly beneath the little window, something is piled, no different from the floor of the room in color, filthiness or smell, but possessed of limbs, flesh, and blood, and which therefore, despite everything, deserves to be called a human being. It was Zaita. . . .
>
> If you once saw Zaita you would never again forget him, so starkly simple is his appearance. He consists of a thin, black body, and a black gown. Black upon black, were it not for the slits shining with a terrifying whiteness which are his eyes. Zaita is not a Negro; he is an Egyptian, brown-skinned in color. Dirt mixed with the sweat of a lifetime has caked a thick layer of black over his body and over his gown which also was not originally black. Black was the fate of everything within this hole. (54–55)

In the order of presentation, a writer communicates a worldview. The section typifies Mahfouz's approach; he first describes a place, then the inhabitant, and then mixes person and place together. Place shapes a person. In the room, the reader first senses the smell. The lamp's "dim light" provides a path to describe the room's contents. The shelf and the tools of Zaita's trade are described before we see Zaita and learn the use of the tools. Zaita is introduced first as a thing, little different from the other pieces of rubbish in the room. He lives by cruelty: his profession is maiming and disfiguring those who wish to prosper as beggars.

Blackness forms the basis of Zaita's description in the third paragraph. Color seldom plays an important role for Mahfouz, but light and darkness do. The blackness throughout the third paragraph establishes a sense of mystery and human evil. Egyptian readers often find Mahfouz too cynical. He associates Zaita with Egyptians: "Zaita is not a Negro; he is an Egyptian," says the narrator. In this way Mahfouz connects Zaita's hole and Egypt, concluding with the statement, "Black was the fate of everything within this hole." Zaita is not just a character type located in a neutral space; he also represents the politics of a nation in the hole of colonization, teaching her people to be beggars. A teacher might use the passage as an opportunity to recall and situate other dark holes emblematic for both colonizer and colonized.

A final stylistic feature in Mahfouz's description of Zaita's room is the "one tiny window." Mahfouz carefully places Zaita underneath the window. In the original, the phrase تحت الكوة مباشرة (*tahta al kuwwati mubasharatan*; "directly under the opening") is set off by dashes, a device Mahfouz uses for emphasis or further explanation. For Mahfouz, windows are an important symbol. In interviews and café talks, he uses the expression مصر المشربية (*Masr al-mashrabiyya*; "Egypt is a window screened with wood and stained glass"). On the surface, the expression means that Egypt has a history or civilization, referring to this traditional art form. Seen another way, Egypt views the outside world but prevents the outside world from looking in. In this picture of Zaita, Mahfouz's stylistic techniques help develop larger themes in the novel.

Mahfouz's Use of Humor

Despite the cynicism of Zaita's portrait, *Midaq Alley* is rich with carnivalesque humor and satire. The café owner Kirsha is a drug dealer and a homosexual. At one point, his wife, Mrs. Kirsha, goes to Mr. Hussainy, the voice of wisdom in the alley. He tries but fails to convince her husband to hide his homosexuality. Finally she confronts Mr. Kirsha in public:

> "Just you try and move, you filthy wretch!"
>
> She turned once more towards the boy [her husband's boyfriend] and went on: "What has frightened you, you clever fellow? You woman in the clothes of a man! Would you like to tell me what brings you here?"
>
> Kirsha was now standing behind the till, his anger having blocked his tongue, his face pale with fury. She shouted in his face, "If you are thinking of defending your 'friend,' then I will smash your bones to pieces in front of everyone!"
>
> She moved threateningly towards the youth who retreated until he reached Sheikh Darwish. "Do you want to ruin my home, you rake and son of rakes!"
>
> The youth, trembling violently, answered, "Who are you? What have I done so as to . . . "
>
> "Who am I? Don't you know me? I am your fellow-wife . . . "
>
> She fell upon him, punching and slapping him forcefully. His tarboosh fell off and blood flowed from his nose. She then grasped his necktie and pulled it till his voice trailed off in a strangled gasp. (100)

After presenting the reactions of the patrons of the café, none of whom interfered and all of whom were enjoying the scene, Mahfouz describes the battle further. The husband defends the boy:

> "Leave him alone, woman, you have caused enough scandal!"
>
> Her husband's strong grip forced Mrs. Kirsha to release her rival. Her cloak fell to the ground and her blood was now boiling. Her voice rose in a shrill scream as she grasped her husband by the collar and yelled, "Would you hit me to defend your friend, you animal? Bear witness, all you people, against this lecherous villain! . . . You hashish addict! You nincompoop! You filthy lout! You sixty-year-old! You father of five and grandfather of twenty! You bastard! You dumb oaf! I feel like spitting in your dirty, black face!"
>
> Mr. Kirsha, quivering with emotion, stared at her in a fury and yelled back, "Hold your tongue, woman, and take away that toilet of a mouth of yours; you're spraying us all with its filth!"
>
> "Shut your mouth! You are the only toilet around here, you scarecrow, you disgrace, you rat-bag!" (101)

Through unexpected verbal and behavioral excess, humor releases tension caused by deviations from the norm. Egypt of the 1940s saw homosexuality as a moral sickness. Mrs. Kirsha tries to shame her husband to bring him back to his senses.

While the shaming becomes a public spectacle, it conforms to its own norm, that of the ردح (*radh*). In a *radh* ("exchange of insults"), two or more disputatious women hurl epithets in public. As each tries to degrade and expose the other, indirectness and sayings are their weapons. Once the *radh* begins, the spectators are expected not to interfere unless physical violence occurs. Although this *radh* between Kirsha and his wife seems to violate the rule that the dispute should always be between two women, Mrs. Kirsha considers her husband and the boy women. Humor emerges through this confusion of roles and genders. The reversal of the husband's behavior leads to a reversal of the wife's role, as she becomes dominant. The reversal of gender roles also leads to a reversal of normal language use, as language now exposes according to the demands of the *radh*.

Though the translation fails to capture all the verbal play in the *radh*, the humor is preserved. Mrs. Kirsha first attacks the boy, whom she pictures as a rival, but when her "cloak fell to the ground," she turns on her husband. Usually when a *radh* starts, women begin to take off their clothes to prevent men from interfering; disrobing is a message that the women have no more concern for social norms. The loss of the cloak is Mrs. Kirsha's signal that she can do whatever she wants. A public argument is shameful, but Mrs. Kirsha emphasizes the public nature of this fight by calling on the spectators, "Bear witness, all you people, against this lecherous villain!"

Much of the scene's humor lies in the insults Mrs. Kirsha hurls at her husband, on his age, his stupidity, his lechery, his clumsiness, his drug addiction, and even his skin color. The insults create a sense of misrule; they have no logical coherence. In the original, the words are sometimes in the vernacular and other times a translation of the vernacular into the formal. At this point, even the Egyptian reader is forced to translate. The translation captures this sense of strangeness; some of the insults are translated colloquially ("You nincompoop! . . .

You bastard!"), while others retain the foreignness of the original ("You father of five and grandfather of twenty!"). Translation of humor is difficult because humor depends on wordplay or actions that have social or cultural references. Yet Mahfouz's humor explodes in a *jouissance*, a play of language and customs that invites students to participate.

To encourage my students to visualize the events, we act out the scene in class. The exercise calls for some sensitivity, for we are dealing here in part with a stereotyping of homosexuality. At this point I like to introduce some insights from queer theory to contextualize issues of gender crossing and sexual orientation and to help the students see that Mahfouz's satire is directed not at Mr. Kirsha but at the excesses of his wife. We also focus on the style of the scene, to recognize ways in which levels of language, dialogues, public and private language, and images interact in creating humor.

For those who teach Mahfouz, analyzing prose style and approaching issues of translation enrich the classroom experience. The interactions of the elements of style such as the narrator, the dialogues, the sequence of presentation, the settings, images, symbols, and humor all call for the reader to participate actively to construct meaning. As readers interact with the text, they draw on their own experiences and come to understand more fully how they stand in their own culture. While this process obtains in all reading experiences, the effect is heightened in a translation. The style of Naguib Mahfouz in translation is a place where the foreign always emerges, making reading more challenging but ultimately more rewarding.

NOTES

[1] I explore this topic in my dissertation, from which parts of this essay are adapted.

[2] These roles parallel the position of the translator in relation to the text. At certain points, the translator is (or tries to be) objective, focusing on individual words and translating them almost literally. At other points, the translator adds details and extra information as background. In adding explanation, he becomes, like Mahfouz's narrator, a commentator.

[3] This point is made by Mona Takieddine-Amyuni: "Mahfouz's exact and lucid prose depicts the quotidian, trivial actions and feelings of men and women in the Alley. A detached attitude seems to dominate the author as he examines the nature, function, and effect of the society under scrutiny. Yet, beneath the impersonal surface lurk tremendous evil powers. Mahfouz's mastery of Jamesian irony and his skillful blend of cool observation and biting satire, broaden the description of the specific world of the Alley" (25).

[4] Mohammed Albakry discusses this feature in an article on translating the Moroccan writer Muhammad Zefzaf: "Particularly challenging from the translation point of view is handling the extensive use of free direct speech merged with the narration without any overt indication by a reporting clause or a switch to indirect speech."

Christ and the Abrahamic Legacy in *Children of the Alley*

Nabil Matar

It is not often that a novel nearly costs its author his life. But that was the case with Naguib Mahfouz (1911–2006) and his novel أولاد حارتنا (Awlad haritna), translated into English as *Children of Gebelaawi* and, more accurately, *Children of Our Alley*.[1] Fortunately, Mahfouz survived the assassination attempt after a crazed fanatic stabbed him in the neck on 14 October 1994. This essay is divided into two parts. First is a brief history of the novel and its critical reception. Second is a discussion of two questions regarding Christ and the Abrahamic legacy in the imagination of Mahfouz: What Islamo-Arabic precedents about representing the founders of Abrahamic monotheism were available to Mahfouz? How did Mahfouz, a Muslim, interpret Christ?

Children of the Alley was completed in April 1958 in Cairo, where Mahfouz grew up, studied, married and raised a family, worked, lived, retired, and died (al-Naqqash, "Mahfouz"). Mahfouz had finished what would prove to be his masterpiece, the trilogy, around five years earlier. Suddenly, after so many difficult years of inactivity, as he reminisced, he found himself putting pen to paper and starting to write again, not in the realistic vein he had mastered but symbolically and philosophically. On completing the novel, he sent it to be serialized in the *Ahram* newspaper, but as soon as a few installments had appeared, complaints were lodged with the editor, Muhammad Hasanein Haykal. Haykal resisted pressure to discontinue publication. After the novel appeared in full (between 21 September and 25 December 1959), Mahfouz was contacted by a representative of the country's president, Jamal Abd al-Nasser, who informed him that the novel would be banned in Egypt. A Beirut publishing house promptly produced the book from the *Ahram* serialization, without Mahfouz's permission, after which the novel was widely read around the Arabic-speaking world.[2] After its translation into English in 1981, it was read in the rest of the world.[3]

The complaint against Mahfouz rested on his presentation in a fictional work of three biographies that were very similar to the lives of the prophetic founders of monotheism—Moses, Jesus, and Muhammad. Although there is no direct or open allusion to any of the prophetic figures in the novel, the events that Mahfouz describes were inspired by the lives of those men. But he vehemently contested the religious interpretation of his novel, and over a decade after he had finished writing it, he explained that politics rather than religion was at the core of all his works. "In all I write, you will find politics. . . . Even in *Children of the Alley*, which can be described as a metaphysical novel, you will find [the political emphasis in] the feud over the property [وقف; *waqf*]" (al-Ghitani, "Naguib Mahfouz Remembers" 78).[4] In another interview, when asked whether he believed in God, he answered, "I guess so"—a safe way of avoiding a discussion of religion.

When asked whether he prayed or not, he remained silent (Sayigh 81).[5] (It is striking that in *Children of the Alley*, not a single figure prays). Mahfouz later stated that often people are forced to make a choice between religion and socialism, but that in *Children of the Alley*, he presented an alternative. The novel, he added, was addressed to the leaders of the Egyptian Revolution, who, in his view, had lost their ideals:

> I wanted to ask the men of the revolution, do you want to follow the path of the prophets or that of the *futuwwa* [فتوات]? The story of the prophets in the novel is the fictional framework, but the purpose is to criticize the revolution and the social order that arose in its wake.
>
> (qtd. in Mahmoud 244)[6]

The novel describes Mahfouz's disillusionment with the aftermath of the 1952 revolution that had replaced monarchy with a form of socialist democracy under the charismatic but authoritarian leadership of Abd al-Nasser.

Early evaluations of the novel concurred in emphasizing the political interpretation of it. Sasson Somekh, author of the first full-length study in English of Mahfouz, moved the focus away from the religious to the socialist and situated *Children of the Alley* and other novels in the ideological context of Egypt's leftist movements that Nasser challenged in the 1950s. A similar approach emphasizing social criticism appeared in Hilary Kirkpatrick a year later. In *Religion, My Own*, Mattiyahu Peled treated the novel as an "iconoclastic" work, and analyzed it from a "philosophical" angle (173–81). Ironically, it was not until Mahfouz received the Nobel Prize in 1988 that some telepreachers in Egypt restarted the attack on the novel. Although it is unlikely that they had read the novel and the scholarly criticism that had appeared about it,[7] they began to calumniate *Children of the Alley*, an attack that culminated in the vicious words of Sheikh Omar Abd al-Rahman (who is now in a United States prison): "Had we killed Mahfouz when he published *Children of the Alley*, Salman Rushdie would not have raised his head" (qtd. in Mahmoud 14).

As such odious views were expressed, Egyptian and other Arab critics rose to defend Mahfouz and present detailed and nuanced studies of his work. Rasheed el-Enany published *Naguib Mahfouz: The Pursuit of Meaning* in 1993, arguing that the novel presented "a panoramic view of the history of man and religion" without challenging theological beliefs (142). A year later, Mustafa Abd al-Ghani published his نجيب محفوظ: الثورة والتصوف (Naguib Mahfouz: al-thawra wa al-tasawwuf; "Naguib Mahfouz: Revolution and Sufism"), arguing that the novel depicted "the eternal conflict between authority and people in the presence of divine powers that always look on us from on high" (58). But attacks on the novel continued, most pedantically in the "refutation" (رد; *radd*; as in religious disputation) of the novel by Sheikh Abd al-Hamid Kishk. The cleric painstakingly contrasted every "insolent" description of the novel's protagonists with passages from the Qur'an, concluding that the novel was sacrilegious and the author an "atheist" (159).[8] The cover of his book, as it was semiotically analyzed by the Egyptian critic Gaber Asfour, showed the sheikh on the right side standing with a spear-like pen in one hand and the Qur'an in the other (both red in color). He is pointing at the small, crooked figure of Mahfouz cowering with the word "Nobel" (in Arabic and in English) at his feet.[9] The sheikh, who had been a courageous critic of corruption during Sadat's regime (as earlier of Nasser's secular ideology), felt it incumbent on himself to continue his jihad.[10] Fortunately, this enmity subsided, and when Mahfouz died on 30 August 2006, a large number of religious authorities in Egypt as well as members of the Muslim Brotherhood took part in the funeral, showing that the anger at the novel had been forgotten. Actually, a few months earlier, the Azhar, the center of religious authority in Egypt, had given its imprimatur for publishing the novel for the first time in the country (Abu al-Majd).

Even if Mahfouz viewed the novel as a political indictment, the specific choice of the names of the protagonists inevitably points in the direction of an intriguing and courageous interpretation of the founders of the prophetic tradition. So what Islamo-Arabic precedents for representing the founders of Abrahamic monotheism were available to Mahfouz?

There had been only one attempt in Arabic before Mahfouz at writing about the Prophet Muhammad, which appeared in a play by the father of Arabic theater, Tawfiq al-Hakim, in 1936. As al-Hakim described it, *Muhammad, God's Prayer and Peace upon Him* was a "biographical dialogue" (سيرة حوارية; sira huwariyah). The choice of title is important: al-Hakim was unambiguous that he was rewriting the prophetic *sira* in a dramatic dialogue to be enacted on stage. (Whether it was or not enacted, I have not been able to verify.) Still, in the 1930s, it was permissible for a writer to present the hallowed *sira* in a new literary form. It was also permissible to present the figure of Muhammad himself—as a child who travels with his uncle and is seen by the Rahib (monk) of Buhayra; as the amin ("trustworthy") who is consulted by his tribe members regarding the rebuilding of the Kaʿba; as a young merchant who marries Khadija; and as a man, aged forty, who receives the first revelation of the Qur'an from the angel Jibril (Gabriel). Al-Hakim had no qualms about presenting Muhammad as one of the dramatis personae, along with all the major figures of early Islamic history: Abu Bakr, Ali, Hamza, Bilal, and others. All these figures were to appear on stage, presumably impersonated by actors and actresses. The table of contents at the end of the text explicitly described the events in each scene and provided explanatory information about them. For al-Hakim, the Prophet was a marvelous topic for dramatic historicization because there was a massive amount of relatively reliable information about him in the *sira*, the hadith, and other sources. Al-Hakim peremptorily mentioned these sources in a footnote, adding that he had rearranged them, since his play was "neither a historical nor a practical work, but an artistic one" (*Muhammad* 14). For him, unlike for Mahfouz decades later, there was no need to justify the creative process.

Familiar with al-Hakim's work, Mahfouz may have been following in the trajectory that the playwright blazed: of beginning his writing career with material inspired by Egypt's pharaonic past, then turning to Egypt's religious history. But in *Children of the Alley*, Mahfouz was not as explicit as al-Hakim had been. Although he did not explain his purpose in the novel, he clearly did not reimagine the *sira*; rather, his inspiration for the novel derived from another literary tradition in Arabic, the biographical dictionary, which evolved from the *sira*. If al-Hakim could imagine a play about Muhammad, Mahfouz would imagine a biographical dictionary about Moses, Christ, Muhammad, and the Scientist, along with all the men and women and children in their lives.

In the history of Arabic literature, biographical dictionaries were written about people who shared the same profession, jurisprudential school, city or region, century, or other feature. Sometimes these dictionaries were in twenty volumes, sometimes in one. The most significant thing about them is that they provided, as Wadad al-Qadi has shown, "an alternative history of the Muslim community"—alternative to the political chronicle, which was the official voice of a ruling dynasty (33). Flexible in form and unrestricted methodologically, the dictionaries included all sorts of information, from reliable facts to strange hearsay, from precise details to imaginative asides and fictional encounters. As H. A. R. Gibb stated, the biographical dictionaries showed how

> the history of the Islamic community is the contribution of the individual men and women to the building up and transmission of its specific culture; that it is these persons (rather than the political governors) who represent or reflect the active forces in Muslim society in their respective spheres; and that their individual contributions are worthy of being recorded for future generations. (qtd. in al-Qadi 32)

Gibb's definition perfectly fits Mahfouz's achievement in *Children of the Alley*, a one-volume biographical dictionary based on a single region, dynasty, and religious tradition. Mahfouz forced the different founders into one alley (حارة; *hara*), mixing scriptural history with imaginative adjustments. In so doing, he was not far of the mark from some of the authors of the biographical dictionaries who had included biographies of the prophets (Adam, Abraham, etc.), embellishing with anecdotes and interpolations the orthodox narrative about those men. Further, the biographical dictionaries showed that the history of Islam was about men and women—not just فتوات (*futuwwat*; "strong-arm men")—as the stories of Jabal, Rafaʿa, Qasim, and all others involved with them show. As the Qurʾan attests, all the prophets of monotheism are Muslim and therefore comakers of the community of believers. Those men, and not the political institutions, possessed the energy to challenge society and indeed to remake it. Because of their achievements, the narrator of *Children of the Alley*, as he explains at the outset of the novel, recorded their histories for future generations. The narrator reminds his readers that there have been many accounts and stories about his subjects, but that he is now deciding how this information is to be organized and presented. It is not surprising that the novel proved to be Mafhouz's most autobiographical (Hasan 11), as Mahfouz admitted, and one of the three dearest to his heart (the other two being the trilogy and *The Harafish*) (al-Ghitani, "Naguib Mahfouz Remembers" 68). In the biographies of the prophets, Mahfouz saw his own story as well as his *hara*'s.

In telling of the Abrahamic monotheists, Mahfouz created a synthesis of episodes derived from the Hebrew, Christian, and Islamic scriptural legacies. He was able to fuse stories from the lives of the founders of the three monotheisms into a single narrative because the Qurʾan had presented those founders in a divinely ordained sequence. The Qurʾan views Moses, Jesus, and Muhammad (along with all the other prophets that it recognizes, from Adam through David to John the Baptist) as part of the Abrahamic legacy. Abraham in the Qurʾan is a privileged monotheist, and all prophets after him proclaimed the same message of divine oneness. It was thus the Qurʾanic Abraham (but not necessarily the biblical) who furnished the Islamic legacy with a place for the monotheistic prophets who preceded it. Abraham was celebrated from the very beginnings of Islam's revelation. In أخبار مكة (Akhbar Makka; *History of Mecca*), Abu al-Walid al-Azraqi reported statues of Abraham, Jesus, and Mary inside the Kaʿba. When the Prophet returned victoriously to Mecca in AD 630, he headed to the Kaʿba to destroy the pagan idols. But once he saw the statue of Mary with her son in her lap and the statue of Abraham near it, all of them standing near the column closest to the exit, he covered them with his hands, turned to his followers, and said, "Destroy all images except what is under my hands" (al-Azraqi 1: 165).[11] A generation later and thousands of miles away, the Umayyads built domes above the tombs of Abraham and his wife Sara in al-Khalil (Hebron), the city of Ibrahim al-Khalil ("Abraham, the friend of God"). And the Abbasids built the dome above the tomb of Joseph. The Abrahamic legacy has been foundational in the religious culture of Islam.

How did Mahfouz, a Muslim, interpret Christ? Because of this firm place for all the prophets of monotheism in Islam, Mahfouz was able to present a Muslim interpretation of Christ. Intriguingly, Christ rose to special eminence in Arab-Islamic piety in the same years in which Mahfouz was conceiving his novel.[12] Writing *Children of the Alley* in the second half of the 1950s, a time in which he was reading widely in theology, Sufism, and philosophy, Mahfouz turned to the figure of Christ because of the important publications about Christ that had appeared in Egypt a few years earlier. In 1953, the distinguished literary critic ʿAbbas Mahmoud al-ʿAqqad published عبقرية المسيح (ʿAbqariyat al-Masih; "The Genius of the Christ"). In this work, al-ʿAqqad told the story of Christ—interestingly using the "Christ" name that appears in the Qurʾan rather than the other name, "ʿIsa," which is the Qurʾanic replacement of Yassouʿ (Jesus). Al-ʿAqqad presented the ethical mission of Christ, summarized many of his parables and sayings, and described the role played by the disciples. For the Muslim author, the genius of Christ lay in his message, not in the theology that came after:

> The great miracle of Christ is . . . that a man grows up in the house of a carpenter in a sleepy village among a defeated people. With his word, he conquers dominions, including that of the Romans. He will not spend as much time in realizing such a conquest as giants have spent in defeating a single region. (197)

A year later, Muhammad Kamil Hussein wrote a quasi-biographical novel about Christ, which received the *Ja'izat al-dawla* (Government Award) in 1958. The novel focuses on the Passion Week, particularly on the Friday of the Crucifixion. This focus is striking, since the Qur'an does not accept the Crucifixion. Hussein avoided the dilemma of offending Christians by rejecting the Crucifixion and offending fellow Muslims by proclaiming it and ended his novel with the solar eclipse, which is mentioned in the New Testament, and with the elevation (ارتفاع; *irtifa*ʿ) of Christ to heaven (207). Hussein was eager to present as much of a Christian view of Christ as possible, which is probably why he used Greek-Hebrew New Testament names rather than Arabic ones: Jerusalem is *Urushalim*, not *al-Quds*, while *Calfary* and *Juljuta* are transliterated. Like al-ʿAqqad, he used the name al-Masih and not ʿIsa and referred to Christ as a رسول طاهر (*rasul tahir*; "chaste prophet"), a very Qur'anic appellation. He tried to re-create the geographic and human experience of the Passion, providing descriptions of landscapes and people with more imagination than verisimilitude. To explore the teachings of Christ, he presented the arguments of a Sadducee and his wife, who disagree about the "Jew" (214) and his message that الله هو الحب (12; Allah huwwa al-hubb; "God is love"). There is also a Greek magus who appeals to reason (but later submits to faith in the message of Christ) and a group of believers (women, as was the case with those who went to the tomb) who refute both rationalism and Sadducism.

In *Children of the Alley*, Mahfouz does not present the fideistic element that dominates the above-mentioned works by al-ʿAqqad and by Hussein. Instead, his novel tells the story of a mysterious figure, called al-Jabalawi (literally, "of the mountain"), who lives in a glorious mansion (Garden of Eden?) that is part of a وقف (*waqf*; "religious endowment"). When he decides to bequeath his authority to his son Adham (Adam), Adham tries to spy out the deed to the *waqf* at the instigation of his jealous brother, Idris (rhymes with إبليس [*Iblis*; "Satan"]). Al-Jabalawi expels everyone from his mansion into the alley. Later he decides to bring back his grandson, Hammam, to live with him, but Hammam is killed by his brother in a fit of jealousy. One of the managers of the property, Jabal (Moses), is adopted by the Hamdani people. But when he sees one of the people being mistreated, he kills the aggressor and flees, later to return with his wife to the alley to lead the Hamdanis in their struggle against the tyrannical *futuwwat*. He prevails and takes over the alley, ruling harshly but justly until his death.

Children of the Alley positions the message and lives of Jabal and his successors against the *futuwwat*, a curious choice of term for Mahfouz. On the one hand, *futuwwat* was applied in the Middle Ages to Muslim brotherhoods fighting to defend Islam and abiding by codes of chivalry and honor. It was also the term applied to those groups who fought against British domination in Egypt, from 1919 on. The *futuwwat* were not outlaws but fighters for Egyptian independence and autonomy. On the other hand, *futuwwat* could also mean "brawlers" or "hecklers." The novel shows how the *futuwwat* had fallen from their roles as protectors of the alley (the world) to bullies—a reference perhaps to the secret police that came to tyrannize over Egyptian society during Nasser's rule. After the death of Jabal, the *futuwwat* resume their tyranny, whereupon a new figure appears, Rafaʿa, who tells the people that al-Jabalawi asked him to help them. He is a master of magic but is rejected by the alley and so moves to another alley where he gathers many followers. The *futuwwat* plot against him and succeed in killing and burying him. His followers unearth the body and bury it in an unknown spot, as a result of which people believe that al-Jabalawi took the body to his own garden.

Many of the images, actions, and episodes associated with the life of Rafaʿa have parallels in the four Gospels. Mahfouz wrote about a Christ figure using scriptural material from the New Testament and the Qur'an—material that was steeped in a long history of doctrinal interpretation and contestation. The challenge facing him was to reconcile the dissimilar narratives of the New Testament and the Qurʾan, while remaining within the parameters of what was religiously, if not theologically, acceptable to both traditions. Mahfouz was fully aware that his Egyptian and Cairene society contained a mix of Christians and Muslims who would not look kindly at any misrepresentation of Christ—either from a biblical or a Qurʾanic perspective. Still, writing a novel that had its own artistic criteria, he could not help but deviate from the scriptural models: thus Christ learns magic and does not perform the miracles that both the New Testament and the Qur'an relate. Although Mahfouz did not follow the scriptural sources to the letter, neither did he follow in the track of European authors who felt no compunctions about reinventing the Christ figure in a manner completely opposite to that given in the New Testament.[13]

Instead, Mahfouz told the stories of "our" alley, the story of humankind that has "been told and re-told," as the omniscient (but not divine) narrator says at the beginning (7). The narrator sees himself as part of al-Jabalawi's *hara*, writing about the alley because he has witnessed some of its last episodes. The theme of the *hara* had fascinated Mahfouz since 1947, when he wrote *Midaq Alley*. In that novel, he presented through a community in a Cairene cul-de-sac a portrait of human endurance, folly, lust, and continuity. The alley was a microcosm in both its comedy and its tragedy. After all, if Egypt is أم الدنيا (*umm al-dunia*; "mother of the world"), as Egyptians always state, and as the narrator repeats on the first page of *Children*, then its *hara* is the alley of the world. In *Children*, the *hara* is the "whole universe" in which the four protagonists live and die (Yaghi).

Mahfouz opens *Children of the Alley* with the same omniscient narrator he used in *Midaq Alley*, an "I" that described the small Cairo alley with the same observant but nonjudgmental eye as it does the universal children of the *hara*.

The narrator declares his intention to answer the following question: "How was [the *hara*] founded? What about it? Who are the children of our *hara*?" (8). The answer comes in his stories about the prophet-like figures who shaped the history of the *hara*: Jabal, Rafaʿa, and Qasim—men as respected and honored as were the scriptural stories on which they were based. The narrator presents himself as a historian of al-Jabalawi and of al-Jabalawi's actions in the world. He is the sole recorder of the final testament—in 114 chapters, the same number of chapters found in the Qurʾan.

Rafaʿa is the Christ figure. His name derives from the verb that the Qurʾan uses to describe the ascension: رَفَعَهُ اللَّهُ إِلَيْه (rafaʿahu Allahu ilayhi; "Allah raised him [Christ] to Himself" [4.158]).[14] He is born near Muqattam, that mysterious mountain where centuries before, one of the Shiʿite caliphs, al-Hakim bi-Amr Allah, went into occultation. As in both the New Testament and the Qurʾan, Mahfouz has nothing to say about Christ's lost years, and as in the Gospel of Luke, after the first chapter about nativity, the narrative moves quickly to Rafaʿa as a young man, twenty years old, returning to his people to begin his career as a carpenter. When he first appears, he is neither unique nor striking but an average migrant to the *hara*. Mahfouz avoids the thorny issue of the virgin birth, although both the New Testament (at least two Gospels) and the Qurʾan proclaim it. He gives Rafaʿa two parents—unlike the Qurʾanic account, which makes no mention of Joseph—and confirms their flight from the *hara* because of its brutality and the slaughter of its innocents. On thir return to the *hara*, they enter Mahfouz's familiar landscape of Egypt.

Rafaʿa soon learns the art of exorcism. This is no divine gift, just a talent that he acquires from an old woman, who is surprised that a man wants to learn what has been the profession of women. While preparing himself for the role of حكيم *hakim,* with the play on the Arabic word's dual meaning of "physician" and "wise man," Rafaʿa hears the voice of al-Jabalawi speak to him. Al-Jabalawi does not appear, although the narrator tells us that a few imaginative pictures had been made of him (a reference to the iconography of Christianity, unique among the monotheisms). Rafaʿa goes out into the wilderness for meditation and solitude (but does not fast), seeking out the Rock of Hind—the spot where Hammam (Abel, or Habil in Arabic) was murdered by his brother. As he is returning, he hears a voice calling him, as in the Gospel of Luke the voice at baptism in the Jordan River called on "my beloved son" (248). Inspired by the voice, Rafaʿa launches on his mission—to heal people of the عفاريت (*ʿafarit*; "demons") that take possession of them, to serve and to love people with compassion and dignity. Henceforth, and as in the Gospel of Luke, where the most prominent miracles involve exorcism, Rafaʿa dedicates himself not only to working at his father's carpentry shop but also to curing people. He wants to lead people to "true happiness" (260) and away from their greed for the land and from the conflicts that al-Jabalawi's promise of the land produced. He becomes so overwhelmed by his love of people that he turns into one of the مجذوبين (*majzubin*) (261)—those drawn to God in the Islamic Sufi tradition.

It is tempting to go through the account about Rafaʿa and unravel all the analogies with the New Testament, the Apocrypha, and the Qurʾan. Suffice it to say that his dominant characteristic is love—a love that sends him out among the worst thugs and bullies, to bring them happiness. He goes to the poor, even to those who are outside the *hara*—as Christ went to the Gentiles, the sinners, and the unwanted. Like Christ, Rafaʿa is chaste: although the New Testament Christ was surrounded by women, who even covered his expenses, there was not a hint of infamy about his relationship with any of them, including the elusive Mary Magdalene. Similarly with Rafaʿa: despite marrying Yasmina the prostitute, whom he saves from punishment—in a scene that draws on Christ's protecting the prostitute from the stone-throwing rabble—he never touches her. He remains, as the Qurʾan describes him, the purest of the prophets.

The most daunting challenge for Mahfouz regarding the death of Rafaʿa was twofold: first, how to present the murder of Rafaʿa, since the Qurʾan does not accept the Crucifixion (the Qurʾan argues that God sent someone else to replace Christ on the Cross); second, how to exclude reference to the resurrection—an exclusion that Christianity cannot accept. Rafaʿa is clubbed to death—his last cry, يا جبلاوي (Ya Jabalawi; "O mountain man"), is a rerendering of the famous "Eli Eli" that Christ uttered before his death. The killers are Bayyoumi and Khunfus, representing the Roman ruler and the chief rabbi, both of whom collude to kill "love and mercy and healing" (297). Rafaʿa is killed west of the Rock of Hind, as his four followers flee, after one of them, Peter-like, denies him before the crowd. The location of Rafaʿa's death is important for Mahfouz: where the traditional Christian site of the Crucifixion was the same as that of the tree of knowledge (where Adam fell and incurred original sin, Christ died to effect salvation), the rock of Hind recalls the murder of Abel—which is why in paintings of the Crucifixion in Christian iconography a skull lies at the foot of the Cross. Rafaʿa is killed where the first murder occurred: but there is no redemption, just repetition of human cruelty, degeneration, and defeat. His body is taken by his four followers and buried in a secret spot. After that, and as with all religions, the teachings of Rafaʿa are interpreted, misinterpreted, and corrupted by his followers, the Rafaʿites.

The novel continues with accounts about Qasim and ʿArafa (Qasim was the name of the Prophet Muhammad's first son, so Muhammad was known as Abu Qasim; and ʿArafa is from the verb عرفة "to know"). Both men bring hope, but after their deaths the alley returns to its perennial chaos and violence under the *futuwwat*. Significantly, at the end of the account about Rafaʿa (and later, at the end of the novel), Mahfouz's narrator grapples with the paradox of faith and history—and resolves it in favor of history. Such a resolution was not different from the demythologization that was ongoing in Christian exegesis under Rudolph Bultmann, an important twentieth-century theologian, just about the same time that Mahfouz was writing. Indeed it may well be Bultmann's exegetical revolution that inspired the spate of Egyptian biographies of Christ in the 1950s: Bultmann provided the Muslim authors with an alternative to the Coptic or Monophysite view of Christ, which is prevalent in Egypt and views Christ as exclusively divine, not human and divine. Bultmann presented a human Christ that Muslim authors could harmonize with the Qur'an.

But if Bultmann applied his radical-historical criticism to New Testament theology, Mahfouz applied it to the New Testament and Qur'anic composite of biographical narratives. He demythologized the Gospel narratives and projected them onto the daily life of average people in the alley. Bultmann stated that every "theology is an entirely human affair and thus as such has no directly divine significance or function" (21). But he was a theologian who surveyed the historical evolution of doctrine over the centuries and separated myth and human additions from the origins of faith. Mahfouz depicted those origins in their historical context: the Last Supper, for instance, which produces in Christian tradition numerous practices, rituals, articles of faith, and violent disagreements, is presented as a simple dinner that Rafaʿa shared with his four followers and his treacherous ex-prostitute wife. They drink some wine and eat bread, cheese, cucumber, and radishes—common foods in the Middle East for common folk—in an evening of fear and hiding. Mahfouz took the most momentous event in Christian soteriology and showed it as part of the quotidian experience: he showed how unmysterious the event was on which controversial doctrine had built its mystery. The characers have common Egyptian names, like Ali, Hussein, and Shafiʿi (important in Islamic history), but some names are peculiar: Khunfus ("beetle"), Zaytouna ("olive"), Battikha ("watermelon") Hannoura, and Shaldham. The people of the alley are as real, faulty, cruel, and kind as the people of any alley in Egypt or the world. God is mentioned in the novel but does not seem to have much of a role: many characters invoke Allah and رب السماوات (rabb al-samawat; "the God of heavens"), but more by force of habit—as Arabic dialogue with its constant allusion to God shows—than as reference to a supreme power.

The progression of the history of monotheism that Mahfouz depicts in the novel paradoxically transgresses the monotheistic definition of history. Where history in Judaism, Christianity, and Islam is teleological, it has no finality in the alley and provides no venue for humanity to shape or determine its future. There is neither consummation nor evolution, and none of the characters thinks that there is a movement closer to a final alley of heaven. Rafaʿa was one of many who brought hope, fought against injustice, helped the people, cured their ailments, and preached love and peace. But he was defeated and al-Jabalawi did not intervene—nor was al-Jabalawi likely to, since he too could be defeated and killed. As Mahfouz explained in one of his last interviews before his death, *Children of the Alley* demonstrates that if people leave religion (al-Jabalawi) and opt only for science (ʿArafa), then science will turn evil, "allowing the ruler to become despotic and to rob his subjects of their freedom" (Abu al-Majd).

What Mahfouz frighteningly presents in the novel is change without eschatology or teleology. Whereas the monotheistic traditions all pinned their certainty on a Messianic finality, Mahfouz deeschatologized the alley and ended the novel with the certainty of movement without continuity. Here he differs from

Bultmann, for whom eschatology is revealed in the eternal present, in the full realization of the divine here and now. Mahfouz excludes an ending and does not even subscribe to a cyclical history. None of the characters will ever return, and their legacies survive in contiguous but separate alleys, under a brutal and heavily armed overseer. Perhaps with tongue in cheek, Mahfouz presents a linear trajectory that points, as the narrator concludes the novel, to a future when "tyranny [will] be defeated in our *hara*, and light and wonders [will] dawn" (552). How serious Mahfouz is about this future is unclear, since the meaning of the lives and deaths of the characters is unclear. Rafaʿa has been murdered, his disciples dispersed, and his teachings confused. There is no continuity from the life of Jabal to the lives of ʿArafa and Qasim. There has been a succession in time without connectedness, figural or otherwise.

The alley is like the natural order: it will never cease growing, changing, transforming: *natura nascendo.* Meanwhile, the children of the alley continue in trial and error, love and law, brutality and belief. But they are not the children whom Christ called to him—and Mahfouz used in his title the same word that is used in the New Testament: *awlad.* They are children without a promised kingdom, children of our alley.

NOTES

[1] The first translation was by Philip Stewart and published (although completed two decades earlier) in 1981 by Three Continents Press. Stewart later revised his translation by comparing the serialized *Ahram* with the Beirut version. This edition appeared in 1997, by Passeggiata Press. The second translation was by Peter Theroux, *Children of the Alley* (Anchor Books, 1996). In this essay, I translate directly from the Beirut edition, (third printing, 1967).

[2] A popular saying that captures the reading-and-publishing mood of that period is, "The Egyptians write, the Lebanese publish, and the Iraqis read."

[3] For a study of the translations, see Allen, "Impact."

[4] In the light of the reference to the metaphysical novel, it is not surprising that Mahfouz "passionately loved" *Moby-Dick*, as he said (al-Ghitani, "Naguib Mahfouz Remembers" 42).

[5] I am grateful to Muhammad Shaheen for giving me a copy of this rare interview.

[6] See Abdallah, esp. ch. 7, where the critic shows how the "children of our alley are divided into the geniuses of social change and the giants of tyranny" (244).

[7] When captured, the youth who stabbed Mahfouz admitted not having read a single word by the novelist. He was, as he explained, obeying the command of his prince, the notorious Omar ʿAbd al-Rahman.

[8] See his refutation of Mahfouz's depiction of Rafaʿa (Christ) in ch. 13 (271–80).

[9] See Asfour's summary of the history of the controversy around *Children of the Alley* in four articles in *Al-Hayat*.

[10] Two years later, Fauzi M. Najjar wrote a broad interpretation of the novel, arguing for a literary rather than a theological analysis.

[11] A woman from the tribe of Ghassan (a Christian tribe) came on pilgrimage to the Kaʿba, reported al-Azraqi from his uncle, and on seeing the statue of Mary, she swore, "By my mother and father, you are an Arab. So the Prophet ordered the destruction of all the statues except that of Issa and Maryam" (165).

[12] On Christ in twentieth-century Arabic literature, see Jomier; Pinault. Neither article, however, deals with Mahfouz's novel.

[13] In *The Last Temptation of Christ*, Nikos Kazantzakis, writing at the same time that Mahfouz was working on his novel, presented a Jesus living with a woman after his resurrection, raising a family, and challenging the religion that his disciples constructed about him. Kazantzakis had finished his novel before *Children of the Alley*, but it was published only in 1960. When *The Last Temptation of Christ* was turned into a film in 1988, there was massive protest against it by Christian groups in the United States and elsewhere. The film was banned in all Islamic countries. Earlier, in 1929, D. H. Lawrence wrote *The Man Who Died*, a veiled account about Jesus after his resurrection. Lawrence had Jesus going off to mate with the priestess of Isis.

[14] The verse comes after the one that denies the Crucifixion of Christ.

Teaching Mahfouz's "Zaabalawi"

Roger Allen

In this essay I explore ways in which one might introduce Naguib Mahfouz's well-known short story "Zaabalawi" to American students. That such a gesture is appropriate and even useful is, needless to say, a direct consequence of the fact that this eminent Egyptian writer of fiction was the Nobel laureate in literature in 1988, the first and thus far the only Arab author to be so honored and accorded such international recognition.

I myself was involved in the process leading up to that momentous day, 13 October, and I have written about the circumstances, as have a number of other commentators ("Arabic Literature" and "Najib Mahfuz: Nobel Laureate").[1] Although at that time a number of translations of Mahfouz's novels had been appearing in a relatively cheap format from the American University in Cairo Press as the result of a project initiated in 1972 and although a certain number of copies of those translations were held by Columbia University Press in New York, the major work mentioned by the Nobel committee in its citation, the trilogy of novels set in Cairo, was not yet available in English translation. The small reserve of copies of the already translated novels was exhausted on the very day that the name of the Egyptian prizewinner was announced. What was more interesting and involved me to a far greater extent was that the many commentators and columnists who went in search of information about this unknown author from a thus far unrepresented literary culture all expressed to me their surprise that they could find very little reference in English to either his writings or to Arabic literature in general. The only work with any detail about him was the *Encyclopedia of World Literature in the Twentieth Century*, a set of volumes that Ungar, a New York publishing house, had put together a few years earlier. Ungar had asked me to serve as Arabic literatures adviser to the series. In what seems to be a prophetic gesture, it included—for the first time—some modern Arab authors, including Naguib Mahfouz.

Since that day in October 1988, the name of Naguib Mahfouz has come to the fore in the framework of a worldwide readership of fiction. A large number of his fictional works have been translated into most of the languages of the world, and his works have been widely read and anthologized. In retrospect, however, one can begin to ask whether the actual reception of his works in the various cultures of the world has differed in any way from that of other Nobel laureates in literature from non-Western and what I might (riskily) term other tangential literary traditions. The term *tangential* is an obvious and deliberate acknowledgment of what appears to be an inevitable sense of cultural centrality and even hegemony on the part of the publishing industries involved.

After the historical moment when such writers are subjected to the glare of world publicity and the concomitant processes of publication and marketing, what remains and for what reasons? Those are broad questions, involving the complexities of translation as a process of carrying a work of art across a cultural divide; the overt and covert assumptions of cultural expectations on either side of the divide; and the issue as to whether the work is to be judged by the target readership primarily on the basis of its content—what it portrays—and how far it meets or contradicts preconceived notions, or whether the artistic qualities of the original text, and especially its intrinsic cultural features with all their elements of difference, are to be included in the evaluative process.[2] I am not going to tackle those questions here, but I refer to them because they have an immediate impact on the approaches one may wish to adopt in introducing a text such as "Zaabalawi" to students in a comparative literature class devoted to a study of the modes of analysis of contemporary narratology.

Context

So where does this particular short story fit in Mahfouz's overall fictional output? Previous commentators on his works have been eager to identify different phases in his writing career and to link those phases to particular changes in style, technique, and even theme. Mahfouz certainly took great pains to develop his fictional styles and techniques (based to some degree on his awareness of trends in international fiction), but it is difficult to delimit his themes and place them in particular time periods. It is with that thought in mind that I turn to "Zaabalawi."

Mahfouz has now become a world-famous writer of Arabic fiction, but he was also what I would term a *penseur.* It is important for us to recall that he began graduate study at the University of Cairo in philosophy and wrote a number of articles during the 1930s on a variety of topics in that field. He also became involved in the wave of interest in Egyptology and what became known as pharaonism (Egypt's search for a national identity and the linkage of its present to a glorious heritage in ancient times), trends that were prevalent among Egyptian intellectuals during the 1920s and 1930s—not least because of the discovery of Tutankhamon's tomb in Luxor in 1922. Mahfouz's first published book was not in fact a piece of fiction but a translation from English into Arabic of a popular study of ancient Egypt by James Baikie, an English writer. The person who encouraged Mahfouz to continue the development of his talents as a writer was Salamah Musa, an Egyptian Coptic intellectual who had been much influenced by the Fabian socialist movement in England. Thus the young and budding writer of Arabic fiction was a former student of philosophy (and the philosophy of religion) with a lively interest in the history of his homeland, trends in modern political movements, and the search for identity, both individual and national.

That "Zaabalawi" appeared in a collection published in Cairo in 1962 suggests that it was written in the early 1960s. By that time, Mahfouz had published three novels set in ancient Egypt—عبث الأقدار (1939; ʿAbath al-aqdar; *Khufu's*

Wisdom [2003]), رادوبيس (1943; Radubis; *Rhadopis of Nubia* [2003]), and كفاح طيبة (1944; Kifah Tiba; *Thebes at War* [2003])—that received a certain amount of critical attention but were soon superseded by the pathbreaking series of novels beginning with خان الخليلي (1945?; *Khan al-Khalili* [2008]) in which he switched his attention to modern times and the travails of the various classes of Egyptian society, particularly during World War II. These novels would culminate in a major event in modern Arabic fiction, the publication of his trilogy, بين القصرين (1956; Bayn al-qasrayn; *Palace Walk* [1990]), قصر الشوق (1957; Qasr al-shawq; *Palace of Desire* [1991]), and السكرية (1957; Al-Sukkariyyah; *Sugar Street* [1992]). The trilogy, the work for which Mahfouz is best known in the Western world, is not my subject here (see Allen, "Cairo Trilogy"), but significant in a discussion of the place of "Zaabalawi" in his output is that, although the trilogy was completed in April 1952 (i.e., before the Egyptian revolution that took place in July of that year), its size (over 1,500 pages) meant that it was not published in book form until 1956—in other words, until after the revolution. It was an immediate success among reading publics throughout the Arabic-speaking world, but Mahfouz himself has admitted on several occasions that the events of 1952 and their consequences in Egyptian society were sufficiently complex that for some time he felt unable to comment on them in fictional form. Instead he devoted his energies to one of his favorite media, the cinema, writing scenarios for a number of works.

When Mahfouz did begin writing another work in fictional form, called أولاد حارتنا (1959 [1967]; Awlad haritna; *Children of Gebelawi* [1981]; *Children of the Alley* [1996]), it was first published in the newspaper *al-Ahram*, as a series of articles in 1959. To many readers of his previous novels, it came as a surprise: a highly allegorical work in which a thinly disguised series of episodes narrated by a traditional storyteller recounts the history of the major Middle Eastern prophetic figures—Adam, Moses, Jesus, Muhammad, and a figure representing *scientia* (ʿArafah)—all set against the distant control of a mysterious figure, Jabalawi, and the often futile attempts by these leadership figures to control their communities' proclivity to violence. If the critical community was surprised by this work, the religious community, focused on the al-Azhar mosque-university in Cairo, was outraged and demanded the immediate cessation of its publication. When the newspaper's editor, Muhammad Hasanayn Haykal, refused to do so and supported Mahfouz, the tense situation that resulted was resolved only when, following the publication of the complete series of articles in the newspaper, an agreement was reached (in which Mahfouz himself was involved) never to publish this work in book form in Egypt—although an incomplete version of it was published in Beirut in 1967 by Dar al-Adab. That decision was to remain in force for decades and was challenged only after Mahfouz was attacked and almost killed on 13 October 1994—that day being the anniversary of the announcement of his Nobel prize.

In the chronological context into which "Zaabalawi" fits, this controversy was still fresh in the minds of Egyptian and Arab readers of fiction. Mahfouz's change in focus and technique should not have surprised those who were already aware of his long-term intellectual concerns and interests. Thanks to the possibilities of retrospect that are now available to us, we can observe that in subsequent decades (especially after the June war of 1967), Mahfouz was to return frequently to his earlier themes: not only religion, politics, and modernity but also ancient Egypt and the role of history.[3]

The Story

How is one to describe the contents of "Zaabalawi"? At the story's very beginning, the narrator concludes that he must find a person named Zaabalawi. Not only that, but it is also clear, whether we zero in on the Arabic word أخيرا (*akhiran*) or rely on the English word "finally," with which the English version cleverly starts, that we are being introduced to a scenario that is already under way. The beginning, in other words, is a story beginning, not an actual one. Our narrator, it emerges, has a chronic illness for which no one knows a cure. Hence the need to resort to Zaabalawi, whoever he may be. The narrator now leads the reader on a quest—a loaded word, I realize, in the context of the study of narratives, but it is justified here: he needs to locate this mysterious figure about whom his father spoke.

So off we set on a series of visits. The first is to a sheikh, a religious-court lawyer with the appropriate name of Qamar (meaning "moon," a symbol of Islam). His office is in a very Westernized part of the city (Garden City), and he is wearing a business suit. A beautiful perfumed woman emerges from his plushly carpeted room. His response to the narrator's plight and questions is lackadaisical. Other visits take us to a residence at the al-Azhar mosque and to some religious bookstores. All end in failure: no one has seen Zaabalawi recently. The narrator returns home in despair, and time passes. The illness intensifies, so our narrator decides to consult secular authorities. He thus finds himself in the office of the head of the local district (شيخ الحارة [*shaykh al-harah*]—and here one should explain the different meanings of *sheikh* in Arabic), a figure who is dressed in the traditional floor-length *galabiyyah* of Egyptian men but is also wearing a (Western) coat over it. As part of the discussion with this civilian figure, Mahfouz introduces into the story a factor that has been a major source of debate and controversy in the history of all the monotheistic religious communities of the world. The district head suggests that, instead of wandering around Cairo aimlessly in search of this Zaabalawi figure, the narrator needs to go about the quest "using reason" (*God's World* [1962] 162; the English text uses "rationally" ["Zaabalawi" 140]). To help in that process, the sheikh provides the narrator with a tool for such an organized approach, a map.

The narrator now starts on a second series of visits, and each involves a kind of artisan and elicits meaningful comments about Zaabalawi. The narrator is also told that, with his particular illness, "suffering is part of the cure" (166; 142).

He is told to search for Hajj Wanas al-Damanhuri, and he eventually tracks him down at a bar. This supposedly devout returnee from a pilgrimage to Mecca (hajj) surprises the narrator (and perhaps readers as well) by telling him to get drunk before he will agree to talk to him or help him. Once the narrator is sufficiently plastered, he falls asleep and has a spectacular dream. Waking up with a painful head, he learns to his horror that Zaabalawi has just been there but left again. The narrator is in despair but on reflection realizes that at least one thing is now clear: Zaabalawi does exist. The story ends with his vowing to continue his quest.

My summary of the story is incomplete, and deliberately so, but it should provide a basis on which we can now turn to a discussion of the ways in which the story can be read and discussed in a variety of program and course formats.

Teaching the Story

When one is deciding on strategies for introducing this short story in a course syllabus or other pedagogical context, the obvious first question concerns the context, focus, and subject matter of the course in question. The amount of culturally specific detail sketched above may initially appear daunting, indeed to require something akin to a lecture on Cairo, Egypt, Sufism, the role of reason in faith systems, and so on. Some sort of preliminary guide might be needed in a world literature course in which knowledge of the source cultures involved is not expected. All of which begs the question as to whether in fact this is a story that can be read by a "general reader" (of whatever age) without resort to a good deal of background information. I have taught this story in both its Arabic and English versions, to students who know a good deal about Arabic and its literature and even about Cairo and Egypt and to students in a comparative literature narratives class with no such specific knowledge. I have been constantly surprised and gratified by the extent to which regular readers of narrative texts, with some knowledge of the principles of critical analysis, have been able to get a great deal out of this story. Leading students through the process of interpreting the layers of meaning involved and the gradual accumulation of evidence turns out to be fulfilling for everyone.

The best way to approach this text is as a short story. An initial question as to what the story is about usually produces interesting answers, and there will often be intelligent guesses as to who or what the figure of Zaabalawi represents. After some discussion, I like to focus on the story's structure: I ask the readers to look at the first sentence, then at the last. The notion of circularity soon emerges, leading to a discussion of the kinds of narratives that are circular and even to the circular diagrams so beloved of structuralist interpretations of quest narratives and other folkloric genres ("ashes to ashes, dust to dust," as the Hebrew Bible and the Ash Wednesday Christian liturgy remind us all). My more theoretically aware students frequently bring up the famous analysis of Vladimir

Propp (*Morphology of the Folktale*), pointing out that, while this short story does not appear to share the characteristics of a folktale, it has a clearly illustrated sequence—the two series of visits.

I ask the readers to describe the characteristics they have gleaned concerning the figure of Zaabalawi and also to diagnose the illness from which the narrator is suffering (what do the premed students in the class have to say about that?). Through this seemingly analytic approach we begin to broach the less obvious aspect of the allegorical nature of this story, which links it to its immediate predecessor, *Children of Gebelawi*. There are of course many illnesses for which we possess no cure, but what kind of illness is it where suffering is part of the cure? Here we enter the difficult realm of the possibilities (or perhaps, more accurately, the impossibilities) of translation. At what stage in the process of reading this story does the reader of the Arabic version become aware of the nature (and history) of the language and terminology being used? At what stage—if ever—does the reader of the English version discover that, behind neutral English words used in the translated text, there is a lot more going on than first meets the eye? I often suggest to students in my classes that a literary text is one that must be read more than once. The suggestion becomes almost inevitable when readers discover that the text is circular. In a very real sense, the first reading of this story provides readers with the information needed for a necessary second reading.

When agreement is reached that there is more going on in this story than first meets the eye and that the language used is loaded, we can embark on a guided tour through the various visits and fill in, as needed, culturally specific background information. The visits, part of a quest, form a sequence: the first group focuses on people or locations that are or were religious in their purpose; the second resorts to secular authority. Then comes the final encounter with Hajj Wanas. These various stops on the quest road—and I am deliberately using a particular terminology now—can be related to a feature of this story that is characteristic of many of Mahfouz's writings during this period (most notably, *Children of Gebelawi*, *The Thief and the Dogs*, and later *Echoes of an Autobiography*). The terminology is Sufi, that of Islamic mysticism.

The narrator's quest is part of a path or way (طريقة; *tariqah*) followed by the devotee, that being the word used in Sufism to describe the life of the mystic, the quest for communion with the transcendent; the term is used by the various Sufi sects (the Mevlevis, the Rifaʿis, the Shadhilis, and so on). Furthermore, in the literature of Sufism, the process of trying to cancel a concern with this world in order to achieve a state of oblivion (فناء; *fana'*) and encounter the transcendent involves a series of stages (مواقف; *mawaqif*) that devotees go through in order to achieve their goal.[4] Relying at this point on the Arabic version of this story, I note that the text is in fact filled with Sufi terminology: the use of the word "memory" in English is a translation of the Arabic word ذكر (*dhikr*), referring to the Sufi ceremony and practice of repeating the name of God. Often in this story, especially its second section, the people visited invoke God's name when they talk about Zaabalawi; one of them is actually crafting a calligraphic image of the Name. One of the lines of poetry cited in the story is from a famous ode by the great Egyptian Sufi poet Ibn al-Farid (d. 1235). Our surprise when Hajj Wanas demands that the narrator get completely drunk before he will talk to him lessens when we recall that in the tradition of Arabic (and Islamic) mystical poetry, the consumption of wine (and all its concomitant features—the bottle, the wine pourer [ساقي; *saqi*], and the boon companions) represents the communion of devotees with their Lord. It is precisely when the narrator is drunk and unaware of the world around him (in other words, in a state of oblivion, *fana'*) that he has a beautiful dream: a vision of paradise full of verdure and moisture. In the outside world, Zaabalawi has arrived, is present in the bar. The moisture in the narrator's dream is simultaneous with Hajj Wanas's trying to wake him by pouring water over him.

But the meeting is not to be; by the time the narrator wakes up, Zaabalawi has left. The narrator must continue his journey, quest, path, but now, as he notes, with a greater sense of conviction. In having Zaabalawi leave, Mahfouz is illustrating the need for the narrator to continue his search on the symbolic level; he is also commenting on the situation in Egypt at the time of his writing. Zaabalawi used to be a renowned and popular figure but is now pursued "by the police on a charge of false pretenses" (166; 143). No wonder that he does not linger in any one place. As we look back to the 1960s from the perspective of today, when Islamic groups in Egyptian society and the public display of belief are playing an increasingly prominent role, the accusations of false pretenses remind us of the diminished role that religious belief (or at least its outward manifestation) played in Nasser's Egypt.

Mahfouz, writer, philosopher, intellectual, and believer, in "Zaabalawi" is adding yet another strand to the works in which he explores the problems of modernity, nationhood, and society and the varying ways in which the continuing debate over the relative roles of faith and human reason can be explored in a modern, socialist system. "Zaabalawi" is one of his most successful forays into this debate, which is of significance not only to his culture but also to others. From a reading of the story emerge a number of discussion points, giving us a superb example of how a work of relatively few pages can provoke a great deal of thought.

NOTES

1 For another commentary on the circumstances surrounding Mahfouz's nomination for the Nobel Prize, see Espmark. See also my more general writings on Mahfouz ("Najib Mahfuz" [1989], "Najib Mahfuz" [1990], "Najib Mahfuz and World Literature," "Najib Mahfuz and the Nobel Prize," "The Cairo Trilogy," and "Naguib Mahfouz").

2 We appear to be in a postorientalism era (the reference being, of course, to Edward Said's renowned work; e.g., see Irwin, *Dangerous Knowledge*. Among factors that can be

raised in this context are the much explored influence of the *Arabian Nights* on European culture and its view of the Middle East and the ongoing love affair with ancient Egypt and the pharaohs, reflected in part in the decision by the American University in Cairo Press to publish a large amount of Mahfouz's fictional writing set in the pharaonic period (see Stock).

3 Among works that evoke discussion of religious themes, I would cite in particular حكايات حارتنا (1974; Hikayat haratina; *Fountain and Tomb* [1988]), رحلة ابن فطومة (1982; Rihlat Ibn Fattumah; *The Journey of Ibn Fattouma* [1993]), and أصداء السيرة الذاتية (1995; Asda' al-sirah al-dhatiyyah; *Echoes of an Autobiography* [1997]). For works with strong Egyptological ties, I would cite العائش في الحقيقة (1985; Al-ʿa'ish fi al-haqiqah; *Dweller in Truth* [2000]) and أمام العرش (1983; Amam al-ʿarsh; *Before the Throne* [2009]).

4 Muhammad al-Niffari (d. 965) wrote a work under the title *Book of Stations* (Mawáqif).

Homage to Ibn al-Fârid: Nostalgia in "Zaabalawi"

Michael Beard

The same story taught in two different courses may take on different appearances. A course in a national literature, for instance, is likely to show a centripetal drift in its assignments, to focus on developing traditions, on influences that evolve from one generation to the next and help define a common style, tracing fields of force that connect writers—the way the novel changes across the nineteenth century, the way poets look back at their predecessors as shapers of a tradition. It is a context likely to make any individual work seem part of a dialogue. In classes organized to sample world literature, the emphasis is likely to fall on variety, and individual works may seem far-flung, disconnected, and solitary. In world literature courses, we watch traditions evolve separately, sometimes aware of one another, sometimes not, and any given assignment is likely to be the only representative of that literary tradition the students will read. A course in the Egyptian short story, or (a more likely phenomenon) in the Arab short story, has the option of showing how the styles evolve from, say, the *Thousand and One Nights* or the مقامات (*Maqâmât*; "Assemblies") of al-Hamadhânî to the short stories of Yahya Haqqi and Latîfa al-Zayyât. In such a course, Mahfouz might take more than one role, perhaps as a realist or perhaps as an experimental voice. In the wider context of a world literature course, students are likely to experience Mahfouz as the single Arab writer, the representative of his culture. Juxtaposed with other short narratives by, say, James Joyce, Lu Xun, Albert Camus, or Gabriel García-Márquez (all frequently anthologized writers), Mahfouz's works become willy-nilly characteristically Arab and Mahfouz becomes the sole representative of his tradition.

Both approaches have their advantages: read against a global backdrop, Mahfouz's attention to social detail may emphasize his role as an observer of Cairo life, whereas in a course on Arab writers, we may be more likely to see how Mahfouz was a stylistic innovator. Arab writers often mention the distinctiveness of his voice, what a challenge it was for young writers to come up with a new narrative idea, hoping that Mahfouz hadn't already thought of it. It would be misleading to imagine him a typical Arab writer, though his influence has been so considerable that the reader looking back may feel in retrospect that Mahfouz is typical. There is a bon mot that the evolution of Mahfouz's style, from the historical romances of the early 1940s and the leisurely realist works, which reach their terminal point with the trilogy (1956 and 1957), to the experiments that begin with أولاد حارتنا (1959; Awlad haritna; *Children of Gebelawi*), recapitulate the history of the Western novel from Balzac to Kafka. I don't know whether this recapitulation makes his an original voice, retracing through his own vision a track built into the logic of narrative, or a derivative one, but it certainly draws our attention to his stylistic development. From the 1960s to the end of his career, that development is marked by constant narrative experiment.

The short story "Zaabalawi" (1962; زعبلاوى) will seem in the context of a course on Arab writers a point on the path of his unfolding stylistic experiments. In the global setting, it is likely to provide us a kind of guidebook, an opportunity for a reverie on the map of Cairo. It is my suspicion that students in American universities, even if they have only a rudimentary sense of Egyptian culture and its complexities, even if they are not drawn to Mahfouz's vision or his aesthetic identity, are likely to appreciate the variety of neighborhood settings, of dress, and of cultural identity.

"Zaabalawi" has taken on a particular prominence among his stories, in part from the accident that it is so frequently anthologized, in part because it gives us a brief and vivid sketch of a layered and charming city, in part because it represents an interesting moment of change in Mahfouz's career (more inventive and less predictable). It has been my experience that students are struck forcibly by the narrative arc. The story begins by creating a powerful effect of suspense: the narrator, who is afflicted with an unstated sickness and cannot be helped by doctors, seeks a Sufi saint who may be able to cure him. Then we are refused the anticipated sense of closure. I say "struck forcibly," because I want a term that includes two reactions: a reader can read the story as a statement of affirmation (yes, we discover that the spiritual figure Zaabalawi exists) or as a statement of unresolved, Kafkaesque frustration (we don't know whether or not the narrator will connect). The opening sentence, "Finally I became convinced that I had to find Sheikh Zaabalawi" (اقتنعت أخيرا بأن على أن أجد الشيخ زعبلاوي; Iqtanaʿtu ʾakhîran biʾan ʿalayya an ʿajida al-Shaykh Zaʿbalâwî [1; 136]), echoes the closing one, "Yes, I have to find Zaabalawi" (نعم، على أن أجد الزعبلاوي; Naʿm, ʿalayya an ajida al-Zaʿbalâwî [14; 150]). A reader can experience this repetition as a satisfying symmetry or as a feeling of being stuck painfully in place.

There is no doubt of the force with which Mahfouz brings the reputation of Zaabalawi into the foreground: the popular song about him, recalled from the narrator's childhood, is the first event of the story, and the testimonial from the narrator's father is the second. The quotation from the (fictional) popular ballad is itself surprising, because it's not a recorded song but a ballad sung in the streets—a traditional practice that characterizes an age now lost, something like the teahouse that storytellers lamented in *Midaq Alley*. The theme of the quest emerges between two terminal points: the reputation of Zaabalawi and the emphasis on the narrator's illness. (The father's testimony establishes that Zaabalawi can cure sickness—"Were it not for him I would have died miserably..." [1; 136]). So the opening page gives us two terminal points of the quest, its goal, Zaabalawi, and the initiating cause, the narrator's illness. Students can be frustrated never to be told the nature of his illness, but it can hardly be called an oversight on the part of the author. When Maggie Nassif interviewed Mahfouz in 1998 (Mahfouz, Interview), she asked specifically what is "that illness for which no one possesses a remedy" (1; الداء الذي لا دواء له عند أحد; al-dâʾu al-ladhi lâ dawâʾa lahu ʿind ahad [136]). Mahfouz evaded answering, to an extent that seems almost comic. We learn at turning points in the story that there is pain (ألم; *alam*) involved. The word *alam* is physical pain, but even here one feels that a figurative reading is a possibility.

Once the theme of a quest narrative is established, the story can be summarized by listing the places in Cairo where the narrator searches for Zaabalawi, each of them significant and worth a gloss. Indeed, the reader visiting Cairo could use the story as a guide to the city more than forty years after its publication. There are formal details that organize it in terms so accessible and universal that the point may come across no matter from what cultural background the reader approaches it. The first stop in the narrator's search for Zaabalawi, the office of Sheikh Qamar, a municipal authority, is a setting appropriate to a Westernized character, and this Westernization is emphasized by the detail that the office is in the traditional part of town whereas the sheikh lives in Garden City. Mahfouz makes it clear from the context that Garden City is a Westernized suburb, yet if the teacher informs a class that the term in Arabic consists of the English words "Garden City" (transcribed as جاردن سيتي), it brings the motif into high relief. (Note that the northern boundary of Garden City is just south of the Nile Hilton Hotel in downtown Cairo.) If in addition one has a map that shows its location, south of Tahrir Square, between Qasr al-ʿAinî Street and the river, it has a visual impact that Mahfouz's first readers would appreciate immediately.

The next informant is in the al-Azhar district to the north ("The Birgawi Residence" [3; 138]), one of the most important areas of traditional Cairo. Yet the real quest seems to begin as the narrator remembers "the local sheikh of the district" (4; 138), who is described in terms that combine realism and a figurative image with equal intensity: "His office was in the nature of a small shop, except that it contained a desk and a telephone, and I found him sitting at his desk, wearing a jacket over his striped galabeya" (4; 139). The image of a character wearing a half-traditional, half-Western outfit, a djellaba with a Western jacket (the Arabic جاكتة [*jâkita*] is a loan word from English), is realistic (it is a perfectly possible mix of styles) and iconic. One can even imagine a class discussion about traditional clothing. The word "galabeya" will not be found in most dictionaries (though it will show up in a *Google* search), so it might be worth a gloss for students who have not seen those traditional robes. (The word in Arabic, by the way, is جلباب [*jilbâb*], an etymological relative that is oddly described as a woman's dress in Hans Wehr's dictionary of Arabic. It might be appropriate to compare the term *burnoose*, itself an Arabic term [برنس] with an interesting etymology, since it comes from Greek *birros*, the same robe, more or less, but with a hood.) It is this liminal character, the local sheikh, who draws the map that allows us to visualize the narrator's quest in detail.

As the narrator penetrates further into the traditional districts, his next two informants are artists: the calligrapher Hassanein in the Umm al-Ghulam district (where the tomb of Barsbay al-Bagasi is often part of architectural tours [Parker, Sabin, and Williams 225]) and the musician Shaykh Gad, both of whom speak of Zaabalawi as an inspiration in their art. The theme of traditional Cairo as the place where spirituality is to be found has taken on an additional dimension, because spirituality is also preserved in the traditional arts. One could imagine a commentary for American students, for whom a calligrapher has skills we might attribute to a graphic designer, that explains how calligraphy functions differently in a society using the Arabic script. Now that computer graphics have begun to generate so much calligraphy, this may have changed, but it wasn't long ago that signs on storefronts and posters in the street that pushed the possibilities of the Arabic script were striking and even visionary in their invention and their ability to surprise.

Yet if there is a hierarchy of the arts in Mahfouz's writing, music takes precedence. One sometimes hears that Mahfouz studied playing the قانون (*qânûn*) early in his career because he felt that to learn improvisation would help him as a creator of plots. One doesn't have to read many of his stories—his ability to produce surprising variations—to find the anecdote convincing (see Moosa 14). The visit to Shaykh Gad, whom the narrator finds in the Tambakshiyya district, is in fact the focal point of the narrative, the place where we learn about attributes of Zaabalawi in the most specific way. The conversation with the musician, having hesitancies and seemingly inconsequential details, slows the story down and grounds it in a new sense of the immediate. The opening of their discussion establishes that Shaykh Gad has no better map than the narrator's other informants (though he will provide the clue of seeking Zaabalawi through Haj Wanas, which leads to the climax of the story). What changes for the reader is something in the grain of the narrative, an audible shift of gears. After his famous, frequently cited comment about Zaabalawi's inaccessibility, "Such are saints or they would not be saints" (7; 142), the conversation takes an odd, musical turn:

> He took up the plectrum and began plucking soft strains from the strings. Lost in thought, I followed his movements. Then, as though addressing myself, I said, "So my visit has been in vain."
>
> He smiled, laying his cheek against the side of the lute. "God forgive you," he said, "for saying such a thing of a visit that has caused me to know you and you me!" (8; 142–43)

We are trained as readers of fiction to see each event as functional, justified by its contribution to a unified effect, but here a character in the story insists that simply meeting the narrator has a function. In the next moment, he begins to sing a quotation from the poetry of ʿUmar ibn al-Fârid.

Ibn al-Fârid, one of the most important figures in the poetry of Sufism, developed the paradoxical connection between spiritual intoxication and drunkenness. There is even a Sufi group (a branch of the Qâdiriyya order) said to derive its authority from his teachings (Trimingham 271). The footnote that identifies the quotation from his poetry in *The Norton Anthology of World Literature* is brief ("From a poem by the medieval mystic poet Ibn al-Farid, who represents spiritual ecstasy as a kind of drunkenness" [Lawall, *Norton Anthology* 2535]), but expanding the context of that reference can be a useful step in reading the story closely. It is also useful to discuss the pronunciation of the poet's name (ابن الفارض). Differences between the English alphabet and the Arabic are an obstacle to our reading his name correctly. The five-letter name *Farid* in Roman letters can represent two different names. Farîd, having a short *a* and the accent on the second vowel, a long *ee* sound, is a not uncommon name derived from a stem meaning "singular," "unparalleled." The Fârid of the name Ibn al-Fârid, seen less frequently, has its accent on the long *a* sound, and it concludes with a *d* sound we don't have in English. (Standard transcription would add a dot under the *d*. It is the *d* in the name of the month Ramadan.)

A. J. Arberry includes in his *Arabic Poetry: A Primer for Students* a poem of Ibn al-Fârid whose opening introduces a series of paradoxical figures of speech that characterize Sufi poetry with remarkable economy:

شربنا على ذكر الحبيب مُدامةً
سكرنا بها من قبل ان يُخْلَق الكرم

Sharibnâ ʿalâ dhikri al-habîbi mudâmatan
Sukirnâ bi-hâ min qabli an yukhlaqa al-karmu (127)

Arberry's translation is precise if rhythmically awkward: "We drank upon the remembrance of the Beloved a wine wherewith we were drunken before ever the vine was created" (126). One would like to imagine a translation that shows the way شربنا (*sharibnâ*; "we drank") is echoed in سكرنا بها (*sukirnâ bi-hâ*; "we got drunk on it") in the second half of the couplet. And of course no translation will catch the multiple resonances of the word ذكر (*dhikr*; "remembrance"), which include a secular erotic memory (as it comes up so frequently in pre-Islamic poetry) and the remembrance of the divine. A *dhikr* in devotional terms can be a specific ceremony in which a repeated prayer phrase functions something like a mantra in Hinduism. (Homerin's more recent English translation may better capture the poetic effects, though *dhikr* continues to elude us: "In memory of the beloved / we drank a wine; / we were drunk with it / before the creation of the vine" [*ʿUmar ibn al-Fârid* 54].)

There are images implied so subtly and references made so delicately, that I don't have a category to describe them. Underneath the opening image is a pre-Islamic scene of wine drinkers passing a cup around the circle, reciting poems in praise of a woman. It lends itself ironically to the image of Sufis reciting a *dhikr* together, itself a variant of love poetry but in praise of the divine, with the implication that to be in a state of spiritual intoxication is to be transported into the sky. The next line glosses the word مُدامةً (*mudâma*; "a drink") in terms that bring the celestial imagery into focus: in Th. Emil Homerin's version, "The full moon its glass, the wine / a sun circled by a crescent; / when it is mixed, / how many stars appear" (57). The moon is now a wine cup, a crescent that fills with light as the lunar month progresses, as a rounded bowl might fill with fluid, light playing the role of wine. Simultaneously we have the soul filling with light as it grows spiritually. The rest of the poem (forty-two *bayts* or double lines in Arberry's edition, thirty-three in Homerin's translation) elaborates the initial image, circling and deepening it.

Shaykh Gad sings a verse from Ibn al-Fârid, and students should know that Mahfouz uses quotations from poetry not infrequently to mark an important narrative moment. In اللص والكلاب (Al-liss wa al-kilâb; *The Thief and the Dogs*), which came out just a year before "Zaabalawi," the hero Saʿîd Mahran, the thief of the title, sleeps at the center directed by a Sufi sheikh in the scene before the climax, and as the thief listens to recitation of verses from Ibn al-Fârid recited as part of a Sufi ceremony (*Thief* 167–68; *Beggar* 152–53), the reader feels an alternative society profoundly unlike the frantic, uncentered world of the foreground action. His host, the sheikh Ali al-Junaydi, represents a pole of certainty and stillness to balance the constant motion and tortured improvisations of the central character. Homerin reads that scene of recitation as a case where Mahfouz cites Ibn al-Fârid against the grain, suggesting that we hear the *dhikr* ceremonies from Mahran's point of view, not comprehending the devotion going on as he tries to sleep (*From Arab Poet* 95–97). It would be difficult to say whether the reader is more likely to hear this recitation from Saʿîd Mahran's uncomprehending point of view or more sympathetically, as a road untaken, the proof that a more benevolent community exists that we only glimpse. In later writing—حكايات حارتنا (1975; Hiyakat haratina; *Fountain and Tomb*) and ملحمة الحرافيش (1977; Malhamat al-harafish; *The Harafish*)—Mahfouz would use quotations from the Persian poet Hafez with a similar effect, though the Persian quotations look odd transcribed in an Arabic context.

When Shaykh Gad sings in "Zaabalawi," he chooses a verse from Ibn al-Fârid that, we are told, Zaabalawi suggested to him. It is the only quotation from the poet in the story, but it seems to me worth a central place in class discussions:

أدر ذكر من أهوى ولو بملامي
فان أحاديث الحبيب مدامي

Adir dhikra man ahwâ wa law bi-malâmî
fa'inna ahâdîth al-habîbi mudâmî

Denys Johnson-Davies translates with reasonable accuracy: "I make lavish mention, even though I blame myself, of those I love / For the stories of the beloved are my wine" (143), though his version makes the key words a little harder to notice. The word translated as "mention" is *dhikr*; the word *mudâmî* is "my drink," an image we saw in a different form in the wine ode. We saw حبيب (*habîb*; "loved one") there as well. Homerin's translation may be a useful addition to a student discussion: "Pass round remembrance of one I love, / though that be to blame me, / for tales of the beloved / are my wine" (*From Arab Poet* 94). Again, it is easy to see the elements of the traditional wine song as Ibn al-Fârid liked to redefine the image. The command to pass the wine around echoes the earliest wine songs, and the notion that the poet is willing to take on blame prolongs the tension between the two readings, a group drinking literal wine and a group partaking of the *dhikr.*

"Zaabalawi" can be read as an homage to Ibn al-Fârid, and Homerin's observation that Shaykh Gad was in fact the name of the caretaker at Ibn al-Fârid's shrine, starting about the time Mahfouz was writing this story, would fit that argument (*From Arab Poet* 90). If we read in these terms, we might see the concluding scene at the Nigma (or Nijma) Bar, the scene where Shaykh Gad's tip has led the narrator to track down a merchant from the city of Damanhour named Hâg (Hâj) Wanas, as a footnote or addendum rather than as a climax. In that inconclusive, ambiguous confrontation, the traditional imagery of wine and *dhikr* is recapitulated, but we are likely to experience shock, since the wine is literal. For some readers it is a frustrating ending, as we never see Zaabalawi. Hâj Wanas's perverse condition that he won't talk until the narrator is drunk makes the confrontation with the saint indirect: it is not an actual meeting but an ecstatic dream, which comes to the narrator after he has passed out: a fountain in a garden, a hill of jasmine petals, and a conviction of serenity and rightness. He awakens to learn that Zaabalawi was sitting next to him but has just left, that Zaabalawi sprinkled water on him to wake him up, which explains the spray from the fountain in the dream. It would probably require an advanced class to discuss the changes that Ibn al-Fârid's paradoxes undergo in the barroom scene, but I like to imagine an unusually accomplished and articulate class working out the details of the transformation—how the once scandalous imagery of the circle of wine drinkers, reformatted as Sufi congregants reciting the *dhikr,* is changed to become a scene in the Nigma Bar where the holy man approaches the person who has literally passed out. The concluding scene, where the narrator runs out into the street and fails to track down the object of his quest, is oddly reminiscent of the final scene in Fyodr Dostoevsky's *Notes from Underground,* where Liza's departure leaves Dostoevsky's unnamed narrator similarly empty.

I mention Dostoevsky because he and Mahfouz, at least the Mahfouz of "Zaabalawi," have at least one important feature in common. Religion for both writers is more than a theme; it is a shaping force, a prop on which the narrative relies. Such reliance can be an obstacle for contemporary readers but should be acknowledged. One could read "Zaabalawi" as a standard quest to locate a fictional individual, but we can't ignore the power of the assumption, necessary to the story, that there are people of power, intermediaries between the world of human beings and the divine realm. There is no doubt that writers in the twentieth century, as in every other period, are often believers, but it becomes increasingly rare to see in the work of canonical writers commitment to religious vision as the dynamic element that pulls the reader in—rare at least in world literature anthologies. Western equivalents might be in a European setting, Pär Lagerkvist (the 1951 Nobel laureate); in the United States, Walker Percy or Flannery O'Connor, though in Percy and O'Connor the religious vision takes some effort to locate because the device of irony can hide it. Mahfouz is a writer who fits uneasily into anthologies of his historical period for just this reason.

Miramar and Postcolonial Melancholia

Elliott Colla

In class, I always ask students which American author Naguib Mahfouz was thinking about when he wrote his 1967 novel *Miramar*. Usually I am met with a long silence. But when we break it down a bit—noting the novel's radical experimentation in solipsistic subjectivity, its crumbling community, and the centrality of a female character who is talked about but does not have her own interior voice—some students begin hazarding guesses. When we add to that list the theme of loss and the defeats of the past, at least one student soon comes up with the right answer: William Faulkner. I normally do not like fishing like this, but in this case there is a point: not to test the knowledge of students but to emphasize that literature is a conversation, often between languages, cultures, and historical moments, and that if we can reconstruct the contours of that meandering conversation, we often find that many foreign works are not so foreign after all. The payoff is two-fold: it gives us preliminary rubrics for reading works of literature from distant traditions; it estranges us from those works we thought we know and allows us to read them fresh.

Following Jabra Ibrahim Jabra's 1961 translation of *The Sound and the Fury*, there was a small boom of Arabic rewrites, explicitly adapting themes and structures of the American novel to Algeria, Iraq, Palestine, and Egypt.[1] For his part, Mahfouz distanced himself from the American writer, saying, "Faulkner makes things more complicated than they need be" (qtd. in Hafez, "Naguib Mahfouz"). Yet, despite his disavowal, Mahfouz thought highly enough of *The Sound and the Fury* to borrow from it while writing *Miramar*. Like Faulkner's work, *Miramar* tells the story of the dissolution of an intimate community brought together, but also torn apart, by their affection for a girl. Like the American text, Mahfouz's novel is narrated through the fragmented perspectives of disintegrating characters.

It is not surprising that Mahfouz turned to Faulkner, for like other Arab authors, he was at that moment moving away from realist styles and intensely exploring psychology and voice. As an experiment with radical shifts of perspective, monadic interiority, and idiosyncratic verbal expression, *Miramar* stands alone in Mahfouz's body of work. I do not want to overstate the overlap between *Miramar* and Faulkner, for the novel is very much Mahfouz's own, and it emerged directly from the Egyptian context. Nonetheless, *Miramar* draws and expands on many basic elements in Faulkner's work—and it seems useful to pair the two novels in any reading. This usefulness works in both directions, because when Faulkner's works are paired with rewrites from other contexts, we can begin to see how Faulkner was read outside the United States as a writer speaking eloquently about colonial loss and defeat—about colonialism as a set of ongoing aftermaths. Long before critics in American studies began to recognize how he addressed the tragic consequences of white imperial expansion across North America, Third World writers like Mahfouz saw the postcolonial aspect of his writing and fully appropriated it to speak about their own experiences in the wake of colonialism. Notably, this Faulknerian strand of writing about colonialism was acutely attuned to the melancholic shades of that history. For students of Faulkner in my class, Mahfouz's novel thus becomes an object lesson in seeing the postcolonial arguments in his work, even if such strands are still, even now, not always evident to his most astute American critics.

It has often been said that *The Sound and the Fury* is about the search for lost objects of desire, but this observation does not say all that there is to be said. If loss structures Faulkner's narrative, recovery does not. Rather, his text and its Arabic rewrites, like *Miramar*, register loss first and foremost and then in their peculiar style of inward-focused narration compound and concentrate that sense of loss. The result is not that there is an originary moment of loss incurred by the characters at the beginning of the novel that leads them to search for compensation or redemption. We come to know about their loss only after the fact. We are never outside the realm of "the aftermath."

In this essay, I consider *Miramar* as a unique literary event that, more than any other Egyptian novel of its time, was concerned with Egyptian colonial and postcolonial history as a set of disappointments and losses. *Miramar* recapitulates not just the losses produced by colonization but also those of the nationalist movement and Egypt's revolutions. The resulting narrative is not about gains and redemptions but about compounded defeats and further setbacks. In this regard, the novel needs to be understood as somewhat out of step with the national canon at the time. In early 1967, when Mahfouz wrote *Miramar*, the political field of the Arab world was dominated by nationalist discourses of anti-imperialist struggle, and the Egyptian literary field was very much still under the sway of social realism and the Sartrean doctrine of "engaged literature" (Badawi, "Commitment"). Not long after the 1967 defeat, Arab nationalist discourse would lose its confidence—and social realist dogma would lose its hold over literary sensibilities. Although written before the cataclysmic event of the defeat, *Miramar* belongs spiritually to the period of self-critical writing that followed in the 1970s (Ajami, *Arab Predicament*).

For all these reasons, *Miramar* seems a useful text to revisit the place of melancholia in postcolonial discourse. Loss, mourning, and melancholia have figured surprisingly little in postcolonial theory (notable exceptions are Eng and Kazanjian; Khanna; and Scott). Indeed, although colonization has arguably most often been experienced in terms of loss and defeat—at least for those colonized—the tone of many of the theoretical traditions that reflect on this legacy has often been buoyant and even triumphalist. There have been, no doubt, concrete political and methodological reasons for this disjuncture. On the one hand, the exigency of political solidarity with Third World national liberation—and an interest in discovering resistance and subversion wherever possible—has led many theorists to focus on the possibilities of redemption rather than loss. Nationalist investments in narratives of progress—the story that colonial decline would be replaced by postindependence renaissance—have usually also further precluded the laborious recounting of loss. On the other hand, in postcolonial theory the methodological strategies of poststructuralism, in particular its routine disbelief of linear narratives or figures of presence-absence, have also meant that many claims about loss were rejected out of hand as mere constructions (Appiah, "Post-colonial"). Those critics who dwell too long on loss invite dismissal as nostalgics. As Nauman Naqvi recently argued, nostalgia has a long, unsavory history as a medical term, a diagnostic weapon designed to pathologize those subjects who refuse to relinquish attachments to places, times, and objects stolen or destroyed by colonial modernity. Together, these habits worked to transform the problem of loss into something else: in the first instance, by renarrating colonial loss as the condition for postcolonial redemption; in the second, by lightening the weight of loss on philosophical grounds.

Mahfouz's novel offers a melancholic meditation on the recent colonial and nationalist history of its context. To illustrate this, I explore the problematic of national allegory in *Miramar*, the significance of its setting in Alexandria, its relation to Egyptian discourse on revolution, and its citations of Qur'anic discourse. I conclude with a few words on the novel's powerful but ambiguous critique of Nasserism to argue that, as *Miramar* shows, to ruminate on loss and defeat is not to become defeatist or passive. Rather, it is to seek another sort of victory, the kind of knowledge that only the defeated can hope to gain.

Miramar *as National Allegory*

Miramar tells the story of the dispersal of a small group of lodgers from an Alexandria pension sometime around 1962. In colonial times, the Miramar Pension was respectable, but now—a decade after Egypt's 1952 revolution, which brought national independence—it has fallen on hard times and attracted people struggling on their way up or on their way down. The cast of lodgers seems strange at first glance. I have always found this strangeness to be a great point of entry into thinking about the choices Mahfouz made to represent a diversity of generations, class origins, and ideologies in the novel. Five men, three young and two old, have arrived in the city as exiles, dreamers, or schemers. There are three sons of the post-1952 generation: Hosni Allam, an aristocratic playboy who maintains his privilege by parroting the slogans of the revolution; Mansour Bahi, who, after abandoning his former comrades to the secret police, has taken up a new career in state radio; and Sarhan al-Beheiri, whose rise from humble origins owes everything to his joining the ranks of the revolution. There is the ridiculous and reactionary old aristocrat, Tolba Marzouq, whose fortune and career were ruined by the 1952 revolution. There is Amer Wagdi, the patriot of the earlier 1919 revolution whose liberal nationalist ideals, no less than the politics of the old comprador aristocracy, were rejected by the new revolution. The two women in the novel are Zahra, the peasant girl working as a servant at the pension and whose sultry image adorns the cover of the Maktabat Misr edition of the book, and Mariana, proprietor of the pension. Though Mariana is the novel's only native Alexandrian, she is ethnically Greek, not Egyptian.

The next salient aspect of the novel may be self-evident to Egyptian readers but not to those who are not steeped in modern Arabic letters. *Miramar*, like so many of Mahfouz's other novels, is a national romance. I usually devote some time to explaining what national romance means. As both Doris Sommer and Jean Franco developed this concept with regard to genres of Latin American novels, the national romance tells a certain kind of social allegory that is clear to its readers, in which the libidinal competition between men for the affection of a woman stands in for class, race, and regional competitions in the nation. In Egypt, the novelistic canon is built on a kind of narrative that resembles the Latin American—but with significant differences. Egyptian novels, as in visual and popular political culture at large, often represent the abstract idea of the nation through the recognizable character of a virtuous peasant girl. In *Miramar*, this reading is made all the more obvious by the peasant girl's name, Zahra ("flower"), for it is her virtue and flower that are at stake throughout the novel. Following the work of Beth Baron (*Egypt*) and Lisa Pollard, we might call this modernist tradition, dating from the late nineteenth century, "Egypt as woman."

The national romance of *Miramar*, like that of other novels by Mahfouz, is about the competition of men not so much for a woman as for the body and heart of the nation. Marriage, in this allegory, becomes the emblem for the union between the nation and those modern nationalists who would gently and lovingly govern her. In the earlier colonial context of winning Egypt from the clutches of overbearing European suitors, this allegory was powerful—and remains so even to this day.[2] But two dynamics render the reading of national romance problematic in this novel. For one thing, while there are assignations and while a man wins the girl's heart and body, there is no uniting of lovers. The romance ends not with marriage but with the tragic death of a would-be suitor. This resolution causes all sorts of problems for reading the allegory of the nation, since it suggests that although Egypt has given her body and soul to a lover, no one wins her.

At the novel's end, Zahra finds her good name has been compromised and prepares to return to the village whose backwardness she tried to flee. Only at this point do the characters realize that it was not the pension that brought them together: their triangulated, "homosocial" (Sedgwick) affection for Zahra made them a "knowable community" (R. Williams 164–81) of men. But that is not the only problem that Mahfouz's novel poses for reading it as a straightforward allegory. There is another national romance of sorts: the two older men, Tolba Marzouq and Amer Wagdi, vie for the heart and body of the old Greek proprietor, Mariana. Her name too suggests allegory (she is associated throughout with a statue of the Virgin Mary, and her name has echoes of the colloquial Arabic for "saint" (مار, *mar*) just as it resonates with the name of the pension (*Miramar*) and Latinate words for "sea" (*mar*). Her name also points to Marianne, symbol of

French republicanism and, by extension, of the francophone imprint of Egyptian cosmopolitanism. *Miramar* thus suggests that one might have a patriotic love for two separate Egypts: on the one hand, Egypt as a young peasant from the countryside; on the other, Egypt as an old cosmopolitan Greek from maritime Alexandria.

Alexandria

Another aspect of the novel that is not self-evident is its place in a history of modern Alexandrian literature. Even a cursory presentation of this context helps students grapple better with the novel's significance. During the twentieth century, the city of Alexandria produced a disproportionate amount of melancholic writers, by which I mean simply writers more interested in exploring loss than gain or redemption. For Constantine Cavafy, the city's palimpsest history gave the city a permanent presence in absence that invited melancholic rumination, an insistence that an attachment to loss itself was superior (or more beautiful) than the attachment to any actual object of desire. For E. M. Forster, Lawrence Durrell, André Aciman, and others of the late colonial era, Alexandria was associated with the seeping away of empire and dissolution of cosmopolitan privilege. In their writing, Alexandria is productive of the kind of dreaming of the past that Paul Gilroy has called "postcolonial melancholia," that longing for lost empire that persists even in an era of multiculturalism. For Mahfouz as for other Egyptian writers, like Edwar al-Kharrat and Ibrahim ʿAbdel Meguid, Alexandria became a site for producing another kind of melancholic writing that was also about the late colonial era. These Egyptian writers tend to be not only emphatic about the loss of cosmopolitan Alexandria but also deeply ambivalent about the supposed gains of national independence.

Mahfouz authored more than thirty-five novels and a dozen collections of short stories—the vast majority of which take place not only in Cairo but actually in the Cairene neighborhood of Gamaliyya. *Miramar* is his only work set in Alexandria. And while Alexandria has a long list of twentieth-century writers who have lived there or called it home—in addition to the names already mentioned—Durrell, Forster, and Cavafy—we could add Stratis Tsirkis, Robert Solé, Jacques Hassoun, and Giuseppe Ungaretti (Halim, "City," "Alexandria Archive," and "Forster"; Hirst and Silk; Ostle; Starr). But the city was neither home nor place of residence for Mahfouz. He was not an Alexandrian writer at all but a writer of Cairo for whom Alexandria was another city. So, I tell students, the choice of Alexandria for his novel raises questions.

Before writing *Miramar*, Mahfouz spent twenty years writing realist novels in the third person. Moreover, his fictional world had been founded on the "chronotope" of the حارة; (*hara*; "urban alley") (Bakhtin, *Dialogic Imagination*). In Mahfouz's hands, the alleyway of Cairo sets the stage where different class backgrounds, lifestyles, temporalities, ideologies, and aspirations meet one another and usually clash violently in the process. While in *Miramar* there is no alleyway, the novel does take place in a similar kind of time-space—the pension—which allows for the exploration of clashes between different backgrounds and worldviews. But in contrast to the knowable, semipublic community of the alleyway, the choice of a pension turns Mahfouz's fictional voice inward. A pension is a semiprivate space inhabited by characters who speak in fragmented interior monologues—and it is unclear whether they know or will ever know one another in a meaningful way. This shift to Alexandria was productive for Mahfouz in that it marks the first time the author experimented with radical shifts in perspective, interior monologue, and the fragmentation of the self. Likewise, in contrast to the permanent, nearly timeless feel of the alleyway in Mahfouz's other novels, the feel of the Miramar pension is temporary and fleeting. More, the pension is already passed, already gone.

The novel depicts Alexandria itself as already passed, already gone. The pension is but a shadow of its former self, and the places of the city—the cabarets, cafés, restaurants, and stores—are all in the process of changing hands throughout the novel, as their foreign and minority owners prepare to leave for Europe. Alexandria in Mahfouz's novel draws on the cosmopolitan elements that feature so large in the work of non-Egyptians on the city. The historical context and setting of the novel are significant in this regard, since at the moment depicted in the novel, the early 1960s, Alexandria loomed large in the nationalist imagination as a place badly in need of purification, decolonization, and nationalization.

Egyptian nationalists were not deluded in associating the city with colonial legacies. The French occupation of Egypt in the late eighteenth century began with this city. After the boom of the 1860s, as Egyptian cotton filled the gap left when American production collapsed, Alexandria served as the local base of operations for European financial and trade networks doing business in the expanding Egyptian economy (Reimer). Soon after opening, the Alexandria bourse became a central node in the global economy, and merchants and financiers set up shop and settled in the city. Bust soon followed boom, and European creditors, backed by their governments, descended on Egypt to recoup their debts. In perhaps the first organized restructuring of a modern state, the Egyptian government was forced to hand over its economic and development affairs to experts imposed on them by France and England. It was in Alexandria, not Cairo, where much of the drama played out.

Alexandria soon became a flash point again, this time as the restructuring efforts failed and descended into military conflict. Ethnic Egyptian officers soon revolted against the Turko-Circassian political elites who had granted so many concessions to European creditors. In the process, they created one of the first parliamentary governments in Africa but quickly came into confrontation with British troops dispatched to protect European financial interests. The invasion began with an industrial-scale bombardment. An Englishman who watched the event from sea wrote that the bombardment "commenced on Tuesday July 11, 1882 at seven in the morning. From where [we were] anchored we could see the whole thing quite clearly through our glasses. To a civilian who had never seen warfare the spectacle was magnificent" (qtd. in Mitchell 128). As one historian of bombing technologies has described it, "The British navy shelled Alexandria from sunrise to sunset. During the night, the city was transformed into a sea of fire" (Lundqvist 18). A French witness to the destruction, Admiral Aube, was less enthusiastic about the event. Concerned about the precedent it was setting, he asked, "Is it now fair game . . . for the navy to bombard the enemies' undefended coastal cities?" (qtd. in Lundqvist 19). Under European leadership, the twentieth century would answer his question in the affirmative.

Soon after, British marines went ashore, armed with Gatling guns. After a week of mopping up resistance, Alexandria was secured. Thus began seventy-four years of direct British rule in Egypt. Through no fault of its own, Alexandria figured large in this colonial legacy. The bombardment of the city had flattened the old Ottoman port, a swath of land miles long and roughly half a mile deep. As we know from our own times, such events bring with them reconstruction opportunities and real estate speculation. Humanitarian and reconstruction contractors came from all over the Mediterranean, from the Dalmatian coast, from Marseilles, from Sicily and Malta. The modern center of Alexandria as we know it today was built on land cleared by this bombardment. What was once crowded harbor frontage eventually became an area of sweeping corniches, broad boulevards, open squares, and the kind of fin de siècle high-rises ubiquitous throughout cities of the eastern Mediterranean.

If Alexandria had had an association with Western finance and trade before the British occupation, this tie was now strengthened, though for reasons more complicated than mere colonial penetration. Historically, Alexandria had been home to large nonethnic Egyptian communities: Greeks most famously, but also Syrians, Sephardi and Mizrachi Jews, Maltese, Sicilians, French and North Africans (Ilbert, Yannakakis, and Hassoun). Under a complicated set of laws inherited from the Ottomans, non-Muslim, non-Egyptian communities enjoyed special legal privileges that were further bolstered by British divide-and-rule policies. As the Egyptian national liberation movement developed, these rights increasingly became a point of contention. Given the large numbers of nonnationals residing permanently in Alexandria, the city became a symbol of colonial extraterritoriality on Egyptian soil. The very multiculturalism, cosmopolitanism, and hybridity celebrated by some Alexandrian authors became, in the eyes of nationalists, a set of problems to fix.

National Liberation(s)

Other historical references in the novel can be effectively and economically presented to great effect in the classroom. In official history, Egypt has had no less than three moments of national liberation from modern colonial rule: the 1882 Urabi Revolt, the 1919 revolution, and finally the 1952 revolution. Alexandria figured importantly in each of these moments. In 1882, it was a center of military conflict and defeat. In 1919, it was the site of a popular uprising against British (and foreign) presence in the city, but it was also key symbolically. When the national figurehead, the Sorbonne-educated lawyer Saad Zaghloul, was expelled from the peace talks in 1918 by the British, he returned to Egypt to press his case there. Soon after, he was expelled from Egypt by the colonial authorities, and it was this expulsion that shifted the movement from legalistic strategies to a more immediate and public form of politics. Zaghloul remained in exile for weeks as the country, now radicalized, took to the streets. Forced to relent, the British allowed him to come back, and his return to Alexandria was celebrated as a national holiday. After Zaghloul's death, Parliament funded a number of massive memorials of his figure—including one in central Alexandria near the spot where Zaghloul returned to Egypt following his exile.

But by the 1950s, Zaghloul's Wafd Party had become so associated with the compromises and corruption of colonial rule that the leaders of the next revolution could eliminate it without much popular complaint (J. Gordon 14). In the wake of the 1952 coup d'état, the legacy of the 1919 revolution was shown to be ambiguous. It did not matter that the earlier revolution had been a mass undertaking whereas the later one involved only a handful of junior officers acting in secret. After 1952, 1919 and its liberal values were shown to be dinosaurs. This issue returns us to the character of Amer Wagdi, the core conscience of Mahfouz's novel, who is associated with this earlier revolution: he is described as a mummy in the novel, and for him the world is inhabited by ghosts of the failed revolution and especially by the specter of long-dead Zaghloul.

Alexandria was not a battleground during the 1952 revolution, but the presence of large numbers of nonnationals in the city became a focus of nationalist attention as the new military junta came into conflict with the lingering fact of British and French empire in nearby Cyprus and Algeria, and as Egypt moved into greater confrontation with Israel, rightfully perceived as a legacy and client of European imperialism. The process of nationalizing the Egyptian economy only intensified this conflict. As Joel Beinin has argued, this conflict was exacerbated by the Lavon Affair, in which Egyptian Jews, conscripted by Israel, set off bombs in Alexandria and Cairo in the hope of destabilizing the Nasser regime. In the wake of this campaign of terror, Egyptian police arrested hundreds of Egyptian Jews on suspicion of having dual loyalties. Jewish-owned properties and businesses were also seized by the state. These events, in turn, helped spark the 1956 Suez War. During this same period, the new state began to insist that Egyptian citizens own controlling shares in large-scale business and industry. By 1961, the year in which land reform and economic nationalization laws came into full effect, most of the cosmopolitan business communities had either fled or been expelled from the country. The city center of Alexandria was especially affected by these departures: businesses and buildings had been sold for a pittance, and large numbers of rural immigrants moved into the vacuum.

Miramar is thus set in an overdetermined time and location. The novel takes place directly in the former colonial center of town and is filled with references to the changing landscape of Alexandria, to Trianon, Panayoti, Genevoise, Metro, Café de la Paix, Windsor, and Miramar. Greek restaurants, French cabarets, Italian stores, and even small pensions are sold as their owners take flight. Streets and buildings empty and peasants rush in from the nearby Delta.

The city in Mahfouz's novel marks the aftermath of three moments of revolution, 1882, 1919, and 1952—now understood to mean three moments of defeat. In reverse order, the departure of Alexandria's cosmopolitan classes by 1961 marks the excesses and failures of a revolution that itself marked the defeat of the revolution of 1919. The level ground of central Alexandria, with its empty broad streets and open squares, suggests that the city was built on the rubble of 1882. In this account, national liberation does not compensate or redeem the losses of colonial rule; it rather compounds and extends them. It is better to mourn than celebrate.

God's Voice

Students reading in translation might feel they can skip over the references to Qur'anic discourse in the novel. I hope I have convinced my students not to, since this is where much of the action is, so to speak. Though the novel is narrated in fragments of interior monologue, the core perspective of the text belongs to ʿAmer Wagdi, whose very name suggests the perseverance of conscience. Throughout his monologues, he recites passages from the Qur'an, remembering his youthful education at al-Azhar and taking comfort from the holy word. Verses from the Sura of the Beneficent recur most often throughout the novel, forming a clear and repeating refrain. They are the closing words of the novel as well, its coda:

1. The Beneficent
2. Hath made known the Qur'an.
3. He hath created man.
4. He hath taught him utterance.
5. The sun and the moon are made punctual.
6. The stars and the trees adore.
7. And the sky He hath uplifted; and He hath set the measure,
8. That ye exceed not the measure,
9. But observe the measure strictly, nor fall short thereof.
10. And the earth hath He appointed for (His) creatures,
11. Wherein are fruit and sheathed palm-trees,
12. Husked grain and scented herb.
13. Which is it, of the favours of your Lord, that ye deny?

(Pickthall, sura 55)

No other Arabic novel from this period includes so much Qur'anic language as *Miramar*, and no other novel ends simply with a direct quotation from the holy text. The passage is well known, and its message—acknowledging God's creative power, His gift of revelation, and the necessity of remembering His generosity—embodies core parts of what the classical commentator al-Zarkashi would call "the sciences of the Qur'an" (1: 17). I draw attention to the last line cited here, which is also the last line of Mahfouz's novel: "So which of your Lord's favors will you deny?" In the Sura of the Beneficent, this phrase is repeated no fewer than thirty-one times. Noting the emphatic quality of the interrogative (استفهام التقرير; *istifham al-taqrir*), some authoritative commentators insist on its status as a rhetorical affirmative and point to a saying (hadith) of the Prophet Muhammad that supports this interpretation (al-Mahalli and al-Suyuti 532). According to this hadith,

> the Prophet was once reciting the Sura of the Beneficent to a group of believers, and when he completed it, he chided, "What is wrong with you? Why are you so silent? Verily the jinn are more responsive than you! Each time I recite this verse to them, *So which of your Lord's favors will you deny?*, they answer, 'Not one of your graces, our Lord, do we deny, for all praise belongs to You.'" (532–33)

The recurring question of this sura carries the demand for an emphatic response from the listener, the expectation that anyone hearing it must voice a resounding "No, we will not deny Your graces."

This reading points to some essential differences between the Qur'anic text of the quotation and the novel in which it is embedded. The novel tradition is based in forms of reading that do not depend on vocalization. In contrast, the Qur'an means little without voice breathing life into its letters. By including this quotation at the end of his novel, Mahfouz is not only asking a well-known question posed by the Holy Word; he is also begging his readers to recite it out loud—in their reading of the novel to move from the silent to the spoken word. Indeed, to remain silent in the face of this question is tantamount to the act of denial denounced in the Qur'anic quotation.

What is the context in which this demand is made on the reader? The Qur'anic passages are filtered through the character of Amer Wagdi, an old liberal nationalist who throughout the novel has been silent witness to a number of violent and absurd events, most of which have to do with a compounding set of losses: the loss of a young woman's innocence; the murder (or suicide) of one of the lodgers; the dispersal of the small temporary community of the pension; the collapse of old and new nationalist dreams of dignity and autonomy; and, above all, the loss of the cosmopolitan city of Alexandria itself, undone by the mechanics of nationalization. There is thus a great degree of irony in the command to remember God's graces, for this is a novel of defeat, corruption, and loss, not one of creation and beneficence. And yet: each time these defeats intrude on the psychic life of the character, the Qur'an appears as consolation and also command—a command to remember and remain attached to "the favors of creation" despite their disappearance and loss. With this recitation and command to remember aloud, the mostly silent character finds his voice, and the words happen to belong to God. This novel, which so radically experiments with partial perspective and the incomplete quality of interior voice, ends with the omniscient, omnipresent voice of God. If there is consolation in this, it is that of bearing witness and nothing more.

In his study of C. L. R. James, *Conscripts of Modernity*, David Scott makes the case that much critical theory on colonialism has worked to obscure our understanding of colonial history rather than to illuminate it. This blindness occurs not because of a moral failure on the part of critics but because we have not been paying sufficient attention to the generic dynamics of our stories. Calling anticolonial literature "a classic instance of the modern longing for total revolution" (6), Scott asks:

> Does anticolonialism depend upon a certain way of telling the story about the past, present, and future? Does the political point of anticolonialism depend on constructing colonialism as a particular kind of conceptual and ideological object? Does the moral point of anticolonialism depend on a certain narrative form, a certain rhythm, and a certain conception of temporality? (7)

He answers his question:

> [A]nticolonial stories about past, present and future have typically been emplotted in a distinctive narrative form . . . with a distinctive story-potential: that of *Romance*. They have tended to be narratives of overcoming, often narratives of vindication, they have tended . . . to tell stories of salvation and redemption. (7–8)

Scott's intervention invites us to rethink the confrontation (or set of tensions) that emerged between commitment ideology of the postindependence era and novels like *Miramar*. Mahfouz's novel is not unique in this regard. Arab rewrites of Faulkner allowed a different kind of emplotment than those of the social realist epics sanctioned by commitment ideology during the 1960s. In *Miramar*, the Faulknerian strand allowed Mahfouz to take a normative genre, the national romance, and turn it into an elegy. At the same time, the tragic quality of this minor tradition did not shy away from political thinking, nor did it amount to a rejection of the anticolonial politics of contemporary national liberation movements.

Mahfouz found probably his clearest political voice in this novel. For the first time he was able to condemn the political tyranny of Nasserism directly. Amer

Wagdi recites verses from the Sura of the History, which retells the well-known confrontation between Moses and Pharaoh:

1. Ta. Sin. Mim.
2. These are revelations of the Scripture that maketh plain.
3. We narrate unto thee (somewhat) of the story of Moses and Pharaoh with truth, for folk who believe.
4. Lo! Pharaoh exalted himself in the earth and made its people castes. A tribe among them he oppressed, killing their sons and sparing their women. Lo! he was of those who work corruption.
5. And We desired to show favour unto those who were oppressed in the earth, and to make them examples and to make them the inheritors . . .

(Pickthall, sura 28)

The moment is as remarkable as it is fraught, for the reference to Pharaoh points to the present political time of the novel as much as it does to the distant past. Medieval commentaries routinely point to Pharaoh as a recurring Qur'anic figure—perhaps the central figure—of tyranny and human arrogance over the ages (Colla, *Conflicted Antiquities*). Yet, by the late 1950s, *Pharaoh* had also become a term with special meaning in modern Egypt: it was the epithet that the Muslim Brothers used to refer to President Gamal Abdel Nasser, associating the hubris of his rule with that of arrogant pagan rulers. Again, the connection to Alexandria is suggestive, for it was in that city that a Muslim Brother nearly succeeded in assassinating Nasser in 1954, an event that set in motion a brutal campaign against the organization and its sympathizers.

Most novels of this period, Mahfouz's included, pursue an implicitly secular agenda. Indeed, literature in general, and the novel in particular, played a prominent role in the broad social-cultural project of النهضة (*al-Nahda*; "the awakening" or "renaissance") modernity that sought to replace received religious traditions with new ones. For these reasons, it is rare to find sustained discussion on issues of Muslim morality or theology in Egyptian novels. It is even rarer to find the Qur'an quoted verbatim as often as Mahfouz does in *Miramar*. But the text allows Mahfouz to say that the world is composed of loss and that Nasser is a tyrant, to say things that under the late Nasserist regime no one might say publicly.

Miramar emplots its politics along a set of points that departs sharply from the nationalist consensus. It calls us to think of colonialism's legacy melancholically and to consider modern Egypt as an aftermath. The invitation is troubling, since it suggests that the broad social investments in national liberation and decolonization were ill founded or bound to fail. We are asked to sit in defeat as it bears witness to the lessons that only defeat can offer. In this, it echoes Reinhart Koselleck's analysis of defeats from another time and place:

> [The] defining experience [of the defeated] is that everything turned out other than they hoped. They labor under a greater burden of proof for

> having to show why events turned out as they did—and not as planned. Therefore they begin to search for middle- or long-term factors to account for and perhaps explain the accident of the unexpected outcome. There is something to the hypothesis that being forced to draw new and difficult lessons from history yields insights of longer validity and thus greater explanatory power. History may in the short term be made by the victors, but historical wisdom is in the long run enriched more by the vanquished. . . . Being defeated appears to be an inexhaustible wellspring of intellectual progress. (qtd. in Schivelbusch 4)

It may be that defeat leads to greater insight than victory. *Miramar* suggests that the best way, for now, to tell the story of colonialism and national liberation is to begin, and even end, with loss.

NOTES

[1] On Faulkner's reception in France, Latin America, and the Arab world, see Aboul-Ela, *Other South*; Azouqa; Casanova; Hafez, "Divergent Civilizational Experiences"; Jabra; and Yousef.

[2] Familial and romance allegories of nation are by no means limited to Latin America or Egypt. See also Dominguez; Hunt.

Miramar: A Pension at the Intersection of Competing Discourses

Hala Halim

The Arab world's only Nobel laureate in literature, Naguib Mahfouz tends to function in the global arena as synecdochic of the vastly varied literatures of the region, the whole often perceived in realist terms. Proposing a number of approaches to the teaching of Mahfouz's *Miramar* (1967), a novel that multiplies the angles of approach to a discrete set of events through the points of view of four different narrators, would then seem to be doubly fitting. The passage of the Arabic novel to the American classroom through English translation (1978) and its entry into *Weltliteratur* space through its author's having won the Nobel (1988) are processes that one would need to foreground and problematize at the outset in a world literature course. Next, the political context of this novel, published on the eve of the June 1967 war and set in the early 1960s, should be provided in relation to the text's critique of the 1952 revolution in Egypt. This context sets the stage for a discussion, drawing on Mikhail Bakhtin, of *Miramar's* chronotope, as one that perfectly supports this polyphonic novel, with its dialogic, heteroglot environment, where the centripetal force of an authoritarian nation-state is undercut by the centrifugal orchestration of heterogeneous discourses (*Dialogic Imagination*). In making the argument that polyphony and heteroglossia in *Miramar* are an emphatic appeal to pluralism, I would then go on to account for the two women figures who are central to the action although neither is accorded a narrative. I would frame the issue of the two women in terms of *Miramar's* intertextual dialogue with two traditions of allegory: in relation to the nation and in relation to cosmopolitanism. Finally, I would posit that the choice of Alexandria is highly motivated in that it reinforces *Miramar's* criticism of the Nasser regime.

In a world literature course, where often only one text from a given culture is included, the burden of representation that a novel from the "Middle East" is made to carry has become all the more fraught since 2001. Surveying the politics of translation of Arabic texts and of their consumption in area studies, Magda al-Nowaihi, in an essay written before September 11, identifies students' interest in the material as a desire "to comprehend how each text 'reflects' Arab reality," the "mimetic model of simple reflection [being] almost unbeatable when encountering foreign texts."[1] Her recommendation that

> part of the answer is not simply to give the students more, and more accurate, information, but to make them aware of their own positionality vis-à-vis the material they are reading, of how the material reaches them, how they consume it, and how their consumption of it is a power-allocating activity (28)

is just as viable, if not more so, when it comes to the representation of Arabic texts in a world literature course today. When presenting a translated Arabic, or Arab anglophone or francophone text in class, I have found it useful to enlist recent critical interventions informed by reception theory and translation studies that have analyzed the various processes of coercion that texts from the region undergo to meet the preconceptions of the global arena. Essays analyzing such processes in the context of north African literature and Arab women feminists, while specific, yield insights into the broader dynamics of the reception of Middle Eastern literatures in the United States. In class discussion, students may now adopt a degree of self-reflexivity toward their multiply mediated encounter with Mahfouz's *Miramar* (on translation from Arabic, see Toler; Amireh; and Kahf).

It is worth recalling that Mahfouz's winning of the Nobel was heralded at the time in various constituencies concerned with Arab cultures as a signal that the translational "embargo" on Arabic literature would be lifted. In 1990, Edward Said used the phrase "embargoed literature" to designate the ideologically freighted nonreception of Arabic literature in the United States, taking Mahfouz, pre- and post-Nobel, as his starting point ("Embargoed Literature"). There was no interest in translating Mahfouz in the United States before he won the Nobel (translations of some of his texts into English were available in Egypt and England), but after he received the award, Doubleday started publishing translations of his novels that

> with one exception . . . were exactly the ones that had been available all along in England, some quite good but most indifferent or poor. Clearly, the idea was to capitalize on and market his fame, but not at the cost of a retranslation. (98)[2]

If taught in English translation, the edition of *Miramar* likely to be read in class is the Doubleday one, first published in 1993 but reproducing the text of the translation—by Fatma Moussa-Mahmoud (edited and revised by Maged el-Kommos and John Rodenbeck)—published by Heinemann in 1978 and later in Egypt by the American University in Cairo Press.[3] Apart from a different cover and blurb about the author, there are two significant differences between the two editions: the Doubleday edition omits John Fowles's introduction to the novel and the explanatory endnotes by Omar el Qudsy, and no new introduction or set of endnotes replaces them.[4]

The permutations that the English translation of *Miramar* underwent in its different editions can be framed in terms of Lawrence Venuti's argument that "multiple determinants" in the Anglo-American context favor "the contemporary dominance of transparent discourse" and privilege "a fluent domesticating method that masks both the translator's work and the asymmetrical relations—cultural, economic, political—between English-language nations and their others worldwide" (17, 38). Venuti's recommendations are to make the translator visible through a strategically "foreignizing" approach to translation and to read in a "symptomatic" way that elicits discontinuities and "[demystifies] . . . the illusion of transparency in a contemporary English-language translation" (29). His "symptomatic reading" as "an historicist approach" (38) brings greater awareness to students' discussion of the novel, but I would also ask the class to debate the question of foreignizing versus domesticating translation in and of itself. An argument made in response to Venuti is that, in the specific context of Arabic literature and

> in the face of the new wave of Orientalism that constantly portrays alternately the Arab and/or the Muslim as the radically other barbarian ramming the gates of civilisation, it is easy to see how this strategy of "foreignising" a text contributes to this mythology of the radical, dangerous other

as Michael Toler has put it (66), although he considers likewise the perils of a fully domesticating approach.

If the process of repackaging for an American audience the translation of *Miramar*, which was first made for a Heinemann *educational* series, is a domesticating one, it should be noted that the translation per se was left virtually unaltered.[5] Although shorn of introduction and endnotes as emphatic markers of the status of the text as a translation, *Miramar* was translated into English with the expectation that notes would be provided and that the text would contain a certain amount of foreign(ized) elements in a largely fluent matrix that a more domesticating translation would have replaced by equivalents in the target language or retained albeit with the insertion of explanations and glosses in the text. For an example of a translational symptomatic reading, consider the following passage from the second narrative, that of Hosny Allam:

> "It's none of your business! Yes, I'll marry anyone I like! I'll marry Aleya!"
>
> *Ya Sayid! Ya Badawi!* Aleya! The schoolmistress! Has Dream Boy accepted that standing invitation she offers everyone to visit her *en famille*? So he's switched his affections from the scholar to the teacher! *Ferekeeko*, be my witness! Long live the Revolution! Long live the July Ordinances! Alexandria, what a lovely day!
>
> Here is Madame's voice, remonstrating in pidgin Arabic; and the great newscaster himself in the flesh, having condescended to interest himself in the affairs of the commonality. He's sure to find a solution to this rustic imbroglio. *A moi!* Welcome the fray! Action, *Ferekeeko*! Never let events forestall you. (80–81)

There are English idiomatic expressions ("none of your business!") and fluent sentences ("Has Dream Boy accepted that standing invitation she offers everyone . . . "); but at the same time transparency is blocked by the inclusion of transliterated Arabic words. Here I would ask the students if the semantic inaccessibility of the Arabic produces an alienating effect or if it functions as a muted echo of the Arabic speech idiosyncrasies of this narrative voice, an echo made less distancing by the exclamatory, ironic nature of the passage and the suggestion of a polyglot environment (the Greek proprietress of the pension "remonstrating in pidgin Arabic"; the French expressions "*en famille*" and "A *moi!*").

As it happens, there is no French in the Arabic original of Allam's speech, though it is justifiable as a marker of his background as a child of the ancien régime. This addition demonstrates "that there might also be a process of gain," and not solely of loss and violence, in translation (Bassnett and Trivedi 4). But in that case what "canons of accuracy" are at stake in those instances of "foreignizing" in *Miramar* (Venuti 37)? The transliterated exclamation "*Ya Sayid! Ya Badawi!*"—an invocation of a Muslim holy figure—might seem to corroborate Toler's reservation about the pitfall of radical othering (in this case, an other steeped in religiosity) attendant on a foreignizing translational strategy. Then again, the endnote on the invocation glosses the expression as "a homely banality that originally had the character of a pious ejaculation . . . [here] turned . . . to ironic effect" (*Miramar* [1987] 140). *Ferekeeko*, a verbal mannerism of Allam's and glossed in a note as a "slang nomen of no certain lexical origin, modish among the alienated young of the early nineteen-sixties," further provides an "index to both period and class" (138). One interpretation that a symptomatic reading of the occasional foreignizing elements would offer is that the text may have been construed in the process of its rendition as imbued with and dependent on the accents and discourses marking a certain time and place. Such a translational strategy adopted in the first English edition of *Miramar*, of which traces survive in the United States edition, would also provide a point of entry into a discussion of the novel's dialogism and heteroglossia as they bear on its criticism of the revolution.

Allam's parodic exclamations "Long live the Revolution! Long live the July Ordinances!" date the events to the early and mid 1960s, being a reference to the socialist laws promulgated in the summer and autumn of 1961. The laws, codifying and extending previous measures to nationalize the economy through sequestrations and the limiting of large landholdings and private enterprises, allowed "the government [to take] over by decree the entire import trade of the country and most of its export trade, including cotton, as well as local insurance and trading establishments" (Vatikiotis 397). But what does it mean that this mock-heroic tone surrounding the 1952 revolution, with its one-party system and its newfangled socialist ideology, should occur in the interior monologue of a character who, like virtually every other character in the novel is—not least during the Umm Kulthum concert soirée[6] that is the one occasion to bring all lodgers together in a moment of sociability—constantly on his guard lest state security agents overhear him criticize the regime? What does it indicate that such a perspective should be included in a novel published while that same regime is still in power—a few months, indeed, before the war that was to bring about the gradual unraveling of that regime? Quite apart from the relation between the author and the state, how does this situation—which throws into relief issues of freedom of speech and the question of representation, both in the political and artistic registers of the word—inform the narrative strategies adopted in the text?

That the long career of Mahfouz (1911–2006), spanning as it did the monarchical and postrevolutionary periods, brought him up against various forms of censorship, insidious or overt, has been the subject of scholarly analysis. The best-known censorship case occurred after the revolution, centering on أولاد حارتنا (1959; Awlad haritna; *Children of Gebelawi*). Although the serialization of this text in *Al-Ahram* continued to the end despite the furor the novel occasioned among the religious authorities and general public, it was prohibited from publication in book form with the proviso that it could be published outside Egypt. As Marina Stagh has demonstrated, this instance of censorship did not amount to an official governmental ban but was multiply dictated and enforced by various authorities (157–70). Compiling "an archaeology of confrontational moments" in Mahfouz's career, Samia Mehrez adumbrates the "constantly compromised position vis-à-vis authority" of the writer who doubled as a civil servant and who was eventually deserted by "the patronage that [he] had benefited from in the late 1950s and 1960s," a patronage that allowed the publication of such subversive texts as ثرثرة فوق النيل (1966; Thartharah fawq al-Nil; *Adrift on the Nile*) and *Miramar* (19, 18, 28).

These two discussions of Mahfouz's experiences with censorship provide a context for reading *Miramar* that brings out its counterhegemonic and pluralizing underpinnings. A thoroughly apt theoretical fit for this novel with four different narrators who qualify one another's point of view is Bakhtin's work on dialogism and heteroglossia. Approaching *Miramar* through Bakhtin, moreover, would serve not only to elicit the novel's undermining of authoritarianism and grand narratives through its relativizing, "democratizing" strategy but also to preempt students' expectations of the "mimetic model of simple reflection," against which al-Nowaihi warns in her intervention.

Faysal Darraj glossed Bakhtin's theory of the novel as a vision of "democratic writing" (70). But Darraj goes on to question dialogism, arguing that Bakhtin, in his thwarted desire to write a book on democracy, projected onto the novel genre what may properly belong elsewhere (87). He engages Bakhtin's assertion that the genre in its modern form is associated with the opening of national languages onto one another and with their interaction and argues that the Russian overlooks "the conditions that gave birth to the new world"—namely, European capitalism's triumphant imperialism. Positing that dialogue among national languages needs to be predicated on "conditions of equality" and self-determination (88), Darraj brings out the linguistic violence of imperialism and adduces Arab anticolonial interventions that upheld ethnolinguistic national identity.

The examples of Arabic texts Darraj cites in riposte to Bakhtin are mostly drawn from the high noon of imperialism in the region.[7] I would modify Darraj's position by offering that many postcolonial Arabic novels insistently display dialogism and heteroglossia to contest the ethnocentrism and authoritarianism of the postindependence nation-states. This is instantiated in a "stratification" of discourse and registers, often enlisting the diglossic specificity of the Arabic language; in an emphasis on a variously construed heterogeneity; in generic hybridity; in traces of linguistic and cultural signifiers of otherness recuperated, in reconfigured form, from the prerevolutionary period.[8] *Miramar*'s polyphonic form and heteroglossia are a prime example of this postcolonial tendency.

If *Miramar*'s polyphony can be said to have "brought together ideas and worldviews, which in real life were absolutely estranged and deaf to one another, and forced them to quarrel" (Bakhtin, *Problems* 91), then the novel's chronotope that so aptly enables this polyphony should first be introduced. As a wayside inn of sorts and hence meeting place, the pension that gives *Miramar* its title shares an affinity with the road in Bakhtin's discussion (*Dialogic Imagination* 98, 243).[9] Like the road, the pension as a "chronotope of encounter" allows for "the spatial and temporal paths of the most varied people—representatives of all social classes, estates, religions, nationalities, ages—[to] intersect at one spatial and temporal point" (243). Something of a microcosm, Miramar is, in Ibrahim Fathi's words, "a narrow spatial framework capacious enough to flexibly embrace different types who populate the transitional phase, with contradictory interests and ideas perpetually at war" in this "orchestra composed of several tunes" (123, 158). The novel brings together seven main characters: the elderly Greek proprietress of the pension, Mariana, an exemplar of the ethnic hybridity of prerevolutionary Egypt; Zohra, the young peasant woman who has migrated to the city in search of a better life and works as a servant at the pension; Amer Wagdi, the retired journalist with a history of involvement in pre-1952 politics, specifically in the Wafd Party; Tolba Marzuq, the elderly promonarchical gentleman whose land has been sequestered; Hosny Allam, the young propertied libertine; Mansour Bahy, the communist-leaning radio broadcaster who has been uprooted from the movement by his officer brother; and Sarhan al-Beheiry, the deputy head of the accountants department at the Alexandria Textile Mills and whose proregime credentials are established through his involvement in the Arab Socialist Union.

Also reading *Miramar* as presenting a "chronotope of encounter," Husayn Hammuda offers that "the dialectic of separation/connection, which is a main dimension of the novel, starting with the multiple narrators" (111), is embodied in the pension itself. He analyzes this dialectic in terms of the walls and rooms that separate the lodgers in relation to the meeting points in the pension (the hall, the salon, the dining room, the elevator), which in turn mediate closeness and separation (113–14). Hammuda also addresses the characters' contrasting relations to the past, particularly with regard to Miramar, such as Wagdi's nostalgic recollection of the pension as "a refuge replete with memories" (113), Allam's flight to it from his personal history as well as his resentment of being holed up with the elderly in the pension, and Mariana's construing it as her home and workplace (112–13).

I would extend Hammuda's analysis both spatially and temporally. As chronotope, the pension is associated in *Miramar* with a host of similar loci, other urban chronotopes conducive to encounter, given that chronotopes can be "mutually inclusive" (Bakhtin, *Dialogic Imagination* 252). These are cabarets, cinemas, streets, hotel lobbies, tram stations, restaurants, cafés, and tearooms—see the many meetings that occur in the Trianon. The pension and such supporting loci also serve as conduits of eavesdropping on adjacent lives, rumor, gossip, furtive transactions, and intrigue. In this sense, Miramar, together with its adjunct chronotopes, provides an apt spatiotemporal environment for heteroglossia and the tension between the centripetal, centralizing discourse of an authoritarian state and the centrifugal, decentralizing drift of diffusion and dispersal (272).

The déclassé, seen-better-days ambience of the pension also decodes into a web of indexes of socioeconomic transformation and of something akin to a historical *longue durée*. In a "massive old building," the pension's interior—where "the old mirrors, the rich carpets, the silver lamps, and the cut-glass chandeliers are gone, [though] a certain faded elegance lingers still on the papered walls and in the high ceilings, which are adorned with cherubs" (1, 5)—is a record of attrition and of traces preserved. It allows for that "special increase in density and concreteness of time markers—the time of human life, of historical time—that occurs within well-delineated spatial areas" (Bakhtin, *Dialogic Imagination* 250). This is perhaps one reason why the text begins (and ends) with the narrative of the oldest character, Amer Wagdi, and introduces at the outset the two other older characters, Mariana and Tolba Marzuq, who, like Wagdi and like Miramar itself, have sustained a "comedown" from "the good old days" (9, 4).

Signs in the pension's décor of otherness and of a bygone era are the statue of the Madonna and the portrait gallery, including Mariana as a young woman, her mother, her first husband, the English captain killed in the 1919 revolution, and her second husband, the Greek "[c]aviar king" who committed suicide (9). If Mahfouz's "guest-house is similar to one" of the circles "of Dante's inferno" (el-Zayyat 155), the text encourages us to interpret these icons in historical and socioeconomic terms by launching with the narrative of Wagdi. There are contrasting references to Mariana's first husband: the portrait of him seen by her—"He was killed by one of those students. Imagine my slaving for them now! This used to be the pension of quality . . . " (14)—and by Wagdi:

> I sit on my own, staring into the eyes of her first husband, who stares from his gilt frame back at me. I wonder who killed you, and how? How many of my generation did you kill before you came to your end? The generation that outdid all others in the extent of its sacrifice. Those were the days. So many fallen. (13)

These different readings of the past lead us to dialogism and heteroglossia in *Miramar*.[10]

To teach dialogism and heteroglossia in *Miramar*, one could begin with an analysis of each of the four narrative voices, how each refracts a given theme, issue, or motif; how each uses the mutually qualifying, socially and historically determined "languages" in the text. In a discourse analysis of *Miramar*, Angele Botros Samaan emphasizes "the linguistic and stylistic features which functionally distinguish these points of view [of the four narrators], and through the interaction between them to evoke a vivid and complex picture of the revolution" (187). She analyzes the "'mind-style' or 'thought-presentation'" of, as well as interaction between, "two characters viewing" the revolution "from two different angles"—Wagdi and Allam (188).

Samaan adumbrates the metaphor of the sea and dwells on the slow rhythm and choice of words in the opening sentences of Wagdi's first narrative, suggesting that the "distinct mark of the discourse is that it seems steeped in the nostalgically poetic, befitting an old man's way of thinking" (189). As an elderly man who, she argues, is a firm believer in revolutionary change (although Wagdi's revolutions are of 1882 and 1919), he is associated with images of decay and antiquity that connote his "disharmony with the times" (189). By contrast, the consciousness of Allam, who "is both resentful of the revolution and alienated from his own class," is evidenced in the first paragraph of his narrative, in the image of a tumultuous sea, in the "contrastive quality of the rhythm of the sentences" and in "the verbless utterances" (190).

One could read the opening paragraphs of the other narrators in the same way.[11] Bahy begins with words that register the ambivalence and claustrophobia that permeate his account: "'So I'm to stay a prisoner here in Alexandria, to spend the rest of my life trying to justify myself.' With that I said goodbye to my brother and went straight to the Pension Miramar" (87). Bahy's predicament and agon are introduced in the form of his officer brother, whose voice is the most prominent one against which his own is dialogized. Furthermore, these opening words overdetermine Bahy's specific angle of critique of the revolution. His narrative dialogically modulates discordances between the authoritarianism of a military junta with a quasi-socialist orientation and left-wing constituencies—here specifically the communists whose activities were banned and who were imprisoned under Nasser.[12]

Al-Beheiry's narrative begins with "The High-Life Grocery" (129), the English name of the store transliterated in the Arabic original though without the word "grocery," hence more amenable to double entendre. The phrase, beyond its denotative import, places a marker on al-Beheiry's upward mobility (see also Tarabishi, "Symbolism" 111). The rest of the paragraph, with its paean to commodities in the store, foreshadows his objectifying view of Zohra in the superimposition of her face on the goods he is coveting: "I'd seen her as I was scrutinizing the prices on the wine bottles in the window: my eyes passed over the barrel of olives . . . and lit on the profile of her nut-brown face . . . " (129).

Students should be urged to trace the markedly heteroglot environment of *Miramar* in and across the different narrative voices. They should note generational speech fads (Allam's "*Ferekeeko*"); the incorporated discourse of a given genre as it changes over time (Wagdi's journalistic style, now dated [6, 11, 140]); the register of a given class (the disgruntled civil servant, as seen in al-Beheiry's conversation with Ali Bakir [133]); and the worldview of a certain group (the communists, seen in stock witticisms, as in Fawzi throwing out, "Good idea. Let's go and see a capitalist film!" [91]). There are also the fragments of speech belonging to other figures, sometimes unidentified, enmeshed in each narrative, that make for internal dialogism. These are occasionally italicized in the English translation (the voices of Bahy's older brother and his old comrades, as well as the various unidentified Wafdist pashas in obsessively recollected dialogue with Wagdi).

Discussion of heteroglossia underscores *Miramar*'s variously articulated undermining of the monological, authoritarian postrevolutionary regime and the novel's emphatic thematization of democracy. Here one should bring to the fore the Wafd Party and the novel's recurrent references to it. The most important of several political parties in Egypt in the first half of the twentieth century, parties that were dissolved in the wake of the 1952 revolution, the Wafd had a mixed legacy. In its early stages an influential, anticolonial, liberal, and secular movement, the Wafd was later tainted by internecine conflict, corruption, and compromise with the British authorities.[13] Inasmuch as the 1952 revolution is subjected to unsparing criticism in this novel, the Wafd is evoked only to be dialogically refracted through the different narrative voices. I would argue that, through and beyond all the contending discourses that surround it in *Miramar*, the Wafd functions as an index to or key marker placed on democracy and the multiparty system.[14]

Granted, the text taps into the nostalgia that surrounded the Wafd in its earlier moment of promise and the charisma of its leader, Saad Zaghloul, most visibly in the discourse of the oldest narrator. Despite having left the Wafd in disenchantment with its later complicity with the British (17), Wagdi continues to uphold Zaghloul as an exemplar, a paragon of egalitarianism who privileged his peasant origins in the face of the Turco-Circassian elite (27), a model of valor and self-abnegating dedication to the nationalist cause (8, 103). Wagdi notes mournfully that Zaghloul's legacy has been reduced to "a couple of statues as . . . memorial" (8). Yet the icon of Zaghloul, whom "the older generation worshipped," is dialogically undermined in Bahy's narrative, where a presumably communist interlocutor, in a fragment of recollected dialogue, remarks, "*What good are such idols? He* [Zaghloul] *stabbed the true workers' revolution to death at its birth*" (96), thereby eliciting the Wafdist nationalists' bourgeois allegiances at the expense of subalternity. This view in turn will be counterpoised by a voice commenting, "I can't deny [the revolution's] overwhelming power. But I believe that when the Wafd died, the Egyptian masses died too" (163). The orchestration of the different perspectives on the Wafd does not leave out its opponents (monarchists, in the figure of Tolba Marzuq [17, 57]), its later complicity with the British (17), and the corruption of some of its leadership (41), even in Wagdi's own narrative.

That very orchestration of views on the Wafd's legacy underscores that the 1952 revolution's official history muted, sometimes altogether erased, earlier oppositional movements. As one character puts it, "All right, we all believe in the Revolution, but the past wasn't a total blank!" (76). In the film *Miramar*, an adaptation of the novel made two years later (1969), there are only a few fleeting references to the Wafd, apart from a slightly more extended one to Saad Zaghloul.[15] Mahfouz's criticism of such elisions is clear in this passage from Wagdi's first narrative:

> I seized this opportunity and took him with me at once on a voyage back into history, leading him to events that *should never have been forgotten*. We reviewed the parties one by one, the pros and cons of the People's Party and the National Party; the Wafd and how it resolved long-standing contradictions—and why, after all that, I had shifted away into independence, why I supported the Revolution. (33; emphasis added)

The anti-amnesia listing of the parties gestures toward a legacy of pluralism that was laid to waste after the revolution, a legacy that is itself not spared the dialogism of *Miramar*.

But what of the two main women characters in this novel, Zohra and Mariana, on whom much of the action pivots but to whom no extended narratives are granted? Does the text thus silence them, or does it problematize the muting of their positionalities, precisely by having their words relayed by others? Critics have proposed that Zohra is an allegorical figure, and I would suggest that Mariana too can be read that way. Evidence of allegorical markers placed on either figure is not lacking: "I caught a glimpse of Zohra. She's the one who really represents the Revolution" (144; trans. modified); "My dear Mariana, *you* are Alexandria . . . " (3).[16] Are the allegorical interpretations of the women as secure as they may seem? What does it mean that Zohra is cast as representative of the 1952 revolution and Mariana of Alexandria?

Miramar is in intertextual dialogue with canonical tropes of two literary traditions of feminization and thus offers a polyvalent intervention. In one instance, the text engages a largely but by no means solely Egyptian tradition of feminization (Egypt as feminized); in the other, a primarily Western tradition (Alexandria personified as a woman). While the first tradition is informed by concerns with the nation, the second is framed by a discourse I have elsewhere called "Alexandrian cosmopolitanism."

Two critical studies can be adduced to situate Zohra as part of the longstanding tradition of feminizing Egypt. In *Egypt as a Woman*, Beth Baron analyzes a range of iconographic representations of the nation (such as sculpture, cartoons, and photography), informed by local notions of honor and kinship in dialogue with Western traditions, to elicit various nationalist agendas, male and female, at work in the feminization trope. Tackling literature specifically, Samah Selim argues that "'the national feminine' is absolutely central in twentieth-century Egyptian fiction" (*Novel* 20) and that the "contest over the right to 'possess' or discipline this national feminine . . . inscribes a set of questions about the destiny of the nation itself" (21). A writer of urban novels, Mahfouz had resorted to the trope of a feminized Egypt in the form of the sexually precocious, upwardly mobile Hamida, who becomes a prostitute working for British officers in World War II Cairo, in زقاق المدق (1947; Zuqaq al-midaqq; *Midaq Alley*) (see Selim, *Novel* 21). *Miramar*'s Zohra (whose name signifies "blossom"), the peasant woman who has migrated to the city, intertextually intervenes in the canonical trope of the nation as a rural woman to lay bare the emptiness of the revolution's promise of greater social justice and amelioration of the subaltern's condition.

If it was the peasant and the worker who, in quasi-socialist fashion, were cast as the primary addressees and beneficiaries of the revolution, certain undeniable rights and benefits having been secured for them, this orientation did not prevent the silencing of the subaltern masses nor the revolutionary leaders from arrogating power and privilege for themselves. Zohra's escape from the village with its "misery" and feudal mores to the modern city where, as she puts it, "love is. Education. Cleanliness. And hope" (43) represents the postrevolutionary possibilities of enfranchisement held out to the subaltern even as it enacts, in the young woman's capacity as symbol of Egypt, the country's would-be transition from an agrarian society to industrialization. That she attributes these possibilities to the revolution is manifested in the portrait of President Nasser hanging in her room (63); in her praying for the revolution (144); and in her firm belief, regarding class differences, that "[t]imes have changed. Haven't they?" (39).

It is specifically in Zohra's relationship with al-Beheiry that the text delivers its most mordent criticism of the revolution (see Tarabishi, "Symbolism" 110). If Zohra is symbolic of Egypt, al-Beheiry represents the revolution's rising class. Reading further in an allegorical key that modulates on the persistence of class stratification in postrevolutionary times, one should consider al-Beheiry's telling reflection the first time he meets Tolba Marzuq, missing from the English translation, that "[Marzuq] belongs to that class which we should, in some sense, inherit" (*Miramar* [1979] 224). The change of regime has not effected an egalitarian leveling of class differences; it has replaced the old elite by a new one at the helm—a state of affairs spelled out in a fragment of recollected dialogue in Bahy's narrative ([1993] 95). This change is allegorically enacted in al-Beheiry's love for but desire to exploit Zohra: he refuses to marry her, his social inferior, because his credo is, "What's the good of going into [marriage] if it doesn't give me a push up the social ladder?" (154).

Does Zohra's lack of a full-fledged narrative participate in or attest to the silencing of the subaltern? And how do we factor in the series of strong decisions that she makes: refusing to be married off against her will, leaving the village, withstanding pressure from her family to return, getting an education, rejecting two more marriage proposals, refusing to be used by al-Beheiry (see also Tarabishi, "Symbolism" 121–22)? To what extent do her actions, as corroborated by others' voices, register an agency that belies this silence? In raising these questions, I would encourage students not to think of them as either/or propositions but to entertain the possibility of a polyvalent, critical intervention by *Miramar* into this trope. To that end, I would put out for discussion two interpretations of the question of allegory, silence, and agency in relation to Zohra.

Georges Tarabishi astutely argues that while Zohra/Egypt functions as a mirror for others' ideological and class positionality,[17] the text does not reduce the character to a passive symbol. The young woman possesses, alongside her symbolic dimension, an irreducible realistic one. Her fierce insistence on being the decision maker in her life counters and deconstructs the process of symbolization (Tarabishi, "Symbolism" 120). Nehad Selaiha reads "this voiceless character . . . as the only truly free spirit and the real protagonist who morally defines the other characters by their attitudes to her" and suggests that

> [s]ubtly, without shattering the realistic credibility of the character, Mahfouz builds Zohra into a glorified, idealised symbol of Egypt as he would like it to be, and he could not have achieved this had he made her one of the narrators. Her silence was useful in another direction too: as it identifies her with the silent majority of Egyptians who were denied freedom of speech, it acts as a satirical comment on Nasser's politics and his rhetoric of freedom. (2)[18]

To read Mariana as Alexandria or a particular Alexandria is to elicit an abiding trope in much modern Western literature about this city. While the feminization of Alexandria is resonant with that of nations and cities, in the case of this Mediterranean city it acquires additional site-specific layers. The city's name is already a feminization of Alexander's. The city is represented in Hellenistic art, such as mosaics, by a female figure and associated with renowned historical women, including Hypatia but more markedly Cleopatra. Alexandria in the hands of modern Western writers would furthermore take on the orientalist overtones of an odalisque. While never yielding a single emblematic figure, such as France's Marianne or Mexico's La Malinche, Alexandria as a woman would be cast as a Cleopatra-like courtesan (see Halim, "City" and "Forster"). This representation is at its most visible in Lawrence Durrell's *Alexandria Quartet* (see Pinchin; Halim, "City" and "Alexandria Archive"), a novel Mahfouz has said he was acquainted with (Massoud 91) and with which his *Miramar* has been compared (Fathi 124, 134–38; Massoud).[19]

That the female figure allegorical of Alexandria in literary texts is either Greek or portrayed with recourse to Hellenic tropes reflects "Alexandrian cosmopolitanism." This was a Eurocentric discourse about Alexandria in the late nineteenth century and first half of the twentieth that revived Hellenistic Alexandria as a golden age. Something of an "invented tradition," it was fed by a variety of tributaries, the most important of which was the pressing into service of the Greek community as the arch or link between modern and Hellenistic Alexandria, thus conferring legitimacy on quasi-colonial conditions.[20]

The discourse of Alexandrian cosmopolitanism furthermore elided the Arabo-Islamic period, ciphered as a moment of decline, a move that in later critics and writers is paralleled by the elision of a post-Suez, postindependence Alexandria, likewise considered a city in decline, in this case fallen victim to nationalism.

Silenced in and excluded from this Eurocentric dominant narrative of cosmopolitanism are the Egyptians who constituted the majority of the city's population and its labor force—which betrays the extent of the collusion of this cosmopolitanism with colonialism (see Halim, "Alexandria Re-inscribed," "On Being," "Alexandria Archive" [3, 12], and "Forster" 242–43 and the references cited there).

It is precisely out of this discourse that Mariana, Mahfouz's latter-day exemplar par excellence, says of Alexandria, "But *we* created it." Mariana says this about the postindependence Alexandria she denigrates: "It's all changed. The streets nowadays are strewn with litter." (trans. modified). Wagdi's reply—"My dear, it had to be claimed by its people" (8)—situates *Miramar* as part of postcolonial literature that "writes back" to colonial discourse (Ashcroft, Griffiths, and Tiffin), in this case Alexandrian cosmopolitanism. In the process of writing back through the figure of Mariana, the text adds dimension to her.

Both Mariana and the statue of the Madonna beneath which she is often seen seated act as signifiers of an ethnic otherness that was rapidly being removed from the country at the time. Further examples of ethnic otherness are seen in the Maltese madame, the Greek owner of High-Life Grocery, the Armenian prostitute, and the Italo-Syrian prostitute. In a musical motif that amplifies *Miramar*'s polyphony, the text sympathetically observes the effect of reverse dispossession on Alexandrians of European origin. With Mariana at the radio listening to the European program, the reader tunes in to the melancholy remembrance of time past and a gilded youth played off the Greek lyric about a young girl's notions of a desirable suitor (74). In a similar musical vein, Azza Kararah has read the Umm Kulthum concert, and Mariana's devotion to it, as "a requiem" to the strains of which "she bids farewell to the Alexandria of her youth," analogous to the moment when Mark Antony hears the mystical choir passing through Alexandria shortly before the fall of the city and his death, in Constantine P. Cavafy's poem "The God Abandons Antony" (Kararah, "Mariana" 5; on *Miramar*, see also Kararah, "Egyptian Literary Images"). Sympathy with Mariana comes from a most unlikely quarter, al-Beheiry, who reflects that he is "sincerely fond" of her, "not just because she loves our music, but because I like her quick wit and her stories of the past, which she repeats with true unquenchable Greek nostalgia" (145).

Although interested primarily in Cairo, Mahfouz turned his attention to Alexandria in a series of 1960s novels, novellas, and short stories.[21] What was behind the shift in scene from the capital to the Mediterranean city, and why did it occur in the 1960s? If the engagement of some of Mahfouz's earlier texts with Alexandria is limited, confined to a protagonist's short sojourn as a vacationer or transferred civil servant, I would argue that Alexandria in *Miramar* is by no means an arbitrary backdrop. Its choice as a setting is not solely a postcolonial riposte to colonial cosmopolitanism; it is also part and parcel of the novel's critique of the revolution.

Mahmud Amin al-ʿAlim argues that Alexandria in Mahfouz's work is associated with alienation and exile, occasionally affording a given character a belated, qualified self-knowledge and a glimpse of hope, as with Zohra at the end of

Miramar. According to al-ʿAlim, Alexandria in the hands of Mahfouz retains a "Cairene significance," being nothing more than a place of refuge or resort and invariably treated as a symbol of a crisis of "the Cairene petit bourgeois," never acquiring "a living social reality" (468).[22]

My argument is that Alexandria was chosen as the setting of *Miramar* precisely to draw out a site-specific social reality as part of the novel's broader political criticism. Consider the number of restaurants and enterprises that carry European names, having been established and owned by Alexandrians of European origin: the Trianon, the Cecil Hotel, the Windsor Hotel, the Genevoise, Monte Carlo, Atheneos, Café de la Paix, Pastroudis, Delices, Monseigneur, the Palma. These names reinforce *Miramar*'s chronotope of encounter in spaces permeated with historical associations. In so doing, they lend further credence to what in my view is the reason why the novel was set in Alexandria, namely on account of the city's providing an acute symptom of the quasi-socialist economic policies adopted by the Nasser regime, which comprised nationalization and sequestration of large assets and enterprises, including those belonging to foreign nationals. The text would seem to be targeting, if nothing else, the excesses in the execution of these policies.

An atmosphere of panic obtains among Alexandrians of European descent as property changes hands between them and Egyptians. Among such transactions in the novel are the purchase by Mahmoud Abu al-Abbas, the newspaper vendor, of Panayoti's restaurant (134, 161) and Allam's taking the Maltese madame's advice to find a foreigner who is leaving and buy him out (65). Allam purchases not Miramar Café, as Mariana suggests (74), but the Genevoise from its foreign owner (83, 85). Whereas these may be individuals' transactions, the text uses them as a backdrop to bring out "the rank breath of corruption" (88) among symbols of the regime in the application of socialist-inspired policies. Bahy's officer brother bluntly explains that Mariana "*comes from a good family, but she's no saint. Her business has its demands. If I hadn't helped her, her flat and her money would have been confiscated long ago*" (113).

Does the text then lapse into colonial nostalgia? Elsewhere, I have discussed "postcolonial melancholia" in relation to Alexandrian cosmopolitanism, as seen in a plethora of memoirs and fictional texts in European languages by émigré Alexandrians, such as André Aciman and Harry Tzalas, that attempt closure to an unresolved mourning of the city's lost space by denigrating postindependence Egypt. Various factors come into play in this melancholia: a latter-day projection of the discourse of Alexandrian cosmopolitanism, with its elision of all things Arab, onto Egyptian nationalism; the country's decolonization and the post-Suez sequestrations of assets of British and French subjects, among others, to be followed by the socialist-inspired policies of sequestrations and nationalizations and hence the waves of immigration of members of foreign communities and the formation of an Alexandrian diaspora. By contrast, Arabic texts that postdate *Miramar*, such as Youssef Chahine's semi-autobiographical Alexandrian films and the novels of Edwar al-Kharrat and Ibrahim Abdel-Meguid, variously address a multiply determined mourning reinforced by a sense of national defeat by training a keen eye on the relation between cosmopolitanism and colonialism, by appealing to a radically different precolonial archive, or by critically reappraising the postindependence period (see Halim, "Alexandria Re-inscribed," "Cosmopolitan Alexandria," "On Being," "Alexandria Archive" [12, 305, 340–44], "Victoria," "Forster" [243, 271–72], and "Latter-Day Levantinism").[23] *Miramar*, published a few months before the 1967 war, anticipates this variegated landscape of loss.

I would offer that the novel is permeated with competing nostalgias, playing off Mariana's nostalgia against that of others. The novel's opening lines read, "Alexandria. At last. Alexandria, Lady of Dew. Bloom of white nimbus. Blossom of radiance, wet with sky water. Core of nostalgia steeped in honey and tears" (1). The words come from Wagdi's narrative, and it is with a second narrative by Wagdi that the novel closes. It has been suggested that the novel throws its weight behind his voice, vesting it with quasi-authorial accents (Tarabishi, "Symbolism" 115). But one could also argue that, in according Wagdi of all the four narrators a second narrative, the text withholds closure. It does so by making speak the very voice that had harked back to an earlier pluralism pitted against a colonial cosmopolitanism with which it was coextensive while at the same time referring us back to the dialogic commentary on the troubled legacy of that pluralism.

The various approaches to teaching *Miramar* discussed in this essay are addressed to world literature courses, but they are adaptable to the presentation of the novel in other kinds of courses. Novels taught in courses offered to undergraduates majoring in Middle Eastern studies are often taught in translation, hence the questions of translation and reception posed here are just as relevant, and the teacher can offer selected short passages in Arabic for comparison. Other parts of my discussion can be adapted to theme-based seminars. For example, the argument about polyphony and heteroglossia in *Miramar* as a response to the authoritarianism of the postindependence regime and the argument about the novel as a riposte to Alexandrian cosmopolitanism can inform *Miramar*'s presentation in seminars on the postcolonial novel or on cities in literature. In both cases Mahfouz's text could be assigned alongside Durrell's *Alexandria Quartet*. Whatever the framework of the course, the approaches offered here should work against *Miramar*'s being construed as a literary native informant and promote a reading of the text as a highly self-reflexive fiction that calls into question this and other assumptions.

NOTES

All translations from the Arabic are mine, unless otherwise indicated. It remains to be seen how the revolutionary movements in the Middle East of 2011 will influence the reception of Arabic literature in the United States. I thank Waïl Hassan for welcoming my proposal, back in 2006, to write on *Miramar*.

[1] Al-Nowaihi's paper was first presented at the Middle East Studies Association annual convention in 2000. A shorter version of the paper was originally published in *Middle East Studies Bulletin* 35.1 (2001).

[2] For an update on Said's comments regarding translation of Arabic literature, see Altoma.

[3] See Altoma 31 and 68 regarding the publication history of the translation. Unless otherwise indicated, all quotations from the novel use the United States edition. Citations from the notes to *Miramar,* taken from the American University in Cairo Press edition (reproducing verbatim the notes to the Heinemann edition) are marked with the date 1987. In one instance where I translate from the Arabic a phrase missing from the English translation, the citation is marked by the date 1979.

[4] The American University in Cairo Press, which holds the copyright to the English translation, used the Doubleday typesetting of *Miramar* in subsequent editions. Like Doubleday, it omitted Fowles's introduction and el Qudsy's notes, according to Neil Hewison, associate director for Editorial Programs at AUC Press. Denys Johnson-Davies, the first translator of Mahfouz into English, writes, "After Mahfouz had won [the Nobel], *Miramar* continued to be published in an edition produced by the AUC Press and Doubleday, but without Fowles' introduction. Why? The reason no doubt was that the introduction had ended with a long quotation from Naguib Mahfouz in which he modesty expressed the opinion that he ranked among the third rather than the first rank of writers. . . . John Fowles himself is a considerable talent and it is surely of interest to find such a writer praising Mahfouz at a time before he had obtained the endorsement of the Nobel" (66).

[5] American spelling replaced British spelling, and certain transliterated Arabic words such as *fellaha* and *feddan*, as well as a few French words, were deitalicized, changes that indicate that the repackaging of the text for an American audience was informed by a domesticating approach.

[6] For a study on Umm Kulthum, see Danielson.

[7] Among the anticolonial intellectuals cited by Darraj who conceived of language as an arena of resistance are ʿAbdullah al-Nadim and Muhammad al-Muwaylihi (88–89). Darraj does, however, turn to postcolonial Egypt of the 1960s—the time frame of *Miramar*—to demonstrate the nationalist devaluing of foreign languages. Darraj's position on Bakhtin is inconsistent. Despite his suggestion that Bakhtin overstates the case, Darraj goes on to argue that the democratizing conditions the Russian posits for heteroglossia and the emergence of the novel, as in a "Galilean perception of language" (*Dialogic Imagination* 366), are absent in the Arab context (146–48, 154–55). In view of the oppressiveness of the religious as well as political establishment, Darraj argues, the Arab novel was "born handicapped" and, though accruing a modicum of independence premised on its specificity, is an express of "deformed social modernities" (151, 157). He also critiques aspects of al-Kharrat's writing that place the Arab novel outside Bakhtin's conception of the novel (266, 278).

[8] I have discussed some of these features in relation to Edwar al-Kharrat's criticism and novels. See Halim, "Alexandria Archive" 294–371.

[9] Hammuda, in his study devoted to the chronotope in Mahfouz's corpus, also notes the connection between the road and the pension (105).

[10] Hammuda, in his discussion of "chronotopic vocabulary," including pictures, mentions the characters' different readings of portraits that invoke "old times and places" as

part of *Miramar*'s polyphonic structure, although he does not discuss the long historical span of which they serve as markers (164–65).

[11] Moosa also analyzes the opening sentences of the different narrators, comparing them to musical leitmotifs (150–51).

[12] On Egyptian communism, see Botman; al-Saʿid. Mahfouz would later devote a whole novel, الكرنك (1974; Al-Karnak; *Karnak Café*), to the police state aspect of Nasser's regime.

[13] For different discussions of Egypt's prerevolutionary multiparty system and civil society, see al-Sayyid-Marsot; Vatikiotis; and Meijer.

[14] In an interview with Rajaʾ al-Naqqash, Mahfouz makes explicit that his main reproach against the 1952 revolution is its turning its back on democracy and on the Wafd (al-Naqqash, "Naguib Mahfouz" 193–94). Mahfouz says that in *Miramar* he explicitly tackled "the problem of the Socialist Union and class conflict . . . as well as dictatorship, which I criticized trenchantly" (249). Two texts by Mahfouz pre-dating *Miramar* in which the Wafd is a central theme are الثلاثية (1956–57; Al-Thulathiyya; *The Cairo Trilogy*) and السمان والخريف (1962; Al-summan wa al-kharif; *Autumn Quail*).

[15] Directed by Kamal al-Shaykh, *Miramar* (1969) can be assigned alongside the novel. A discussion of cinematic adaptations can flesh out the discussion of the translation of the novel into English. The film, instead of seeking cinematic techniques and narrative approaches to render the novel's polyphony, slices through the text to extricate and situate center-stage Zohra's relationship with Sarhan al-Beheiry. At the end of the film, Zohra does not step into an uncertain future as in the novel; she walks off with the newspaper vendor Mahmoud Abu al-Abbas, who renews his marriage proposal. This happy ending can be read as the film's bid for commercial success. Mariana's history and previous marriages are not represented in the film. Of the four narrators in the novel, the one we learn least about in the film is Wagdi, cast as a benign elderly journalist with a Wafdist past who paternally cares for Zohra. The reference to Zaghloul in the film occurs in a scene based on the novel, in a more motivated setting overlooking the leader's statue. In this scene, Marzuq launches into an attack on the deceased leader, to which Wagdi, in the film but not the novel, responds by passionately defending Zaghloul's integrity. Another reference to the Wafd is at the Umm Kulthum soirée, when al-Beheiry is asked if he had any political involvement before the revolution, and he mentions that he was involved in the Wafd; this episode is culled from another context in the novel. Criticism of the revolution is voiced mainly by Marzuq and Allam, although it mostly provides comic relief and occasionally verges on burlesque. On the other hand, Bahy's authoritarian officer brother is adequately portrayed as a crushing, dishonest figure, although his dubious patronage of Mariana is absent from the film. The film suggests polyglossia by the inclusion of Greek and French words, while the dialogue is rendered, unlike in the novel, in colloquial Arabic. By and large, the historical *longue durée* in the novel is elided in the adaptation.

[16] In the English translation, this sentence ends with "to me," an insertion not present in the Arabic.

[17] Tarabishi reads Mariana as the waning power of the foreign exploiter, Marzuq as representative of the national feudal class, and Allam as the alienated nihilist. He suggests that while the text constructs them as phantom enemies, the true danger to Zohra as Egypt is the enemy within, the opportunist representative of the revolution al-Beheiry.

[18] Selaiha's article is a review of an operatic adaptation of *Miramar*, the libretto for which, in Arabic, was written by Sayyid Hijab.

[19] In a discussion of the Algerian novelist Yacine Kateb's *Nedjma*, Shukri compares both that novel and Mahfouz's *Miramar* to Faulkner's *The Sound and the Fury* and Durrell's *Alexandria Quartet* ("Resistance Hero" 143).

[20] For general references on Alexandria in the modern period, see Ilbert and Yannakakis; Ilbert; and Reimer. On the Greeks of Alexandria, see Kitroeff. For two recent compelling studies on Alexandria that have addressed the city's cosmopolitanism in relation to colonialism, see Re; Butler. I borrow "invented tradition" from Hobsbawm and Ranger, and my use of "subaltern" derives from Spivak and Guha.

[21] Alexandria features to varying degrees in the novels السمان والخريف (1962; Al-summan wa al-kharif; *Autumn Quail*), الطريق (1964; Al-tariq; *The Search*), الشحاذ (1965; Al-shahhadh; *The Beggar*), as well as the title story in the collection دنيا الله (1963; Dunya Allah; *God's World*) and a story from the collection بيت سئ السمعة (1965; Bayt sayy'i al-sum'a; "House of Ill-Repute").

[22] Fathi makes a similar comment (124).

[23] The arguments put forward in this essay are taken from a book manuscript, including a chapter on Mahfouz, on cosmopolitan Alexandria, which I am currently revising and which builds on work done in different forums since the early 1990s. Elaborating on a presentation given at the MLA convention in 2001, "Cosmopolitan Alexandria and Postcolonial Melancholia: The Case of Youssef Chahine," a version of which was published as "On Being an Alexandrian," this book manuscript analyzes representations of loss in relation to Alexandrian cosmopolitanism in dialogue with Freud's "Mourning and Melancholia," Gilroy's *Postcolonial Melancholia*, and Eng and Kazanjian's *Loss*. See also Butler, *Return*.

NOTES ON CONTRIBUTORS

Roger Allen is professor of Arabic and comparative literature at the University of Pennsylvania. He is the author of *The Arabic Novel*, *The Arabic Literary Heritage*, and articles on Mahfouz and other Arab writers. Among his translations from Arabic is Mahfouz's *God's World*, which was mentioned by the Nobel committee in 1988.

Michael Beard is Chester Fritz Distinguished Professor of English at the University of North Dakota. He is the author of *Hedayat's* Blind Owl *as a Western Novel* and coeditor, with Adnan Haydar, of *Naguib Mahfouz: From Regional Fame to Global Recognition*.

Elliott Colla is associate professor in the Department of Arabic and Islamic Studies at Georgetown University. He is the author of *Conflicted Antiquities: Egyptology, Egyptomania, Egyptian Modernity* and has translated Ibrahim al-Koni's *Gold Dust*, Ibrahim Aslan's *The Heron*, and Idris Ali's *Poor*.

Terri DeYoung is associate professor of Arabic in the Department of Near Eastern Languages and Civilizations at the University of Washington. She is the author of *Placing the Poet: Badr Shakir Al-Sayyab and Postcolonial Iraq* and coeditor of *Tradition and Modernity in Arabic Literature*.

Nouri Gana is associate professor of comparative literature and Near Eastern languages and cultures at the University of California, Los Angeles. He is the author of *Signifying Loss: Toward a Poetics of Narrative Mourning*, completing a book on the affective politics of Arab contemporaneity, and editing a collection on the rise of the Arab novel in English and another on the Tunisian revolution.

Hala Halim is assistant professor of comparative literature and Middle Eastern studies at New York University. She is revising a book manuscript entitled "The Alexandria Archive: An Archaeology of Alexandrian Cosmopolitanism." Her translation of Mohamed El-Bisatie's *Clamor of the Lake* won an Egyptian State Incentive Award.

Barbara Harlow is professor of English at the University of Texas, Austin. She is the author of *Resistance Literature*; *Barred: Women, Writing, and Political Detention*; and *After Lives: Legacies of Revolutionary Writing*. She has also edited and coedited several volumes.

Michelle Hartman is associate professor of Arabic literature at McGill University. She is the author of *Joseph, Jesus, and Job: Readings of Intertextual Rescriptings of Religious Figures in Lebanese Women's Fiction* and the translator of Iman Humaydan's *Wild Mulberries* and Muhammad Kamil al-Khatib's *Just like a River*.

Waïl S. Hassan is associate professor of comparative literature at the University of Illinois, Urbana. He is the author of *Tayeb Salih: Ideology and the Craft of Fiction* and *Immigrant Narratives: Orientalism and Cultural Translation in Arab American and Arab British Literature* and the translator of Abdelfattah Kilito's *Thou Shalt Not Speak My Language*.

Maysa Abou-Youssef Hayward is dean of e-learning at Ocean County College. Her research is on translation theory, environmental studies, linguistics, and women's issues in Arab and Arab American literatures.

Nabil Matar is professor of English at the University of Minnesota. He is the author of *Islam in Britain, 1558–1685*, *In the Lands of the Christians: Arabic Travel Writing in the Seventeenth Century*, and *Europe through Arab Eyes, 1578–1727.*

Susan Muaddi Darraj is associate professor of English at Harford Community College and a lecturer at Johns Hopkins University. She edited *Scheherazade's Legacy: Arab and Arab American Women on Writing*. She is the author of a short fiction collection, *The Inheritance of Exile.*

Justin St. Clair is assistant professor of English at the University of South Alabama, where he specializes in contemporary American literature and world literature, with emphasis on the postmodern novel and sound culture studies.

Shaden M. Tageldin is associate professor of cultural studies and comparative literature at the University of Minnesota. She is the author of *Disarming Words: Empire and the Seductions of Translation in Egypt* and of articles on comparative (post)colonial literatures in Arabic, English, and French.

SURVEY PARTICIPANTS

Maysa Abou-Youssef Haywar, *Ocean County College*
Peri Giovannucci, *Macomb Community College*
W. Reginald Rampone, Jr., *South Carolina State University*
Stephen Sheehi, *American University in Beirut*
Joya Uraizee, *Saint Louis University*

WORKS CITED

Abbott, Nabia. "A Ninth-Century Fragment of the *Thousand Nights*: New Light on the Early History of the Arabian Nights." *Journal of Near Eastern Studies* 8 (1949): 129–64. Print.

Abd al-Ghani, Mustafa. نجيب محفوظ: الثورة والتصوف [Naguib Mahfouz: al-thawra wa al-tassawuf; "Naguib Mahfouz: Revolution and Sufism"]. Cairo: Al-Hayy'a al-misriyya al-'ama li al-kitab, 1994. Print.

Abdallah, Muhammad Hasan. الإسلامية والروحية في أدب نجيب محفوظ [Al-Islamiyya wa al-ruhiyya fi adab Naguib Mahfouz; "Islam and Spirituality in the Literature of Naguib Mahfouz"]. n. p.: Dar Qabba', 2001. Print.

Aboul-Ela, Hosam. *Other South: Faulkner, Coloniality, and the Mariategui Tradition.* Pittsburgh: U of Pittsburgh P, 2007. Print.

———. "The Writer Becomes Text: Naguib Mahfouz and State Nationalism in Egypt." *Biography* 27.2 (2004): 339–56. Print.

Abu al-Majd, Ahmad Kamal. أولاد حارتنا لنجيب محفوظ تنال براءتها الإسلامية [Awlad haritna li Naguib Mahfouz tanal bara'ataha al-islamiyyah; "Naguib Mahfouz's *Children of the Alley* Gains Islamic Approval"]. *Al-Hayat* 30 Jan. 2006: 16. Print.

Abu-Lughod, Janet. "The Islamic City—Historic Myth, Islamic Essence, and Contemporary Relevance." *International Journal of Middle Eastern Studies* 19 (1987): 155–76. Print.

Agamben, Giorgio. *Stanzas: Word and Phantasm in Western Culture.* Trans. Ronald L. Martinez. Minneapolis: U of Minnesota P, 1993. Print.

Ahmad, Aijaz. "Jameson's Rhetoric of Otherness and the 'National Allegory.'" *Social Text* 17 (1987): 3–25. Print.

Ajami, Fouad. *The Arab Predicament: Arab Political Thought and Practice since 1967.* Cambridge: Cambridge UP, 1981. Print.

———. "The Humanist in the Alleys." *New Republic* 25 Sept. 2006: 31–33. Print.

al-'Alim, Mahmud Amin. أربعون عاماً من النقد التطبيقي [Arbi'un 'aman min al-naqd al-tatbiqi; "Forty Years of Applied Criticism"]. Cairo: Dar al-Mustaqbal al-'Arabi, 1994. Print.

Albakry, Mohammed. "Linguistic and Cultural Issues in Literary Translation." *Translation Directory*. TranslationDirectory.com, n.d. Web. 9 Jan. 2008.

Allen, Roger. *The Arabic Literary Heritage.* Cambridge: Cambridge UP, 1998. Print.

———. "Arabic Literature and the Nobel Prize." *World Literature Today* spring 1988: 201–03. Print.

———. *The Arabic Novel: An Historical and Critical Introduction.* 2nd ed. Syracuse: Syracuse UP, 1995. Print.

———. "The Cairo Trilogy." *Storia del romanzo.* Turin: Einaudi, 2001. Print.

———. "The Impact of the Translated Text: The Case of Najib Mahfuz's Novels, with Special Emphasis on the Trilogy." *Edebiyat* 4.1 (1993): 87–118. Print.

———. "Literary History and the Arabic Novel." *World Literature Today* 75.2 (2001): 205–13. Print.

———. "Naguib Mahfouz: A Retrospective." Farhat J. Ziadeh Distinguished Lecture. U of Washington, Seattle. 8 May 2004. Address.

———. "Najib Mahfuz." *Dictionary of Literary Biography: Yearbook 1988*. Detroit: Bruccoli, 1989. 3–14. Print.

———. "Najib Mahfuz." *Nobel Laureates in Literature*. Ed. Rado Pribic. New York: Garland, 1990. 251–57. Print. Garland Reference Lib. of the Humanities 849.

———. "Najib Mahfuz and the Nobel Prize: The Historical Context." Beard and Haydar, *Naguib Mahfouz* 28–36.

———. "Najib Mahfuz and World Literature." *The Arabic Novel since 1950: Critical Essays, Interviews, and Bibliography*. Cambridge: Dar Mahjar, 1992. 121–42. Print. Mundus Arabicus 5.

———. "Najib Mahfuz: Nobel Laureate in Literature 1988." *World Literature Today* winter 1989: 5–9. Print.

———. "Translator's Introduction." Mahfouz, *Mirrors* 9–10.

Allén, Sture. "Presentation Speech." *1988: Naguib Mahfouz*. Nobelliterature.com, n.d. Web. 10 Oct. 2010.

Altoma, Salih J. *Modern Arabic Literature in Translation*. London: Saqi, 2005. Print.

Amireh, Amal. "Framing Nawal El Saadawi: Arab Feminism in a Transnational World." *Signs* 26.1 (2000): 215–49. Print.

Anderson, Benedict. *Imagined Communities: Reflections on the Origin and Spread of Nationalism*. 1983. Rev. ed. London: Verso, 1991. Print.

Appiah, Kwame Anthony. "Is the 'Post-' in 'Postcolonial' the 'Post-' in 'Postmodern'?" *Dangerous Liaisons: Gender, Nation, and Postcolonial Perspectives*. Ed. Anne McClintock, Aamir Mufti, and Ella Shohat. Minneapolis: U of Minnesota P, 1997. 420–44. Print.

———. "The Postcolonial and the Postmodern." *In My Father's House: Africa in the Philosophy of Culture*. Oxford: Oxford UP, 1992. 137–57. Print.

Apter, Emily. *The Translation Zone: A New Comparative Literature*. Princeton: Princeton UP, 2006. Print.

al-ʿAqqad, ʿAbbas Mahmoud. عبقرية المسيح [*ʿAbqariyat al-Masih*; "The Genius of the Christ"]. Cairo: Kitab al-Yawm, 1953. Print.

Arberry, A. J. *Arabic Poetry: A Primer for Students*. Cambridge: Cambridge UP, 1965. Print.

Ashcroft, Bill, Gareth Griffiths, and Helen Tiffin. *The Empire Writes Back*. London: Routledge, 1989. Print.

Asfour, Gaber. خطاب التكفير [Khitab al-takfir; "The Discourse of Apostasy Accusations"]. *Al-Hayat* 28 Sept. 2006: 18. Print.

———. ضراوة العاصفة [Dhurwat al-ʿasifah; "Force of the Storm"]. *Al-Hayat* 29 Nov. 2006: 22. Print.

———. "Naguib Mahfouz's Critics." Trans. Ayman A. el-Desouky. Beard and Haydar, *Naguib Mahfouz* 144–71.

———. عاصفة التكفير [Asifat al-takfir; "The Storm of Apostasy Accusations"]. *Al-Hayat* 15 Nov. 2006: 18. Print.

———. حكايات أولاد حارتنا [Hikayat *Awlad haritna*; "The Tales of Children of the Alley"]. *Al-Hayat* 13 Dec. 2006: 18. Print.

El-Aswani, Alaa. "Master."

Azouqa, Aida. "Ghassan Kanafani and William Faulkner: Kanafani's Achievement in *All That's Left to You*." *Journal of Arabic Literature* 31.2 (2000): 147–70. Print.

al-Azraqi, Abu al-Walid. أخبار مكة [Akhbar Makka; "The History of Mecca"]. Ed. Rushdi al-Salih Malhas. Madrid: Dar al-Andalus, n.d. Print.

Badawi, M. M. "Commitment in Contemporary Arabic Literature." *Critical Perspectives on Modern Arabic Literature*. Ed. Issa J. Boullata. Washington: Three Continents, 1980. 23–44. Print.

———. *A Short History of Modern Arabic Literature*. Oxford: Clarendon, 1993. Print.

El-Badri, Hala. "Master."

Bakhtin, Mikhail. *The Dialogic Imagination*. Trans. Caryl Emerson and Michael Holquist. Austin: U of Texas P, 1981. Print.

———. "Forms of Time and of the Chronotope in the Novel: Notes toward a Historical Poetics." Bakhtin, *Dialogic Imagination* 84–258.

———. *Problems of Dostoevsky's Poetics*. Ed. and trans. Caryl Emerson. Minneapolis: U of Minnesota P, 1984. Print. Theory and History of Lit. 8.

Bakr, Salwa. "Master."

Balzac, Honoré de. *Père Goriot*. Trans. Burton Raffel. Ed. Peter Brooks. New York: Norton, 1994. Print.

Barakat, Halim. *The Arab World: Society, Culture, and State*. Berkeley: U of California P, 1993. Print.

Baron, Beth. *Egypt as a Woman: Nationalism, Gender, and Politics*. Berkeley: U of California P, 2005. Print.

———. "Women, Honour and the State: Evidence from Egypt." *Middle Eastern Studies* 42.1 (2006): 1–20. Print.

Barth, John. *Chimera*. New York: Mariner, 2001. Print.

———. "The Literature of Exhaustion." *Atlantic Monthly* Aug. 1967: 29–34. Print.

Bassnett, Susan, and Harish Trivedi. "Introduction: Of Colonies, Cannibals, and Vernaculars." *Post-colonial Translation: Theory and Practice*. Ed. Bassnett and Trivedi. London: Routledge, 1999. 1–18. Print.

بين القصرين [Bayn al-Qasrayn; *Palace Walk*]. Dir. Hasan al-Imam. Gibrail Talhami, 1964. Film.

Beard, Michael. "The Mahfouzian Sublime." Beard and Haydar, *Naguib Mahfouz* 95–105.

Beard, Michael, and Adnan Haydar. "Mapping the World of Naguib Mahfouz." Beard and Haydar, *Naguib Mahfouz* 1–9.

———, eds. *Naguib Mahfouz: From Regional Fame to Global Recognition*. Syracuse: Syracuse UP, 1993. Print.

Beinin, Joel. *The Dispersion of Egyptian Jewry: Culture, Politics, and the Formation of a Modern Diaspora.* Cairo: Amer. U in Cairo P, 2005. Print.

Beinin, Joel, and Zachary Lockman. *Workers on the Nile: Nationalism, Communism, Islam, and the Egyptian Working Class, 1882–1954.* Princeton: Princeton UP, 1987. Print.

Benjamin, Walter. "Left-Wing Melancholy." *Selected Writings: Volume 2, 1927–1934.* Trans. Rodney Livingstone et al. Cambridge: Belknap, 1999. 423–27. Print.

———. *The Origin of German Tragic Drama.* Trans. John Osborne. New York: Verso, 1998. Print.

Between Two Palaces. Dir. Hasan al-Imam. 1964. Film.

The Bible. New York: Oxford UP, 2008. Print. Authorized King James Vers.

Boase-Beier, Jean. "Translation and Style: A Brief Introduction." *Language and Literature: Journal of the Poetics and Linguistics Association* 13.1 (2004): 9–11. Print.

Booth, Marilyn. "On Translation and Madness." *Translation Review* 65 (2003): 47–53. Print.

Borges, Jorge Luis. *Ficciones.* New York: Grove, 1962. Print.

———. "The Translators of *The Thousand and One Nights.*" Trans. Esther Allen. *Selected Non-fictions.* Ed. Eliot Weinberger. New York: Penguin, 1999. 92–109. Print.

Botman, Selma. *The Rise of Egyptian Communism, 1939–1970.* Syracuse: Syracuse UP, 1988. Print.

Boullata, Issa J. "The Case for Resistant Translation from Arabic to English." *Translation Review* 65 (2003): 29–33. Print.

Brennan, Timothy. "The National Longing for Form." *Nation and Narration.* Ed. Homi K. Bhabha. London: Routledge, 1990. 44–70. Print.

Brown, Wendy. *Politics out of History.* Princeton: Princeton UP, 2001. Print.

———. "Resisting Left Melancholia." Eng and Kazanjian 458–65.

Bultmann, Rudolph. *Shorter Writings by Rudolf Bultmann: Existence and Faith.* Trans. Schubert M. Ogden. London: Fontana Lib., 1960. Print.

Burton, Richard. *The Book of the Thousand Nights and a Night.* and *The Supplemental Nights.* 17 vols. Privately published, 1885. Print. Luristan ed.

Butler, Beverley. *Return to Alexandria: An Ethnography of Cultural Heritage Revivalism and Museum Memory.* Walnut Creek: Left Coast, 2007. Print.

Byatt, A. S. Introduction. *The Arabian Nights: Tales from a Thousand and One Nights.* New York: Modern Lib., 2001. xiii–xx. Print.

Calvino, Italo. *If on a Winter's Night a Traveler.* New York: Harcourt, 1981. Print.

Casanova, Pascale. *The World Republic of Letters.* Trans. M. B. DeBevoise. Cambridge: Harvard UP, 2004. Print.

Césaire, Aimé. *Et les chiens se taisaient: Tragédie (arrangement théâtral).* 1956. Paris: Présence Africaine, 1989. Print.

Charulata. Dir. Satyajit Ray. 1964. Gala Entertainment, 2004. DVD.

Chatman, Seymour. "Parody and Style." *Poetics Today* 22.1 (2001): 25–39. Print.

Cole, Juan. *Napoleon's Egypt: Invading the Middle East.* New York: Palgrave, 2007. Print.

Colla, Elliott. *Conflicted Antiquities: Egyptology, Egyptomania, Egyptian Modernity*. Durham: Duke UP, 2007. Print.

———. "Multiplying Mahfouz." Rev. of *Naguib Mahfouz: The Pursuit of Meaning*, by Rasheed El-Enany. *Stanford Electronic Humanities Review* 5.1 (1996): n. pag. Web. 19 Sept. 2010.

Cooppan, Vilashini. "World Literature and Global Theory: Comparative Literature for the New Millennium." *Symploké* 9.1–2 (2001): 15–43. Print.

Damrosch, David. *What Is World Literature?* Princeton: Princeton UP, 2003. Print.

Danielson, Virginia. *The Voice of Egypt: Umm Kulthum, Arabic Song, and Egyptian Society in the Twentieth Century*. Chicago: U of Chicago P, 1997. Print.

Darraj, Faysal. نظرية الرواية و الرواية العربية [Nadhariyyat al-riwaya wa al-riwayya al-ʿarabiyya; "Theory of the Novel and the Arabic Novel"]. Casablanca: Al-Markaz al-Thaqafi al-ʿArabi, 1999. Print.

Davies, Humphrey. "Translator's Introduction." Mahfouz, *Thebes* v–xi.

DeYoung, Terri. *Placing the Poet: Badr Shakir al-Sayyab and Postcolonial Iraq*. Albany: State U of New York P, 1998. Print.

Dominguez, Virginia R. *People as Subject, People as Object: Selfhood and Peoplehood in Contemporary Israel*. Madison: U of Wisconsin P, 1989. Print.

Doody, Margaret Ann. *The True Story of the Novel*. New Brunswick: Rutgers UP, 1996. Print.

Dostoevsky, Fyodor. *Notes from the Underground*. Trans. Constance Garnett. 1918. Electronic Text Center, U of Virginia Lib., Feb. 2000. Web. 27 Apr. 2011.

Dryden, John. "On Translation." *Theories of Translation*. Ed. Rainer Schulte and John Biguenet. Chicago: U of Chicago P, 1992. 17–31. Print.

Dubiel, Helmut. "Beyond Mourning and Melancholy on the Left." *Praxis International* 10.3–4 (1990–91): 241–49. Print.

Enani, M. M., ed. *Naguib Mahfouz Nobel 1988*. Cairo: General Egyptian Book, 1989. Print.

El-Enany, Rasheed. *Naguib Mahfouz: Egypt's Nobel Laureate*. London: Haus, 2007. Print.

———. *Naguib Mahfouz: His Life and Times*. Cairo: Amer. U in Cairo P, 2007. Print.

———. *Naguib Mahfouz: The Pursuit of Meaning*. London: Routledge, 1993. Print.

Eng, David, and David Kazanjian, eds. *Loss: The Politics of Mourning*. Berkeley: U of California P, 2002. Print.

Espmark, Kjell. *The Nobel Prize in Literature: A Study of the Criteria behind the Choices*. Boston: Hall, 1991. Print.

Fahmy, Khaled. "The Anatomy of Justice: Forensic Medicine and Criminal Law in Nineteenth-Century Egypt." *Islamic Law and Society* 6.2 (1999): 224–71. Print.

———. "The Police and the People in Nineteenth-Century Egypt." *Die Welt des Islams* 39.3 (1999): 340–77. Print.

Fanon, Frantz. *The Wretched of the Earth*. Pref. Jean-Paul Sartre. Trans. Constance Farrington. New York: Grove, 1963. Print.

Fathi, Ibrahim. العالم الروائي عند نجيب محفوظ [Al-ʿalam al-riwaʾi ʿinda Najib Mahfuz; "Naguib Mahfouz's Fictional World"]. Cairo: Dar al-Fikr al-Muʿasir, 1978. Print.

Fowler, Roger. *Literature as Social Discourse: The Practice of Linguistic Criticism*. Bloomington: Indiana UP, 1981. Print.

Franco, Jean. *Plotting Women: Gender and Representation in Mexico*. New York: Columbia UP, 1989. Print.

Freud, Sigmund. "Mourning and Melancholia." *On Metapsychology: The Theory of Psychoanalysis*. Trans. James Strachey. Ed. Angela Richards. London: Penguin, 1991. 245–69. Print.

———. "On Transience." *Art and Literature*. Trans. James Strachey. London: Penguin, 1990. 283–90. Print.

Gershoni, Israel, and James P. Jankowski. *Egypt, Islam, and the Arabs: The Search for Egyptian Nationhood, 1900–1930*. Oxford: Oxford UP, 1986. Print.

al-Ghitani, Gamal. "From *Naguib Mahfouz Remembers*." Trans. Mona M. Mikhail. Beard and Haydar, *Naguib Mahfouz* 37–51.

———. *The Mahfouz Dialogs*. Trans. Humphrey Davies. Cairo: Amer. U in Cairo P, 2007. Print.

———, ed. نجيب محفوظ يتذكر [Najib Mahfuz Yatadhakkar; "Naguib Mahfouz Remembers"]. Cairo: Akhbar al-Yawm, 1987. Print.

Gilroy, Paul. *Postcolonial Melancholia*. New York: Columbia UP, 2005. Print.

Glissant, Edouard. *Caribbean Discourse*. Trans. J. Michael Dash. Charlottesville: UP of Virginia, 1992. Print.

Goldschmidt, Arthur, Jr. *Modern Egypt: The Formation of a Nation State*. Boulder: Westview, 2004. Print.

Gordimer, Nadine. "Foreword: The Dialogue of Late Afternoon." Mahfouz, *Echoes* vii–xvii.

Gordon, Joel. *Nasser's Blessed Movement: Egypt's Free Officers and the July Revolution*. New York: Oxford UP, 1992. Print.

Gordon, Lady Duff. *Letters from Egypt*. 1865. New York: Praeger, 1969. Print.

Haddawy, Husain. *The Arabian Nights*. New York: Everyman's Lib., 1992. Print.

———. *The Arabian Nights II: "Sindbad" and Other Popular Stories*. New York: Norton, 1996. Print.

Hafez, Sabry. تنظير التجارب الحضارية تفاعل الرؤي الابداعية دراسات في تأثير الصخب والعنف على الرواية العربية [Tanazir al-tajarub al-hadariyya wa-tafaʿul al-ruʾa al-ibdaʿiyya: dirasat fi-taʾthir *al-Sakhab wa-l-ʿunf* ʿala al-riwaya al-ʿarabiyya; "Divergent Civilizational Experiences and the Mixture of Creative Visions: A Study in the Influence of Noise and Violence on the Arabic Novel"]. *Fusul* 3.4 (1983): 215–29. Print.

———. *The Genesis of Arabic Narrative Discourse: A Study in the Sociology of Modern Arabic Literature*. London: Saqi, 1993. Print.

———. Introduction. Mahfouz, *Cairo Trilogy* vii–xxiii.

———. نجيب محفوظ :مصادر ومكونات تجربته الإبداعية [Najib Mahfuz: masadir wa mukawwinat: tajribatuh al-ibdaʿiyya; "Naguib Mahfouz: The Sources and Elements of His Creative Experience"]. *Najib Mahfuz: Atahaddath ilaykum*. Beirut: Dar al-ʿAwda, 1977. Print.

al-Hakim, Tawfiq. *Muhammad*. Cairo: Dar al-Shuruq, 2005. Print.

———. *Return of the Spirit*. Trans. William Hutchins. Washington: Three Continent, 1990. Print.

Halim, Hala. "The Alexandria Archive: An Archaeology of Alexandrian Cosmopolitanism." Diss. U of California, Los Angeles, 2004. Print.

———. "Alexandria Re-inscribed." *Al-Ahram Weekly* 9–15 Mar. 2000: n. pag. Web. 30 June 2009.

———. "The City as Feminine Principle: The Feminization of Alexandria in Durrell's *Clea*, Al-Kharrat's *Ya Banat Iskindiriya*, and France's *Thais*." MA thesis. Amer. U in Cairo, 1992. Print.

———. "Cosmopolitan Alexandria and Postcolonial Melancholia: The Case of Youssef Chahine." 2001. TS.

———. "Forster in Alexandria: Gender and Genre in Narrating Colonial Cosmopolitanism." *Hawwa: Journal of Women of the Middle East and the Islamic World* 4.2-3 (2006): 237–73. Print.

———. "Latter-Day Levantinism; or, 'Polypolis' in the Libretti of Bernard de Zogheb." *California Italian Studies* 1.1 (2010): 1–43. eScholarship, n.d. Web. 28 Apr. 2011.

———. "On Being an Alexandrian." *Al-Ahram Weekly* 11–17 Apr. 2002: n. pag. Web. 28 Nov. 2008.

———. "Victoria into Victory." *Victoria College: A History Revealed*. Ed. Sahar Hamouda and Colin Clement. Cairo: Amer. U in Cairo P, 2002. 187–243. Print.

Hammuda, Husayn. في غياب الحديقة :حول متصل الزمان -المكان في روايات نجيب محفوظ [Fi ghiyab al-hadiqa: hawla muttasal al-zaman / al-makan fi riwayat Najib Mahfuz; "In the Absence of the Garden: The Time-Space Continuum in the Novels of Naguib Mahfouz"]. Cairo: Madbuli, 2007. Print.

Hasan, Mahir Abd al-Munʿim. نجيب محفوظ في حوار جديد مع الشرق الأوسط [Naguib Mahfouz fi hiwar jadid maʿa *al-Sharq al-awsat*; "Naguib Mahfouz in a New Interview with *Al-Sharq al-Awsat*"]. *Al-Sharq al-Awsat*, 13 Apr. 1989. 11. Print.

Hassan, Waïl S. "'La littérature mondiale' et l'enseignement de Naguib Mahfouz aux États-Unis." *Peuples méditerranéens* 77 (1996): 113–29. Print.

———. "World Literature in the Age of Globalization: Reflections on an Anthology." *College English* 63.1 (2000): 38–47. Print.

Hayward, Maysa Abou-Youssef. "Transformance: Dialogic Translation Theory and Cultural Performance." Diss. Indiana U of Pennsylvania, 1997. Print.

Hijab, Sayyid. *Opera Miramar*. Cairo Opera House; Bibliotheca Alexandrina, n.d. Libretto.

Hirst, Anthony, and M. S. Silk, eds. *Alexandria, Real and Imagined*. Aldershot: Ashgate, 2004. Print.

"Hobbyhorse." *Merriam-Webster's Collegiate Dictionary*. 11th ed. 2003. Print.

Hobsbawm, Eric, and Terence Ranger, eds. *The Invention of Tradition*. Cambridge: Cambridge UP, 1983. Print.

Homerin, Th. Emil. *From Arab Poet to Muslim Saint: Ibn al-Fârid, His Verse, and His Shrine*. Columbia: U of South Carolina P, 1994. Print.

———. *ʿUmar Ibn al-Fârid: Sufi Verse, Saintly Life*. Mahwah: Paulist, 2001. Print.

Hunt, Lynn. *The Family Romance of the French Revolution*. Berkeley: U of California P, 1992. Print.

Hussein, Mahmoud. *Class Conflict in Egypt, 1945–1970*. Trans. Michel Chirman, Susanne Chirman, Alfred Ehrenfeld, and Kathy Brown. 2nd ed. New York: Monthly Rev., 1977. Print.

Hussein, Muhammad Kamil. قرية ظالمة [Qarya dhalima]. Cairo: Matbaʿat Misr, 1954. Print.

Ilbert, Robert. *Alexandrie, 1830–1930: Histoire d'une communauté citadine*. 2 vols. Cairo: Institut Français d'Archéologie Orientale, 1996. Print.

Ilbert, Robert, and Ilios Yannakakis, eds. *Alexandrie, 1860–1960: Un modèle éphemère de convivialité: Communautés et identité cosmopolite*. Paris: Autrement, 1992. Print.

Ilbert, Robert, Ilios Yannakakis, and Jacques Hassoun, eds. *Alexandria, 1860–1960: The Brief Life of a Cosmopolitan City*. Trans. Colin Clement. Alexandria: Harpocrates, 1997. Print.

Irwin, Robert. *The Arabian Nights: A Companion*. New York: Penguin, 1995. Print.

———. *Dangerous Knowledge: Orientalism and Its Discontents*. New York: Overlook, 2006. Print.

———. *For Lust of Knowing: The Orientalists and Their Enemies*. London: Lane, 2006. Print.

Jabra, Jabra Ibrahim. الصخب والعنف [al-Sakhab wa-l-ʿunf; "Noise and Violence"]. *al-Sakhab wa-l-ʿunf*. Trans. Jabra. Beirut: al-Mu'assasa al-ʿArabiyya li-l-dirasat wa-l-nashr, 1983. Print. Trans. of *The Sound and the Fury*, by William Faulkner.

Jacquemond, Richard. "L'affaire Mahfouz, 1959–1994." *Nasser—25 ans*. Spec. issue of *Peuples méditerranéens* 74–75 (1996): 281–92. Print.

Jameson, Fredric. "A Brief Response." *Social Text* 17 (1987): 26–77. Print.

———. *Postmodernism; or, The Cultural Logic of Late Capitalism*. Durham: Duke UP, 1991. Print. Post-contemporary Interventions.

———. "Regarding Postmodernism: A Conversation with Fredric Jameson." Interview by Anders Stephanson. Spec. issue of *Social Text* 21 (1989): 3–30. *JSTOR*. Web. 18 Mar. 2008.

———. "Third-World Literature in the Era of Multinational Capitalism." *Social Text* 15 (1986): 65–88. Print.

Jankowski, James. *Nasser's Egypt, Arab Nationalism, and the United Arab Republic*. Dulles: Rienner, 2001. Print.

Jayyusi, Salma Khadra. "The Arab Laureate and the Road to Nobel." Beard and Haydar, *Naguib Mahfouz* 10–27.

Johnson, Peter. "Retreat of the Revolution in Egypt." *MERIP Reports* 17 (1973): 3–6. Print.

Johnson-Davies, Denys. *Memories in Translation*. Cairo: Amer. U in Cairo P, 2006. Print.

Jomier, Jacques. "Quatre ouvrages en arabe sur le Christ." *Mélanges* 5 (1958): 367–86. Print.

Kahf, Mohja. "Packaging 'Huda': Shaʿrawi's Memoirs in the United States Reception Environment." *Going Global: The Transnational Reception of Third World Women Writers*. Ed. Amal Amireh and Lisa Suhair Majaj. New York: Garland, 2000. 148–72. Print.

Kararah, Azza. "Egyptian Literary Images of Alexandria." Hirst and Silk 307–21.

———. "Mariana 'The Greek Woman' in *Miramar*, by Naguib Mahfouz." 1998. TS.

Kazantazakis, Nikos. *The Last Temptation of Christ*. New York: Simon, 1960. Print.

al-Khafaji, Isam. "The Arab Left after Glasnost: Who's Afraid of Bureaustroika?" *Middle East Report* 167 (1990): 30–34. Print.

Khanna, Ranjana. *Dark Continents: Psychoanalysis and Colonialism*. Durham: Duke UP, 2003. Print.

Kirkpatrick, Hilary. *The Modern Egyptian Novel*. London: Ithaca, 1974. Print.

Kishk, Abd al-Hamid. كلمتنا في الرد على أولاد حارتنا [Kalimatuna fi al-radd ʿala *Awlad haritna*; "Our Response to *Children of the Alley*"]. Cairo: Al-Mukhtar al-islami, 1996. Print.

Kitroeff, Alexander. *The Greeks in Egypt, 1919–1937: Ethnicity and Class*. Oxford: Ithaca, 1989. Print.

Lane, Edward William. *An Account of the Manners and Customs of the Modern Egyptians*. 1860. New York: Dover, 1993. Print.

Laplanche, J., and J. B. Pontalis. *The Language of Psycho-analysis*. Trans. Donald Nicholson-Smith. New York: Norton, 1973. Print.

Lawall, Sarah. "Naguib Mahfouz and the Nobel Prize: Reciprocal Expectations." Beard and Haydar, *Naguib Mahfouz* 21–27.

———, ed. *The Norton Anthology of World Literature*. 2nd ed. New York: Norton, 2002. Print.

Lawrence, D. H. *The Man Who Died*. New York: Knopf, 1931. Print.

Leeke, Jane. "A Novel Reading: Literature and Pedagogy in Modern Middle East History Courses in Canada and the United States." MA thesis. McGill U, 2005. Print.

LeGassick, Trevor. Introduction. Mahfouz, *Midaq Alley* [1992] v–xii.

Lundqvist, Sven. *A History of Bombing*. New York: New, 2003. Print.

al-Mahalli, Jalal al-Din, and Jalal al-Din al-Suyuti. تفسير الجلالين [Tafsir al-Jalalayn; "Al-Jalalyn Exegesis"]. Damascus: Dar Ibn Kathir, 2005. Print.

Mahfouz, Naguib. *Arabian Nights and Days*. Trans. Denys Johnson-Davies. New York: Doubleday, 1995. Print.

———. *The Beggar [and] The Thief and the Dogs [and] Autumn Quail*. New York: Anchor, 2000. Print.

———. الشحّاذ [Al-shahhadh; *The Beggar*]. المؤلفات الكاملة [Al-muʾallafat al-kamila; Complete Works]. Vol. 4. Beirut: Maktabit Lubnan, 1991. 317–74. Print.

———. *The Cairo Trilogy: Palace Walk [and] Palace of Desire [and] Sugar Street*. Trans. William Maynard Hutchins, Olive E. Kenny, Lorne M. Kenny, and Angele Botros Samaan. New York: Knopf, 2001. Print.

———. *Children of Gebelawi*. Trans. Philip Stewart. Pueblo: Passeggiata, 1997. Print.

———. أولاد حارتنا [Awlad haritna; *Children of the Alley*]. Beirut: Dar al-Hayah, 1967. Print.

———. *Children of the Alley*. Trans. Peter Theroux. New York: Anchor, 1996. Print.

———. *The Dreams*. Trans. Raymond Stock. Cairo: Amer. U in Cairo P, 2005. Print.

———. *Echoes of an Autobiography*. Trans. Denys Johnson-Davies. New York: Doubleday, 1997. Print.

———. دنيا الله [Dunya Allah; *God's World*]. Cairo: Maktabat Misr, 1962. Print.

———. *God's World: An Anthology of Short Stories*. Trans. Akef Abadir and Roger Allen. Minneapolis: Bibliotheca Islamica, 1973. Print.

———. Interview by Maggie Nassif. *Middle Eastern Literatures*, forthcoming.

———. أتحدث إليكم [Atahaddathu ilaykum; "I Speak to You"]. Beirut: Dar al-ʿawda, 1977. Print.

———. *The Journey of Ibn Fattouma*. Trans. Denys Johnson-Davies. New York: Anchor, 1993. Print.

———. زقاق المدق [Zuqaq al-midaqq; *Midaq Alley*]. Cairo: Maktabat Misr, 1947. Print.

———. *Midaq Alley*. Trans. Trevor LeGassick. New York: Random, 1992. Print.

———. ميرامار [Miramar; *Miramar*]. Cairo: Maktabat Misr, 1979. Print.

———. *Miramar*. Trans. Fatma Moussa-Mahmoud. Ed. and rev. Maged el Kommos and John Rodenbeck. Notes by Omar al Qudsy. Introd. John Fowles. London: Heinemann, 1978. Cairo: Amer. U in Cairo P, 1987. New York: Doubleday, 1993. Print.

———. *Mirrors*. Trans. Roger Allen. Cairo: Amer. U in Cairo P, 1999. Print.

———. "Naguib Mahfouz." Interview by Charlotte El Shabrawy. *Paris Review* 123 (1992): 1–24. Print. Art of Fiction 129. File last accessed 8 July 2007. PDF file.

———. *Naguib Mahfouz at Sidi Gaber: Reflections of a Nobel Laureate, 1994–2001: From Conversations with Mohamed Salmawy*. Cairo: Amer. U in Cairo P, 2004. Print.

———. ليالي ألف ليلة [Layali Alf Layla; "The Nights of a Thousand Nights"]. Cairo: Maktabat Misr, 1982. Print.

———. "Nobel Lecture." Trans. Mohamed Salmawy. Nobelprize.org, 1988. Web. 28 Sept. 2010.

———. حول العرب والعروبة [Hawl al-ʿarab wa al-ʿurubah; "On Arabs and Arabness"]. Cairo: Al-dar al-misriyyah al-lubnaniyyah, 1996. Print.

———. حول الثقافة والتعليم [Hawl al-thaqafah wa al-taʿlim; "On Culture and Education"]. Cairo: Al-dar al-misriyyah al-lubnaniyyah, 1990. Print.

———. حول التحرر والتقدم [Hawl al-taharrur wa al-taqaddum; "On Emancipation and Progress"]. Cairo: Al-dar al-misriyyah al-lubnaniyyah, 1996. Print.

———. حول العدل والعدالة [Hawl al-ʿadl wa al-ʿadalah; "On Justice and Fairness"]. Cairo: Al-dar al-misriyyah al-lubnaniyyah, 1996. Print.

———. حول العلم العمل [Hawl al-ʿilm wa al-ʿamal; "On Knowledge and Work"]. Cairo: Al-dar al-misriyyah al-lubnaniyyah, 1996. Print.

———. حول الدين والديمقراطية [Hawl al-din wa al-dimuqratiyyah; "On Religion and Democracy"]. Cairo: Al-dar al-misriyyah al-lubnaniyyah, 1990. Print.

———. حول التدين والتطرف [Hawl al-tadayyun wa al-tatarruf; "On Religiosity and Extremism"]. Cairo: Al-dar al-misriyyah al-lubnaniyyah, 1996. Print.

———. حول الشباب والحرية [Hawl al-shabab wa al-hurriyyah; "On Youth and Freedom"]. Cairo: Al-dar al-misriyyah al-lubnaniyyah, 1990. Print.

———. بين القصرين [Bayn al-qasrayn; *Palace Walk*]. 1956. Cairo: Maktabat Misr, 1988? Print.

———. *Palace Walk*. Trans. William Maynard Hutchins and Olive E. Kenny. New York: Anchor-Doubleday, 1991. Print.

———. *Thebes at War*. Trans. Humphrey Davies. New York: Anchor, 2003. Print.

———. اللص و الكلاب [Al-liss wa al-kilab; *The Thief and the Dogs*]. Cairo: Maktabat Misr, 1961. Print.

———. *Voices from the Other World*. Trans. Raymond Stock. New York: Anchor, 2000. Print.

———. "Zaabalawi." *Modern Arabic Short Stories*. Ed. and trans. Denys Johnson-Davies. London: Oxford UP, 1966. 137–47. Print. Trans. of زعبلاوي.

Mahmoud, Sayyid. أبطاله كانوا هناك [Abtaluhu kanu hunak]. *Al-Hayat* 1 Sept. 2006: 15+. Print.

Massad, Joseph A. *Desiring Arabs*. London: U of Chicago P, 2007. Print

Massoud, Mary. "Mahfuz's *Miramar*: A Foil to Durrell's *Quartet*." *Images of Egypt in Twentieth-Century Literature*. Ed. Hoda Gindi. Cairo: Dept. of English Lang. and Lit., U of Cairo, 1991. 91–99. Print.

"A Master and His Mantle." Poll by Nader Habib, Pierre Loza, and Engy El-Naggar. Spec. issue of *Al-Ahram Weekly On-line*. Ed. Hala Halim. Al-Ahram, 31 Aug.–6 Sept. 2006. Web. 17 June 2007.

Mehrez, Samia. *Egyptian Writers between History and Fiction: Essays on Naguib Mahfouz, Sonallah Ibrahim, and Gamal al-Ghitani*. Cairo: American U in Cairo P, 1994. Print.

Meijer, Roel. *The Quest for Modernity: Secular Liberal and Left-Wing Political Thought in Egypt, 1945–1958*. London: Routledge, 2002. Print.

Meyer, Stefan. *The Experimental Arabic Novel: Postcolonial Literary Modernism in the Levant*. Albany: State U of New York P, 2001. Print.

Mikhail, Mona. "Existential Themes in a Traditional Cairo Setting." Beard and Haydar, *Naguib Mahfouz* 81–94.

———. *Studies in the Short Fiction of Mahfouz and Idris*. New York: New York UP, 1992. Print.

Milson, Menahem. *Najib Mahfuz: The Novelist-Philosopher of Cairo*. New York: St. Martin's, 1998. Print.

Miramar. Dir. Kamal al-Shaykh. General Company for Cinema, 1969. Film.

Mitchell, Timothy. *Colonising Egypt*. Cambridge: U of Cambridge P, 1988. Print.

Moosa, Matti. *The Early Novels of Naguib Mahfouz: Images of Modern Egypt*. Gainesville: UP of Florida, 1994. Print.

Mouloudi, Francka. *Naguib Mahfouz: The Passage of the Century*. First Run; Icarus Films, 1999. Film.

Moussa-Mahmoud, Fatma. "Depth of Vision: The Fiction of Naguib Mahfouz." *Third World Quarterly* 11.2 (1989): 154–66. Print.

———. "Master."

Naguib Mahfouz, 1911–2006. Amer. U in Cairo P, n.d. Web. 9 Oct. 2010.

Naguib Mahfouz: Biography. Nobelprize.org, n.d. Web. 10 Oct. 2010.

al-Nahhas, Hashim. نجيب محفوظ على الشاشة [Najib Mahfuz ʿala al-shasah (1945–88); "Naguib Mahfouz on the Big Screen"]. 2nd ed. Cairo: Al-hayʾah al-misriyyah al-ʿammah li al-kitab, 1990. Print.

Najjar, Fauzi. "Islamic Fundamentalism and the Intellectuals: The Case of Naguib Mahfouz." *British Journal of Middle Eastern Studies* 25 (1998): 139–68. Print.

al-Naqqash, Rajaʾ. محفوظ وأولاد حارتنا [Mahfouz wa *Awlad haritna*; "Mahfouz and *Children of the Alley*"]. *Al-Sharq al-Awsat* 28 May 1988. 18. Print.

———. نجيب محفوظ صفحات من مذكراته وأضواء جديدة على أدبه وحياته [Najib Mahfuz: safahat min mudhakkiratih wa-adwaʾ jadidah ʿala adabih wa-hayatih; "Naguib Mahfouz: Pages from His Memoirs"]. Cairo: Markaz al-Ahram li-al-Tarjamah wa-al-Nashr, 1998. Print.

Naqvi, Nauman. "The Nostalgic Subject: A Genealogy of the 'Critique of Nostalgia.'" Centro Interuniversitario per le Ricerche sulla Sociologia del Diritto, dell'Informazione e delle Instituzioni Giuridiche, Sept. 2007. Web. 28 Sept. 2010. Working Paper 23.

Nasser, Gamal Abdel. فلسفة الثورة [Falsafat al-thawrah; *The Philosophy of the Revolution*]. Cairo: Dar wa matabiʿ al-shaʿb, 1954. Print.

Nida, Eugene. *Toward a Science of Translating*. Leiden: Brill, 1964. Print.

al-Niffari, Muhammad. *The Mawáqif and Mukhatabat of Muhammad Ibn ʿAbd al-Jabbar Al-Niffari, with Other Fragments*. Ed. and trans. Arthur John Arberry. London: Luzac, 1978. Print. Trans. of مواقف ومخاطبات محمد ابن عبد الجبار النفاري [Book of Stations].

al-Nowaihi, Magda. "Unheard in English." *MIT Electronic Journal of Middle East Studies* 4 (2004): 23–29. Web. <:http://web.mit.edu/cis/www/mitejmes/>.

Ostle, Robin. "Alexandria: A Mediterranean Cosmopolitan Center of Cultural Production." *Modernity and Culture from the Mediterranean to the Indian Ocean, 1890–1920*. Ed. Leila Fawaz, C. A. Bayly, and Robert Ilbert. New York: Columbia UP, 2001. 314–29. Print.

Parker, Richard B., Robin Sabin, and Caroline Williams. *Islamic Monuments in Cairo: A Practical Guide*. 3rd ed. Cairo: Amer. U in Cairo P, 1985. Print.

Peled, Mattiyahu. *Religion, My Own*. New Brunswick: Transactions, 1983. Print.

Pickthall, Muhammad M. *The Meaning of the Glorious Qurʾan: Text and Explanatory Translation*. New York : Muslim World League, 1977. Print.

Pinault, David. "Images of Christ in Arabic Literature." *Die Welt des Islams* 27 (1987): 103–25. Print.

Pinchin, Jane Lagoudis. "Durrell's Fatal Cleopatra." *Modern Fiction Studies* 28.2 (1982): 229–36. Print.

Poe, Edgar Allan. "The Thousand-and-Second Tale of Schehrazade." *Entire Tales and Poems of Edgar Allan Poe: Photographic and Annotated Edition*. Ed. Andrew Barger. New York: Bottletree, 2006. 364–73. Print.

Pollard, A. W. *Chaucer's* Canterbury Tales*: The Squire's Tale*. New York: Macmillan, 1899. Print.

Pollard, Lisa. *Nurturing the Nation: The Family Politics of Modernizing, Colonizing, and Liberating Egypt, 1805–1923*. Berkeley: U of California P, 2003. Print.

Powell, Eve M. Troutt. *A Different Shade of Colonialism: Egypt, Great Britain, and the Mastery of the Sudan*. Berkeley: U of California P, 2003. Print.

Propp, Vladimir. *The Morphology of the Folktale*. Trans. Lawrence Scott. Austin: U of Texas P, 1968. Print.

al-Qadi, Wadad. "Biographical Dictionaries as the Scholars' Alternative History of the Muslim Community." *Organizing Knowledge: Encyclopaedic Activities in the Pre-Eighteenth Century Muslim World*. Ed. G. Endress. The Hague: Brill, 2006. 23–75. Print.

Raymond, André. *Cairo*. Trans. Willard Wood. Cambridge: Harvard UP, 2000. Print.

Re, Lucia. "Alexandria Revisited: Colonialism and the Egyptian Works of Enrico Pea and Giuseppe Ungaretti." *A Place in the Sun*. Ed. Patrizia Palumbo. Berkeley: U of California P, 2003. 163–96. Print.

Reimer, Michael J. *Colonial Bridgehead: Government and Society in Alexandria, 1807–1882*. Oxford: Westview, 1997. Print.

"Revolution." *American Heritage Dictionary*. 4th ed. 2000. Print.

Rushdie, Salman. *Haroun and the Sea of Stories*. New York: Penguin, 1991. Print.

———. *Midnight's Children*. 1980. New York: Penguin, 1991. Print.

Said, Edward W. "The Cruelty of Memory." *New York Review of Books* 30 Nov. 2000: 46–50. Print.

———. *Culture and Imperialism*. New York: Knopf, 1993. Print.

———. "Embargoed Literature." *Between Languages and Cultures*. Ed. Anuradha Dingwaney and Carol Maier. Pittsburgh: U of Pittsburg P, 1995. 97–102. Print.

———. *Orientalism*. New York: Vintage, 1979. Print.

———. *"Reflections on Exile" and Other Essays*. Cambridge: Harvard UP, 2000. Print.

al-Saʿid, Rifʿat. تاريخ الحركة الشيوعية المصرية [Tarikh al-haraka al-shuyuʿiyya al-misriyya; "History of the Egyptian Communist Movement"]. 5 vols. Cairo: Sharikat al-Amal, 1987. Print.

Salih, Tayeb. *Season of Migration to the North*. Trans. Denys Johnson-Davies. New York: New York Rev. of Books, 1969. Print.

Samaan, Angele Botros. "Linguistic Features and the Point of View in *Miramar*." Enani 185–92.

Sayigh, Samir. الأدب, الحرية, الثورة [Al-adab, al-huriyah, ath-thawrah; "Literature, Freedom, Revolution"]. *Mawaqif* 1 (1968–69): 72–87. Print.

al-Sayyid-Marsot, Afaf Lufi. *Egypt's Liberal Experiment, 1922–1936*. Berkeley: U of California P, 1977. Print.

Schivelbusch, Wolfgang. *The Culture of Defeat: On National Trauma, Mourning, and Recovery*. New York: Picador, 2003. Print.

Schölch, Alexander. *Egypt for the Egyptians!* London: Ithaca, 1981. Print.

Schwenger, Peter. *The Tears of Things: Melancholy and Physical Objects*. Minneapolis: U of Minnesota P, 2006. Print.

Scott, David. *Conscripts of Modernity: The Tragedy of Colonial Enlightenment*. Durham: Duke UP, 2004. Print.

Sedgwick, Eve Kosofsky. *Between Men: Literature and Male Homosocial Desire*. New York: Columbia UP, 1985. Print.

Selaiha, Nehad. "A Happy Marriage." *Al-Ahram Weekly* 15–21 Dec. 2005. Web. 28 Sept. 2010.

Selim, Samah. "The Narrative Craft: Realism and Fiction in the Arabic Canon." *Edebiyat: Journal of Middle Eastern Literatures* 14.1–2 (2003): 109–28. *Academic Search Premier*. Web. 19 Sept. 2005.

———. *The Novel and the Rural Imaginary in Egypt, 1880–1985*. New York: Routledge, 2004. Print.

Shakespeare, William. *Hamlet*. Ed. Susanne L. Wofford. Boston: Bedford, 1994. Print.

Shalakany, Amr. "Islamic Legal Histories." Forthcoming.

Shukri, Ghali. نجيب محفوظ : من الجمالية إلى نوبل [Naguib Mahfouz: min al-Gammaliyya ila Nobel; "Naguib Mahfouz: From Gammaliyya to Nobel Prize"]. Cairo: Al-hay ʿa al-ʾamma lil-istiʿlamat, 1988. Print.

———. "The Resistance Hero in the Algerian Novel." Trans. Shafik Makar. *Lotus* 1.4 (1970): 126–50. Print.

Somekh, Sasson. *The Changing Rhythm: A Study of Najib Mahfuz's Novels*. Leiden: Brill, 1973. Print.

Sommer, Doris. *Foundational Fictions: The National Romances of Latin America*. Berkeley: U of California P, 1993. Print.

Spivak, Gayatri Chakravorty, and Ranajit Guha, eds. *Selected Subaltern Studies*. Oxford: Oxford UP, 1988. Print.

Stagh, Marina. *The Limits of Freedom of Speech: Prose Literature and Prose Writers in Egypt under Nasser and Sadat*. Stockholm: Almqvist, 1993. Print.

Starr, Deborah. *Remembering Cosmopolitan Egypt: Culture, Society, and Empire*. New York: Routledge, 2009. Print.

Stewart, Philip. "Awlad Haratina: A Tale of Two Texts." *Arabic and Middle Eastern Literatures* 4.1 (2001): 37–42. Print.

Stock, Raymond T. "A Mummy Awakens: The Pharaonic Fiction of Naguib Mahfouz." Diss. U of Pennsylvania, 2008. Print.

Sutton, Keith, and Wael Fahmi. "The Rehabilitation of Old Cairo." *Habitat International* 26 (2002): 73–93. Print.

Tageldin, Shaden M. "The African Novel in Arabic." *The Cambridge Companion to the African Novel*. Ed. F. Abiola Irele. Cambridge: Cambridge UP, 2009. 85–102. Print.

———. *Disarming Words: Empire and the Seductions of Translation in Egypt*. Berkeley: U of California P, 2011. Print.

Tagore, Rabindranath. *Gora*. Trans. Sujit Mukherjee. Introd. Meenakshi Mukherjee. 1997. New Delhi: Sahitya Akademi, 2006. Print.

El-Tahawi, Miral. "Master."

Taine, Hippolyte. *Histoire de la littérature anglaise*. Vol. 1. 12th ed. Paris: Hachette, 1905. Print.

Takieddine-Amyuni, Mona. "Images of Arab Women in *Midaq Alley* by Naguib Mahfouz and *Season of Migration to the North* by Tayeb Salih." *International Journal of Middle East Studies* 17.1 (1985): 25–36. Print.

Tarabishi, Georges. ألله في رحلة نجيب محفوظ الرمزية [Allah fi rihlat Naguib Mahfouz al-ramziya; "Allah in Naguib Mahfouz's Symbolism"]. Beirut: Dar al-Tibaʿa wa-nashr, 1988. Print.

———. رمزية المرأة في الرواية العربية [Ramziyyat al-marʾa fi ʾl-riwaya al-ʿarabiyya; "The Symbolism of Women in the Arabic Novel"]. Beirut: Dar al-Taliʿa, 1981. Print.

Tinker, John. "Vagrant Sympathies: From Stylistic Analysis to a Pedagogy of Style." *Style* 37.1 (2003). *FindArticles.com*. CBS Interactive Business Network, n.d. Web. 18 Dec. 2010.

Toler, Michael. "The Ethics of Cultural Representation: The Maghribi Novel in Translation." *Journal of North African Studies* 6.3 (2001): 48–69. Print.

Trimingham, J. Spencer. *The Sufi Orders in Islam*. New York: Oxford UP, 1971. Print.

Vatikiotis, P. J. *The History of Modern Egypt*. Baltimore: Johns Hopkins UP, 1991. Print.

Venuti, Lawrence. *The Translator's Invisibility: A History of Translation*. New York: Routledge, 1995. Print.

Vitalis, Robert. *When Capitalists Collide: Business Conflict and the End of Empire in Egypt*. Berkeley: U of California P, 1995. Print.

El-Wardani, Mahmoud. "Master."

Wehr, Hans. *A Dictionary of Modern Written Arabic*. Ed. J. Milton Cowan. Ithaca: Spoken Lang. Services, 1971. Print.

Wichhart, Stefanie. "Intervention: Britain, Egypt, and Iraq during World War II." Diss. U of Texas, Austin, 2007. Print.

Williams, Caroline. "Place and Time in Mahfouz's al-Qahira." Beard and Haydar, *Naguib Mahfouz* 52–60.

Williams, Raymond. *The Country and the City*. New York: Oxford UP, 1973. Print.

Yaghi, Abd al-Rahman. شيخ الحارة في أعمال نجيب محفوظ [Shaykh al-hara fi aʿmal Naguib Mahfouz; "The Alley Chief in the Works of Naguib Mahfouz"]. *Al-Raʾi* [Amman] 9 Dec. 1988: 11. Print.

Yousef, Tawfiq. "The Reception of William Faulkner in the Arab World." *American Studies International* Oct. 1995: 41–48. Print.

Yusuf, Hasan. المفكر الاشتراكي في فكر نجيب محفوظ [Al-Mufakkir Al-ishtiraki fi fikr Naguib Mahfouz; "The Socialist Intellectual in Naguib Mahfouz's Thought"]. Cairo: Dar Al-ʿAlim Al-Thalith, 2005. Print.

al-Zarkashi, Badr al-Din Muhammad ibn ʿAbdallah. البرهان في علوم القرآن [Al-Burhan fi-ʿulum al-Qurʾan; "Qurʾanic Sciences Explained"]. Ed. Muhammad Abu al-Fadl Ibrahim. Cairo: Dar Ihyaʾ al-Kutub al-ʿArabiyya, 1958. Print.

el-Zayyat, Latifa. "Narrative Form in Mahfouz from *The Thief and the Dogs* to *Miramar*." Trans. Nadia El Kholy. Enani 147–58.

Žižek, Slavoj. *Enjoy Your Symptom*. New York: Routledge, 2008. Print.

———. *In Defense of Lost Causes*. New York: Verso, 2008. Print.

INDEX

Modern Language Association of America

Approaches to Teaching World Literature

Achebe's Things Fall Apart. Ed. Bernth Lindfors. 1991.
Arthurian Tradition. Ed. Maureen Fries and Jeanie Watson. 1992.
Atwood's The Handmaid's Tale *and Other Works.* Ed. Sharon R. Wilson, Thomas B. Friedman, and Shannon Hengen. 1996.
Austen's Emma. Ed. Marcia McClintock Folsom. 2004.
Austen's Pride and Prejudice. Ed. Marcia McClintock Folsom. 1993.
Balzac's Old Goriot. Ed. Michal Peled Ginsburg. 2000.
Baudelaire's Flowers of Evil. Ed. Laurence M. Porter. 2000.
Beckett's Waiting for Godot. Ed. June Schlueter and Enoch Brater. 1991.
Beowulf. Ed. Jess B. Bessinger, Jr., and Robert F. Yeager. 1984.
Blake's Songs of Innocence and of Experience. Ed. Robert F. Gleckner and Mark L. Greenberg. 1989.
Boccaccio's Decameron. Ed. James H. McGregor. 2000.
British Women Poets of the Romantic Period. Ed. Stephen C. Behrendt and Harriet Kramer Linkin. 1997.
Charlotte Brontë's Jane Eyre. Ed. Diane Long Hoeveler and Beth Lau. 1993.
Emily Brontë's Wuthering Heights. Ed. Sue Lonoff and Terri A. Hasseler. 2006.
Byron's Poetry. Ed. Frederick W. Shilstone. 1991.
Camus's The Plague. Ed. Steven G. Kellman. 1985.
Writings of Bartolomé de Las Casas. Ed. Santa Arias and Eyda M. Merediz. 2008.
Cather's My Ántonia. Ed. Susan J. Rosowski. 1989.
Cervantes' Don Quixote. Ed. Richard Bjornson. 1984.
Chaucer's Canterbury Tales. Ed. Joseph Gibaldi. 1980.
Chaucer's Troilus and Criseyde *and the Shorter Poems.* Ed. Tison Pugh and Angela Jane Weisl. 2006.
Chopin's The Awakening. Ed. Bernard Koloski. 1988.
Coleridge's Poetry and Prose. Ed. Richard E. Matlak. 1991.
Collodi's Pinocchio *and Its Adaptations.* Ed. Michael Sherberg. 2006.
Conrad's "Heart of Darkness" and "The Secret Sharer." Ed. Hunt Hawkins and Brian W. Shaffer. 2002.
Dante's Divine Comedy. Ed. Carole Slade. 1982.
Defoe's Robinson Crusoe. Ed. Maximillian E. Novak and Carl Fisher. 2005.
DeLillo's White Noise. Ed. Tim Engles and John N. Duvall. 2006.
Dickens's Bleak House. Ed. John O. Jordan and Gordon Bigelow. 2009.
Dickens's David Copperfield. Ed. Richard J. Dunn. 1984.
Dickinson's Poetry. Ed. Robin Riley Fast and Christine Mack Gordon. 1989.
Narrative of the Life of Frederick Douglass. Ed. James C. Hall. 1999.
Duras's Ourika. Ed. Mary Ellen Birkett and Christopher Rivers. 2009.
Early Modern Spanish Drama. Ed. Laura R. Bass and Margaret R. Greer. 2006.

Eliot's Middlemarch. Ed. Kathleen Blake. 1990.
Eliot's Poetry and Plays. Ed. Jewel Spears Brooker. 1988.
Shorter Elizabethan Poetry. Ed. Patrick Cheney and Anne Lake Prescott. 2000.
Ellison's Invisible Man. Ed. Susan Resneck Parr and Pancho Savery. 1989.
English Renaissance Drama. Ed. Karen Bamford and Alexander Leggatt. 2002.
Works of Louise Erdrich. Ed. Gregg Sarris, Connie A. Jacobs, and James R. Giles. 2004.
Dramas of Euripides. Ed. Robin Mitchell-Boyask. 2002.
Faulkner's As I Lay Dying. Ed. Patrick O'Donnell and Lynda Zwinger. 2011.
Faulkner's The Sound and the Fury. Ed. Stephen Hahn and Arthur F. Kinney. 1996.
Fitzgerald's The Great Gatsby. Ed. Jackson R. Bryer and Nancy P. VanArsdale. 2009.
Flaubert's Madame Bovary. Ed. Laurence M. Porter and Eugene F. Gray. 1995.
García Márquez's One Hundred Years of Solitude. Ed. María Elena de Valdés and Mario J. Valdés. 1990.
Gilman's "The Yellow Wall-Paper" and Herland. Ed. Denise D. Knight and Cynthia J. Davis. 2003.
Goethe's Faust. Ed. Douglas J. McMillan. 1987.
Gothic Fiction: The British and American Traditions. Ed. Diane Long Hoeveler and Tamar Heller. 2003.
Poetry of John Gower. Ed. R. F. Yeager and Brian W. Gastle. 2011.
Grass's The Tin Drum. Ed. Monika Shafi. 2008.
H.D.'s Poetry and Prose. Ed. Annette Debo and Lara Vetter. 2011.
Hebrew Bible as Literature in Translation. Ed. Barry N. Olshen and Yael S. Feldman. 1989.
Homer's Iliad *and* Odyssey. Ed. Kostas Myrsiades. 1987.
Hurston's Their Eyes Were Watching God *and Other Works.* Ed. John Lowe. 2009.
Ibsen's A Doll House. Ed. Yvonne Shafer. 1985.
Henry James's Daisy Miller *and* The Turn of the Screw. Ed. Kimberly C. Reed and Peter G. Beidler. 2005.
Works of Samuel Johnson. Ed. David R. Anderson and Gwin J. Kolb. 1993.
Joyce's Ulysses. Ed. Kathleen McCormick and Erwin R. Steinberg. 1993.
Works of Sor Juana Inés de la Cruz. Ed. Emilie L. Bergmann and Stacey Schlau. 2007.
Kafka's Short Fiction. Ed. Richard T. Gray. 1995.
Keats's Poetry. Ed. Walter H. Evert and Jack W. Rhodes. 1991.
Kingston's The Woman Warrior. Ed. Shirley Geok-lin Lim. 1991.
Lafayette's The Princess of Clèves. Ed. Faith E. Beasley and Katharine Ann Jensen. 1998.
Works of D. H. Lawrence. Ed. M. Elizabeth Sargent and Garry Watson. 2001.
Lazarillo de Tormes *and the Picaresque Tradition.* Ed. Anne J. Cruz. 2009.
Lessing's The Golden Notebook. Ed. Carey Kaplan and Ellen Cronan Rose. 1989.
Works of Naguib Mahfouz. Ed. Waïl S. Hassan and Susan Muaddi Darraj. 2012.
Mann's Death in Venice *and Other Short Fiction.* Ed. Jeffrey B. Berlin. 1992.

Marguerite de Navarre's Heptameron. Ed. Colette H. Winn. 2007.
Medieval English Drama. Ed. Richard K. Emmerson. 1990.
Melville's Moby-Dick. Ed. Martin Bickman. 1985.
Metaphysical Poets. Ed. Sidney Gottlieb. 1990.
Miller's Death of a Salesman. Ed. Matthew C. Roudané. 1995.
Milton's Paradise Lost. Ed. Galbraith M. Crump. 1986.
Milton's Shorter Poetry and Prose. Ed. Peter C. Herman. 2007.
Molière's Tartuffe *and Other Plays.* Ed. James F. Gaines and Michael S. Koppisch. 1995.
Momaday's The Way to Rainy Mountain. Ed. Kenneth M. Roemer. 1988.
Montaigne's Essays. Ed. Patrick Henry. 1994.
Novels of Toni Morrison. Ed. Nellie Y. McKay and Kathryn Earle. 1997.
Murasaki Shikibu's The Tale of Genji. Ed. Edward Kamens. 1993.
Nabokov's Lolita. Ed. Zoran Kuzmanovich and Galya Diment. 2008.
Works of Tim O'Brien. Ed. Alex Vernon and Catherine Calloway. 2010.
Works of Ovid and the Ovidian Tradition. Ed. Barbara Weiden Boyd and Cora Fox. 2010.
Poe's Prose and Poetry. Ed. Jeffrey Andrew Weinstock and Tony Magistrale. 2008.
Pope's Poetry. Ed. Wallace Jackson and R. Paul Yoder. 1993.
Proust's Fiction and Criticism. Ed. Elyane Dezon-Jones and Inge Crosman Wimmers. 2003.
Puig's Kiss of the Spider Woman. Ed. Daniel Balderston and Francine Masiello. 2007.
Pynchon's The Crying of Lot 49 *and Other Works.* Ed. Thomas H. Schaub. 2008.
Works of François Rabelais. Ed. Todd W. Reeser and Floyd Gray. 2011.
Novels of Samuel Richardson. Ed. Lisa Zunshine and Jocelyn Harris. 2006.
Rousseau's Confessions *and* Reveries of the Solitary Walker. Ed. John C. O'Neal and Ourida Mostefai. 2003.
Scott's Waverley Novels. Ed. Evan Gottlieb and Ian Duncan. 2009.
Shakespeare's Hamlet. Ed. Bernice W. Kliman. 2001.
Shakespeare's King Lear. Ed. Robert H. Ray. 1986.
Shakespeare's Othello. Ed. Peter Erickson and Maurice Hunt. 2005.
Shakespeare's Romeo and Juliet. Ed. Maurice Hunt. 2000.
Shakespeare's The Tempest *and Other Late Romances.* Ed. Maurice Hunt. 1992.
Shelley's Frankenstein. Ed. Stephen C. Behrendt. 1990.
Shelley's Poetry. Ed. Spencer Hall. 1990.
Sir Gawain and the Green Knight. Ed. Miriam Youngerman Miller and Jane Chance. 1986.
Song of Roland. Ed. William W. Kibler and Leslie Zarker Morgan. 2006.
Spenser's Faerie Queene. Ed. David Lee Miller and Alexander Dunlop. 1994.
Stendhal's The Red and the Black. Ed. Dean de la Motte and Stirling Haig. 1999.
Sterne's Tristram Shandy. Ed. Melvyn New. 1989.
Stowe's Uncle Tom's Cabin. Ed. Elizabeth Ammons and Susan Belasco. 2000.
Swift's Gulliver's Travels. Ed. Edward J. Rielly. 1988.
Teresa of Ávila and the Spanish Mystics. Ed. Alison Weber. 2009.

Thoreau's Walden *and Other Works*. Ed. Richard J. Schneider. 1996.
Tolstoy's Anna Karenina. Ed. Liza Knapp and Amy Mandelker. 2003.
Vergil's Aeneid. Ed. William S. Anderson and Lorina N. Quartarone. 2002.
Voltaire's Candide. Ed. Renée Waldinger. 1987.
Whitman's Leaves of Grass. Ed. Donald D. Kummings. 1990.
Wiesel's Night. Ed. Alan Rosen. 2007.
Works of Oscar Wilde. Ed. Philip E. Smith II. 2008.
Woolf's Mrs. Dalloway. Ed. Eileen Barrett and Ruth O. Saxton. 2009.
Woolf's To the Lighthouse. Ed. Beth Rigel Daugherty and Mary Beth Pringle. 2001.
Wordsworth's Poetry. Ed. Spencer Hall, with Jonathan Ramsey. 1986.
Wright's Native Son. Ed. James A. Miller. 1997.